Women in Law Enforcement Careers

A Guide for Preparing and Succeeding

❖

VIVIAN B. LORD

University of North Carolina–Charlotte

KENNETH J. PEAK

University of Nevada, Reno

PEARSON

Prentice
Hall

Upper Saddle River, New Jersey 07458

Library of Congress Catologing-in-Publication Data

Lord, Vivian B.
   Women in law enforcement careers : a guide for preparing and succeeding / Vivian B. Lord, Kenneth J. Peak.
      p. cm. -- (Prentice Hall's women in criminal justice series)
   Includes bibliographical references and index.
   ISBN 0-13-119129-2 (pbk.)
   1. Policewomen--Vocational guidance--United States. 2. Law enforcement--Vocational guidance--United
States. I. Peak, Kenneth J., 1947-II. Title. III. Series.

HV8143.L68 2004
363.2'023'73--dc22

2004053158

Executive Editor: Frank I. Mortimer, Jr.
Associate Editor: Sarah Holle
Production Editor: Lynn Steines, Carlisle Publishers Services
Production Liaison: Brian Hyland
Director of Production and Manufacturing: Bruce Johnson
Managing Editor: Mary Carnis
Manufacturing Buyer: Cathleen Petersen
Design Director: Cheryl Asherman
Senior Design Coordinator: Miguel Ortiz
Cover Designer: Anthony Inciong
Cover Photo: Ronnie Kaufman, Corbis
Composition: Carlisle Communications, Ltd.
Printing and Binding: Phoenix Book Tech Park

Pearson Education Ltd.
Pearson Education Singapore, Pte. Ltd.
Pearson Education Canada, Ltd.
Pearson Education—Japan

Pearson Education Australia PTY, Limited
Pearson Education North Asia Ltd.
Pearson Education de Mexico, S.A. de C.V.
Pearson Education Malaysia, Pte. Ltd.

10 9 8 7 6 5 4 3 2 1
ISBN: 0-13-119129-2

Dedications

———————————————— ❖ ————————————————

To my daughter, Alana, as she considers what career frontier she will climb and achieve.

—VBL

To Tiff, Oli, and their newborn son, "The Fourth," whose genetic makeup from both sides of the family tree should inevitably have him playing "cops and robbers" by his first birthday.

—KJP

Prentice Hall's
Women in Criminal Justice Series

Series Editor

Roslyn Muraskin, Ph.D.

❖

The Female Homicide Offender: Serial Murder and the Case of Aileen Wuornos
Stacey L. Shipley and Bruce A. Arrigo
ISBN: 0–13–114161–9

The Incarcerated Woman: Rehabilitative Programming in Women's Prisons
Susan Sharp
ISBN: 0–13–094067–4

It's a Crime: Women and Justice, Third Edition
Roslyn Muraskin
ISBN: 0–13–0482000–5

With Justice for All: Minorities in Criminal Justice
Janice Joseph and Dorothy Taylor
ISBN: 0–13–033463–4

Women in Law Enforcement Careers: A Guide for Preparing and Succeeding
Vivian B. Lord and Kenneth J. Peak
ISBN: 0–13–119129–2

Contents

❖

About the Authors

❖

Vivian B. Lord is chair of the Department of Criminal Justice at the University of North Carolina–Charlotte, with adjunct professor appointments in the Public Policy Doctoral Program and the International Studies departments. Dr. Lord received her Ph.D. in psychology from North Carolina State University and is licensed as a practicing psychologist in North Carolina. She is the current chair of the Police Section, Academy of Criminal Justice Sciences, and a past president of the North Carolina Criminal Justice Association. Dr. Lord is editor of the recently published *Policing and Suicide by Cop: Inducing the Police to Shoot* (2003) and is the author of 30 journal articles, academic book chapters, and technical reports exploring primarily topics on women in policing, law enforcement selection, ethics, law enforcement assisted suicide, comparative law enforcement systems, occupational stress, and workplace violence. Her career in policing began as a patrol officer and continued as a detective in a municipal police department in North Carolina. She subsequently instructed, then managed the Justice Services Division of the North Carolina Justice Academy, the state police academy, which is responsible for basic law enforcement training curricula and in-service training for police and sheriff agencies.

Kenneth J. Peak is professor and former chair of the Department of Criminal Justice at the University of Nevada, Reno (UNR). He entered municipal policing in Kansas in 1970 and subsequently held positions as criminal justice planner; director of the Four-State Technical Assistance Institute, Law Enforcement Assistance Administration (and concurrently instructing at

Washburn University of Topeka); director of university police, Pittsburg State University; and assistant professor at Wichita State University. He began at UNR in 1983, where he was named "Teacher of the Year" by the Honor Society and also served as acting director of public safety. He has authored or coauthored 14 textbooks on general policing, community policing, justice administration, and police supervision and management, and two historical books on bootlegging and temperance. He has also published more than 50 journal articles and additional book chapters on a wide range of justice-related subjects. He has served as chairman of the Police Section, Academy of Criminal Justice Sciences, and president of the Western and Pacific Association of Criminal Justice Educators. He received two gubernatorial appointments to statewide criminal justice committees while in Kansas and holds a doctorate from the University of Kansas.

Acknowledgments

This book is the result of the professional collaboration of several people at Prentice Hall. First, we wish to express our gratitude to Frank Mortimer, our acquisitions editor, who realized that this book would fill a gap in the policing literature and brought it to fruition; to his great credit, Frank believes that some books simply ought to be published because of a "social responsibility" to do so. Also, we wish to acknowledge the efforts of Dr. Roslyn Muraskin, series editor for Prentice Hall, as well as our production editor, Lynn Steines, whose expertise and efforts were certainly essential in all phases of bringing the book to closure. Furthermore, copyeditor Pam Rockwell improved the final product immensely. The authors also wish to acknowledge the invaluable assistance of Alex Del Carmen (University of Texas–Arlington, Arlington, TX), Connie Koepf (University at Buffalo, Buffalo, NY), and Allen Cowan (www.cowan-pi.com), whose reviews of the early manuscript resulted in many beneficial changes. Also, Mike Goo of the Washoe County (Nevada) Sheriff's Office, who provided excellent photographic assistance, certainly deserves mention. A final debt of gratitude is owed to all the female law enforcement officers at Charlotte–Mecklenburg Police Department and to all the female officers specifically named in the book for interviews and photographic assistance.

Introduction

Overview to Women in Law Enforcement Careers

Roslyn Muraskin

Series Editor

❖

When we speak of equality of the sexes, we understand that though on paper it *sounds* good, the reality is that it does not exist. Vast disparities still exist. Women are still "deprived of access to many measures and markers of social worth, including dignity, respect, resources, security, authority, credibility, speech, power and full citizenship" (MacKinnon, 2001, p. 2).

In the early 19th century we lived in a country that consisted mainly of agricultural communities. Police departments as we know them did not exist. When the city of Philadelphia in 1833 organized the first police force in this country, the organizers never envisioned the kind of forces we have today, or that there would be women police officers. The motto during the 19th and most of the 20th centuries was "Help wanted—women need not apply" (O'Connor, 2003, p. 441).

A feminist movement that had started when our Constitution was first written was rejuvenated when the all-important case of *Reed v. Reed* was decided in 1971. The case simply indicated that sex-based classification was subject to strict scrutiny under the 14th Amendment to our Constitution under the equal protection clause. There was to be no discrimination unless a rational reason was given. Although there was hope that the ensuing case, *Frontiero v. Richardson* (411 US 677, 1973) would establish that *sex* was a suspect classification, it failed to do so because of the plurality decision. The role of American women was brought even more to the forefront. "The issue was: Are women going to be able to compete in a police career on an equal footing with their male counterparts? The resounding answer from the police organizational culture in the United States was clear, direct and powerful. **No!**" (O'Connor, p. 443). Women were officers as far back as 1905 when the Indianapolis Police Department, taking a historic step, assigned two female officers to patrol on an equal basis with their male counterparts. But women were not as yet given credibility in the law enforcement profession.

Women were not wanted as full partners in the world of policing. After laws banning women from police work were overturned by the courts, we found ourselves in the latter part of the 20th century watching women entering the profession of law enforcement. Could women perform as well and equally with the men? The answer has been answered overwhelmingly with one word, **YES!** But to this day when we think of policing we think of police*men* not police*women*.

We still think of women as not being able to handle deadly force, yet all of the research proves the opposite. The fact is that few female and male police officers need to use deadly and excessive force in their jobs. Females tend to be less corrupt than their male counterparts, and they are less involved in cases of brutality. "Women police are often better at defusing and de-escalating potentially violent confrontations with citizens . . . " (Harrington and Lonsway, 2004, p. 497).

This work, *Women in Law Enforcement Careers: A Guide for Preparing and Succeeding,* discusses the problems that women have faced as they prepare for such careers and how to overcome these barriers. The media would have us believe that high-speed chases and shootings are a daily occurrence. This is not factual. Police on a daily basis probably spend about 80–90 percent of the time on noncriminal or service functions.

Physical ability has been found not to be the determinant in the proper performance of police duties. Jumping over six-foot walls is not the norm. Knowledge is more important and the use of it in the world of policing is of utmost importance. Stereotypes still exist as does physical ability testing, but these have become just that, stereotypes, and have little to do with the world of policing today. Female police officers have had to learn to accept and then to fight back in cases where they are verbally assaulted by other officers, and have also learned to fight back when their backup doesn't show up.

Challenges face the police*women* of the 21st century, but then women have always had to face such challenges. The current national economy warrants employing and recruiting women and minorities. There is a shift to community-oriented policing, and there are women today who will be the "first"—the first to have broken through the legal barriers in both large and small agencies. Once all obstacles are removed, equality will not be far behind.

This work reads almost as a "how-to-do-it" text. It discusses the main points in preparing for a career in law enforcement and how to succeed. This text, as part of the continuing women's series in criminal justice, will succeed because there are mentors who are writing and letting the female officers know how to do it and how to deal with certain situations. Through the use of this text, present and future female officers will learn how to become full participants in law enforcement, and then some. The police door is legally open to women; now take a deep breath and participate in a very rewarding career.

REFERENCES

Harrington, Penny, and Kimberly A. Lonsway (2004). "Current Barriers and Future Promises for Women in Policing," in *The Criminal Justice System and Women,* Barbara Raffel Price and Natalie J. Sokoloff, eds. Boston: McGraw Hill.

MacKinnon, Catharine (2001). *Sex Equality*. New York: Foundation Press.

O'Connor, Martine (2003). "Early Policing in the United States," in *It's a Crime: Women and Justice,* Roslyn Muraskin, author/editor. Upper Saddle River, NJ: Prentice Hall.

Foreword

Margaret M. Moore

Director, National Center for Women and Policing

Feminist Majority Foundation

❖

Plunging into a law enforcement career is not attractive to most women. Why? I have asked myself that question for many years. A law enforcement career is a "good fit" for women, though traditionally occupied by men. Research has shown that women officers use a style of policing that relies less on physical force and more on communications skills. And any good cop will tell you that policing is about "talking with people." Police departments do not reach out specifically to women and, in fact, some discourage women from applying to law enforcement agencies by presenting an aggressive and authoritarian image, an image based on the outdated paramilitary model of law enforcement.

Women have demonstrated that they are often far better at defusing potentially violent situations and are less likely to become involved in a citizen's complaint, or civil lawsuit for excessive use of force. Women have changed the way police respond to violence against women in communities. Women officers respond more effectively to domestic violence incidents, which in some police departments can account for approximately half of all of the violent crime calls. The importance of a police agency mirroring the community is vital for the future of policing. Clearly, the positive impact women have on policing is a message that is not being told.

When I asked a veteran New York City detective why he thought more women were not in policing and once there why they did not apply for promotions, he replied, "Encouragement." This was one man's view and, I believe, an accurate one. So, few women are in policing, as evidenced by a recent survey conducted by the National Center for Women and Policing, which found women constitute a national average of 12.7 percent for departments with over 100 sworn officers. It will take decades before gender equity is realized. With gender equity lacking, women are not as visible in the law enforcement profession and role modeling is limited.

Many of the women you will meet in this book will serve as role models and provide the critical and supportive environment necessary to "encourage" you to take the plunge. This veteran group of women speaks to each of you about exploring the possibility of a career in law enforcement. Look at each one as a personalized mentor guiding you through the challenges and rewards of a law enforcement career.

This guide is valuable to those women contemplating such a career because it contains the experiences of a diverse group of women. Not everyone experiences the same career, but many have experienced the same set of circumstances and offer strategies on how to overcome the barriers and take part in the true enjoyment a law enforcement career can bring to your life.

Get to know the value women bring to law enforcement and how positive change will happen as a result. The disparity between the numbers of men and women involved in policing adversely impacts the culture, the operations, and efficacy of law enforcement agencies all over the nation. Given the many difficult challenges facing modern policing, the imperative to hire more women has never been more urgent. As more women choose policing, the policies and practices to keep them there will become part of the culture, and that can only mean a great benefit to the communities they serve.

 **Margaret Moore** entered a law enforcement career in New York City in 1973, where her assignments included serving as an undercover narcotics police officer. In June 1976 she joined the New York Office of the Treasury Department's Bureau of Alcohol, Tobacco and Firearms (ATF), where she was promoted to positions of increasing responsibility, eventually becoming that agency's first woman special agent in charge; she retired in 1999 as the highest-ranking woman agent, the deputy assistant director for science and technology. In that position her responsibilities included oversight of the forensic labs, which successfully linked evidence involving Eric Robert Rudolf to the Atlanta Olympic Park bombing and other notable cases in Atlanta. Ms. Moore is considered an expert on antiabortion extremist violence (domestic terrorism) and conducts training for police departments in the United States, Ireland, and Australia. She joined the Feminist Majority in September 1999 and is the chief point of contact to federal, state and local law enforcement for the National Center for Women and Policing (NCWP), which has offices in Beverly Hills, California, and Arlington, Virginia, and advocates for increasing the number of women in law enforcement and gender equity. The NCWP conducts annual leadership training conferences on women and leadership, police reforms, strategies to increase the numbers of women in policing, and addressing violence against women. In June 1999, Ms. Moore incorporated Women in Federal Law Enforcement, a not-for-profit organization. She serves as the organization's director and develops an annual women's leadership conference that is attended by over 500 representatives from 60 federal agencies. Ms. Moore holds a B.A. in criminal justice from John Jay College of Criminal Justice in New York City and is a graduate of the Federal Executive Institute, Charlottesville, Virginia.

Preface

I [do not] believe in "careers" for women. A great responsibility rests upon woman—the training of children. This is her most beautiful task.

—Mother Jones
U.S. labor organizer, 1925

❖

Mother Jones typifies the historical view of many people toward women's work and might well represent the thinking of many people today in the United States and abroad. But while it is inarguable that the proper "training" and upbringing of children is one of the most serious responsibilities of any parent, it is also clear that today's women seek, obtain, and flourish in careers outside their homes to a far greater extent than Mother Jones could have foreseen.

This book is about women at work, specifically in the very demanding and often dangerous occupation of law enforcement. Although many justifiable, significant hurdles are to be negotiated by people of both genders seeking employment in this occupation, this book takes the reader through the challenges as they more specifically confront females.

During the past 30 years, the proportion of women serving as sworn law enforcement personnel has been growing, as several formal and often subjective barriers to hiring women have been modified or eliminated. Job discrimination lawsuits further expanded their opportunities; however, women remain overwhelmingly employed in the lowest tier of sworn police positions and in the minority in terms of the proportion of women holding top command positions (captain and higher). Obviously, women still have a long distance to travel in order to reach parity with men in this occupation.

First and foremost, police executives must see the value of utilizing women and vigorously recruit, hire, and retain them. Furthermore, as the community-oriented policing and problem-solving (COPPS) strategy continues to expand across the nation and the world, we believe that female officers can play an increasingly vital role in it. Indeed, many experts in the field believe the verbal skills that many women possess can help to usher in a "kinder, gentler organization."

The authors feel that this book serves as a unique and valuable resource for women who are interested in entering the often daunting and veiled world of policing. It also comprehensively addresses—in a blunt, no-nonsense fashion—the kinds of issues, problems, and challenges that these women will likely face in this quest. The book incorporates interviews concerning the careers and backgrounds of approximately 100 female law enforcement officers across the United States. These women are, or have been, employed in federal, state, and local agencies, with patrol duties, specialized and investigative duties, and administrative responsibilities. (Note that the term *law enforcement* is used throughout the text to include federal, state, and local agencies; furthermore, "local" law enforcement includes both municipal police departments and county sheriff's offices.) Although a protocol of structured questions was used with all of the women officers, most respondents provided information beyond that requested by the questionnaire, and the officers were also encouraged to expand on their responses. Most interviews lasted about two hours. The interviews were conducted privately and in their offices, patrol vehicles, and other locations such as public schools.

LEARNING AIDS

Each chapter of this book begins with an overview of the chapter's key terms and concepts. It is recommended that the reader examine these preliminary items prior to reading the chapter to obtain an overall flavor of the contents as well as some insight into more substantive aspects. In addition, at each chapter's end is a section entitled "Reader Learning Outcomes," explaining which of the chapter's main points the reader should understand upon its completion. Other instructional aids include the figures, tables, and exhibits that are included in several chapters. Finally, a listing of relevant websites and addresses is provided in Appendix IV for readers who wish to independently obtain more information about various aspects of women in policing.

The authors bring more than 62 years of combined scholarly and policing backgrounds to this effort; as a result, the book contains a "real-world" flavor not commonly found. From its introduction, written by Margaret Moore, Director of the National Center for Women in Policing, in Beverly Hills, California, through to the final chapter, the reader will receive a penetrating view of what is certainly one of the most difficult and challenging occupations in America. The book is written primarily for women wishing to enter its inner sanctum.

CHAPTER ORGANIZATION AND CONTENTS IN BRIEF

This book is composed of nine chapters. The first four chapters generally establish the nature of the law enforcement field and women's evolution and contemporary status within it. Because many readers will have little knowledge about the levels and structure of law enforcement organizations, the role of the officer or agent, the nature of community policing, and constitutional limitations that are placed on the police, we provide that kind of fundamental information in Chapter 1. Note that the federal law enforcement system has changed dramatically since 9/11 and the creation of the new Department of Homeland Security; therefore, that agency is the centerpiece of this chapter.

Chapter 2 provides a historical overview of women as they began to enter policing, beginning prior to 1920 and continuing up to the present day. The several reforms for, and greater responsibilities that were placed on, women officers are included in this discussion. Chapter 3 reviews the several legislative enactments and court decisions that helped open the doors to women in the workplace generally.

Chapter 4 focuses on the contemporary scene of women in policing, providing a quantitative profile of their representation in various types of agencies, their representation as supervisors and managers, and personal glimpses into their early and present-day lives. An underlying theme is that prospective female law enforcement officers should carefully examine and select an agency for employment, one that has come to appreciate women as important assets to law enforcement.

Next come two wide-ranging chapters that generally explore the trials, tribulations, and successes of women in law enforcement today. Chapter 5 examines the research surrounding female officers' overall performance; the attitudes of male officers, citizens, and the female officers themselves concerning women in policing; how women cope and adapt to the challenges of the job, including occupational stress; some issues that are unique to female officers of color; and female officers' roles in community policing and problem solving.

Chapter 6 details the "hurdle process"—the selection, hiring, and training methods—that are employed by most local law enforcement agencies. This discussion will provide interested persons with a high degree of insight concerning the kinds of tests they would confront upon choosing law enforcement as a career and initiating the hiring process; they will also be better able to begin to prepare themselves for this undertaking, both physically and mentally. Some anecdotal information gleaned from veteran female officers is included.

Chapters 7 and 8 focus on the information obtained in a structured questionnaire of approximately 100 women who are now or have been in the law enforcement field. Their journeys into this traditionally male-oriented and dominated occupation provide much wisdom and advice for others who wish to follow their example. These chapters also underscore the variety of job opportunities that are available to women at all levels of law enforcement.

Challenges of the future are discussed in Chapter 9, including the kinds of general demographic and crime-related changes that are anticipated for the nation and some major future issues that will concern selection and training, community policing, diversity, and the need for greater numbers of women in leadership roles.

Four appendices complement the information that is provided in the foregoing chapters. First, an example of the community-policing and problem-solving strategy appears in Appendix I. Then, to demonstrate what some cities are doing to recruit more women into their police ranks, some successful strategies are shown in Appendix II. To further enlighten the reader about contemporary law enforcement (see Chapter 1) and to augment the discussion of the hiring process in Chapter 6, a sample resume is provided in Appendix III. And, as mentioned earlier, selected police-related websites are listed in Appendix IV.

Chapter 1

Laying the Foundation: An Overview of Law Enforcement

❖

Key Chapter Terms

Blanket waiver
Community-Oriented
    Policing and Problem
    Solving (COPPS)
Discretion
Esprit de corps
GIS

Investigative functions
Moonlighting
Organizational structure
Police groupies
Police role
Residency requirements
Seniority

Sexual misconduct
Shift assignment
Shoot/don't shoot
Stop-and-frisk search
Support functions

Knowledge is power.

—Popular saying

Learn how to be a police(woman), because that cannot be improvised.

—Pope John XXIII

Introduction

This chapter provides a basic introduction to the occupation of law enforcement to prepare the way for the later discussions of this field and the role that women are asked to play in it. Included here are descriptions of law enforcement at the federal, state, and local levels, including their **organizational structure**; the roles and duties of the police, including their use of **discretion** and a look at their work by **shift assignment**; community-oriented policing and problem solving, the dominant strategy used in policing; constitutional limitations that have been placed on the rights and privileges of officers; and the occupational stress that they often endure. In sum, this chapter shows how law enforcement is organized and functions in its attempt to control crime and disorder.

It should be noted that many additional functions of law enforcement officers are examined in later chapters.

FEDERAL LAW ENFORCEMENT AGENCIES

The Department of Homeland Security

The new Department of Homeland Security (DHS), created in 2002, put 180,000 new federal employees to work. The primary enforcement arm of DHS is a newly established Bureau of Immigration and Customs Enforcement (ICE). ICE has a broad mission and vast investigative authority, from terrorist financing, money laundering, and illegal arms dealing to immigration fraud and the smuggling of migrants.[1]

DHS's 23 federal agencies compose five major divisions, or "Directorates":

1. Border and Transportation Security (BTS)
2. Emergency Preparedness and Response
3. Science and Technology (S&T)
4. Information Analysis and Infrastructure Protection (IAIP)
5. Management

In addition to these five directorates, other critical agencies have been newly created or have been folded into DHS, including the U.S. Coast Guard, U.S. Secret Service, and the Bureau of Citizenship and Immigration Services. Figure 1–1 shows the DHS organizational structure and all of its key components.

The Department of Justice

The U.S. Department of Justice is headed by the attorney general and is the official legal arm of the government of the United States. Within this department are several law en-

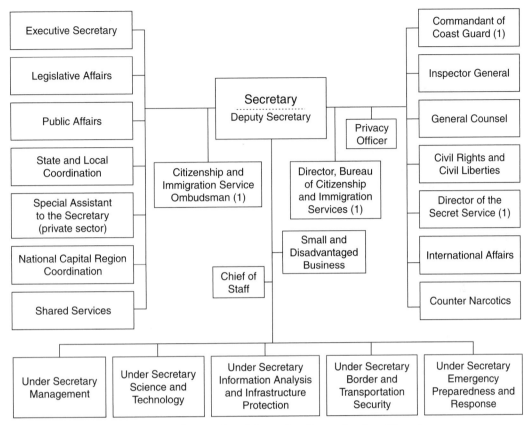

FIGURE 1–1   Department of Homeland Security Organization Structure

forcement organizations that investigate violations of federal laws (see Figure 1–2), some of which are discussed briefly here.

Federal Bureau of Investigation (FBI) The national priorities of the FBI have been modified in major ways since 9/11. Today, the agency's top priorities are to protect the United States from terrorist attack, foreign intelligence operations and espionage, cyber-based attacks, and high-technology crimes. Beyond these, its priorities include combating public corruption, transnational and national criminal organizations, white-collar crime, and significant violent crime and protecting civil rights.[2]

Source: Courtesy FBI.

Alcohol, Tobacco, Firearms, and Explosives (ATF) ATF's general mission is to regulate the production of millions of gallons of beer, wine, and distilled spirits[3] and to reduce the illegal use of firearms and explosives. These regulatory functions extend to tobacco and arson. The ATF is in charge of investigating the character and background of applicants for automatic weapons and of authorizing licenses for firearms dealers, firearms importers and exporters, and ammunition manufacturers.[4] The problem of high explosives has become a major ATF concern as well.

Source: Courtesy ATF.

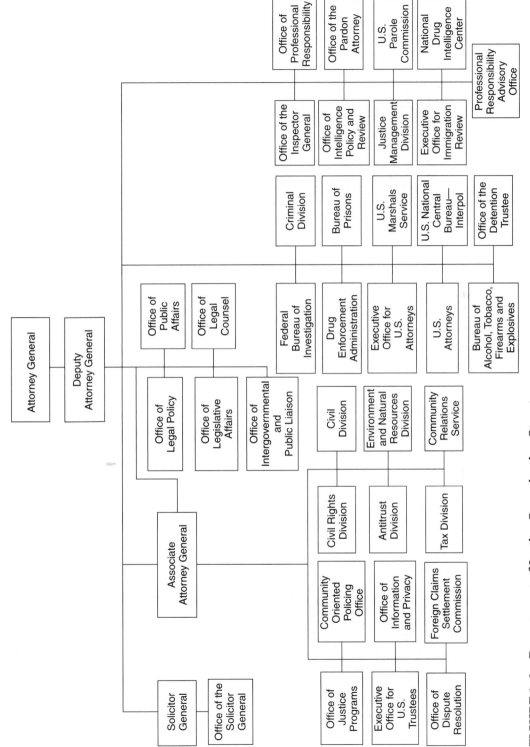

FIGURE 1-2   Department of Justice Organization Structure

Source: Courtesy DEA.

Drug Enforcement Administration (DEA) The major responsibilities of the DEA under the United States Code are (1) the development of an overall federal drug enforcement strategy, including programs, planning, and evaluation; (2) full investigation of violations of all federal drug trafficking laws, including suspects seized with illicit drugs at U.S. ports of entry and international borders; (3) full coordination and cooperation with state and local police officials on joint drug enforcement efforts, as well as with drug enforcement officials of foreign governments; and (4) regulation of the legal manufacture of drugs and other controlled substances.[5]

United States Marshals Service (USMS) Virtually every federal law enforcement initiative involves the USMS. Its agents secure prisoners for trial; protect the courts, judges, attorneys, and witnesses; track and arrest fugitives; and manage and dispose of seized drug assets.[6]

Source: Courtesy USM.

OTHER FEDERAL AGENCIES

Central Intelligence Agency (CIA)

The CIA participates in undercover and covert operations around the world for the purposes of managing crises and the conduct of war. To accomplish its mission, the CIA engages in research and development of high technology for intelligence purposes. With the advent of terrorist attacks in this country, the CIA has created special centers to address such issues as counterterrorism, counterintelligence, international organized crime and narcotics trafficking, and arms control intelligence.[7] The CIA is an independent agency, responsible to the president through its director of central intelligence.

Internal Revenue Service (IRS)

The IRS has as its main function the monitoring and collection of federal income taxes from American individuals and businesses. Since 1919, the IRS has had a criminal investigation division (CI)—employing "accountants with a badge"—that investigates possible criminal violations of income tax laws and recommends appropriate criminal prosecution whenever warranted.[8]

Source: Courtesy IRS.

STATE AND LOCAL LAW ENFORCEMENT AGENCIES

There are now about 17,800 state and local law enforcement agencies in the United States,[9] employing about 708,000 sworn, full-time personnel,[10] of which about 440,000 are municipal employees, 165,000 are sheriff's personnel, and 56,000 are state law enforcement agency employees[11] (the remainder are special jurisdiction personnel, who serve at educational institutions, state capitols, and so forth).

Agents of the 49 state law enforcement agencies (Hawaii has no such agency) are employed in state bureaus. The agents perform routine criminal **investigative functions** and specialized operations, such as investigations of organized crime or livestock brand theft. State investigators often assist local police agencies in investigative matters, such as performing background checks on police applicants.

Municipal police departments have general police responsibilities, including such functions as traffic enforcement, accidents investigation, patrol and first response to incidents, property and violent crime investigation, and death investigation.

The 3,000 sheriff's offices in the country have diverse roles. The following is a list of their functions:

1. Maintenance and operation of the county correctional institutions. Most (about 80 percent) of the nation's sheriff's departments are responsible for operating a jail[12]
2. Service of civil processes (protective orders, liens, evictions, garnishments and attachments), extradition and transportation of prisoners
3. Collection of certain taxes and real estate sales (usually for nonpayment of taxes) for the county
4. Routine order-maintenance duties (enforcing state statutes and county ordinances); arresting offenders and performing traffic and criminal investigations
5. Service as bailiff of the courts

Organizational Structures

Every law enforcement agency, no matter what its size, has a unique organizational structure that divides up the agency's various responsibilities and shows its chain of command. The organizational structure is flexible; it can be modified as resources and needs change. Figure 1–3 shows all of the fundamental functions of a police organization.

Operations (also known as line element) personnel are engaged in active police functions in the field. They may be subdivided into primary and secondary operations elements. The patrol function—often called the "backbone" of policing—is the primary operational element because of its major responsibility for general policing, providing routine patrols, conducting criminal and traffic investigations, and making arrests. The investigative and youth functions are the secondary operations elements.

The **service functions** fall into two broad categories: staff (or "administrative") services and auxiliary (or "technical") services. The staff services usually involve personnel matters and include recruitment, training, promotion, planning and research, community relations, and public information services. Auxiliary services are the kinds of functions that a nonpolice or civilian person rarely sees. They include jail management, property and evidence, crime laboratory services, communications, and records and identification. These

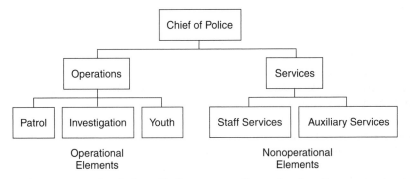

FIGURE 1–3   Basic Law Enforcement Organization Structure

types of services offer many career opportunities for persons interested in police-related work but who, for some reason, cannot or do not want to be a field officer.

Obviously, the larger the agency, the greater the need for specialization and the more vertical the organizational chart will become. With greater specialization comes the need and opportunity for officers to be assigned to different tasks. For example, in a medium-sized department serving a community of 100,000 or more, it would be possible for a police officer with ten years of police experience to have been a dog handler, a motorcycle officer, a detective, and/or a traffic officer while simultaneously holding a slot on the special weapons or hostage negotiation teams.

THE POLICE ROLE

Four Primary Duties

Police officers encounter all manner of situations while engaged in routine patrol—situations that they discover themselves and problems phoned in by citizens. When reduced to fundamentals, however, local law enforcement officers (including municipal police and sheriff's office personnel) may be said to perform four basic functions:

1. Enforcing the laws
2. Performing welfare tasks: a very broad category that includes such functions as handling "attempt to locate" calls, usually involving missing persons, and "attempt to contact" and "be on the lookout" calls, such as an out-of-town individual needing the police to try to locate someone in order to deliver a message; also included are "check the welfare of" calls, where a person hasn't been seen or heard from for some time and relatives are concerned; maintaining or assisting animal control units; reporting burned-out street lights or damaged stolen traffic lights and signs; delivering death messages; and delivering blood to hospitals
3. Preventing crime: patrolling and such tasks as providing the public with information on locks and lighting to reduce the opportunity for crime
4. Protecting the innocent: investigating crimes systematically removes innocent people from consideration as crime suspects[13]

Today, women working in local law enforcement are in both sworn and non-sworn positions—outside on patrol, inside with inmates, in communications, as well as in a variety of other assignments.
Source: Courtesy Washoe County (Nevada) Sheriff's Office.

The American Bar Association's *Standards Relating to the Urban Police Function* identified 11 elements of the **police role**:

1. To identify criminals and criminal activity and, where appropriate, apprehend offenders and participate in court proceedings
2. To reduce the opportunities for the commission of crime through preventive patrol and other measures
3. To aid individuals who are in danger of physical harm
4. To protect constitutional guarantees
5. To facilitate the movement of peoples and vehicles
6. To assist those who cannot care for themselves
7. To resolve conflict
8. To identify problems that are potentially serious law enforcement or government problems
9. To create and maintain a feeling of security in the community
10. To promote and preserve civil order
11. To provide other services on an emergency basis[14]

Use of Discretion

Ours is supposed to be a government of laws and not of people, but that is simply a myth, at least in the manner in which the law is applied. Official discretion pervades all levels and most agencies of government. The discretionary power of the police is awesome.

What determines whether the officer will take a stern approach (enforcing the letter of the law with an arrest) or be lenient (issuing a verbal warning or some other outcome short of arrest)? First, the *officer's attitude* is a consideration. Police, being human, bring to work either a happy or unhappy disposition. Another major consideration is the *citizen's attitude*. If the offender is rude and condescending and denies having done anything wrong, the probable outcome is obvious. On the other hand, the person who is honest with the officer, avoids attempts at intimidation and sarcasm, and doesn't try to the "beat the rap" will normally fare better.[15]

Patrol Work as a Function of Shift Assignment

The nature of patrol work is also related to the officer's particular shift assignment. Following are general descriptions of the nature of the work on each of the three shifts (three eight-hour shifts per day).[16]

The day shift (approximately 8:00 A.M. to 4:00 P.M.) probably has the greatest contact with citizens. Officers may start their days by watching school crossings and unsnarling traffic jams. Also, speeders and traffic accidents are more common in the morning as people hurry to work. School and civic presentations and other such programs are numerous during the day. Most errands and nonpolice duties assigned to the police are performed by day-shift officers, such as unlocking parking lots, escorting people, delivering agendas to city council members, transporting evidence to court, and seeing that maintenance is performed on patrol vehicles, among other tasks. But day shift officers are also more likely to be summoned to such major crimes as armed robberies and bomb threats. Even so, this shift often has lull periods, as most people are at work or in school. Usually officers with more seniority work the day shift.

The "swing" or evening shift (4:00 P.M. to 12:00 P.M.) comes on duty in time to untangle evening traffic jams and respond to a variety of complaints from the public. Youths are out of school and feeling their oats, shops are beginning to close and, as darkness falls, officers must begin checking commercial doors and windows on their beat; new officers are amazed at the frequency with which business people leave their buildings unsecured. Warm weather brings increased drinking and partying, along with noise complaints. Domestic disturbances begin to occur, and the action at bars and nightclubs is beginning to pick up; soon fights will break out. Many major events, such as sports and concerts, occur in the evenings, so crowd and traffic control are often required. Toward the end of the shift, fast-food and other businesses begin complaining about loitering and trash on the premises from teenage gatherings. Arrests are much more frequent than for the day shift, and officers must attempt to take one last look at the businesses on the beat before ending their shift to ensure that none has been burglarized during the evening and night hours. That done, arrest and incident reports often must be completed before officers may leave the station house for home.

The night shift (12:00 P.M. to 8:00 A.M.), known throughout history as the "graveyard" shift, is an entirely different world. Because of its adverse effects on the officer's sleeping and eating habits, this shift is usually worked by newer officers (who also, because of low seniority, work most weekends and holidays), but only long enough for the officer to build enough seniority to transfer to another shift. Few officers actually like the shift enough to want to devote a large number of years of their career working it. (Note that many agencies also have shift rotation, transferring their officers from one shift to another at fixed intervals.)

Officers come on duty fresh, ready for action in those states where bars and taverns legally must close at midnight. From about midnight to 3 A.M. the night shift is quite busy. Traffic is relatively heavy for several hours, and then normally drops off to a trickle. The "night people" begin to come out—those people who sleep in the daytime and prowl at night, including the burglars. The nightly "cat and mouse" game begins between the cops and the robbers. Night shift officers come to know who these people are and their vehicles, preferred crimes, habits, and hangouts. Night shift officers spend much of the night patrolling alleys and businesses, working their spotlight as they seek signs of suspicious activity, open doors and windows in businesses, and unlawful entry. They also watch the residential areas, performing courtesy checks of homes in general or with greater scrutiny where people are away on vacation and have asked the police for a periodic check of their property.

Such patrol is inevitably very eerie in nature. Officers typically work alone under the cover of darkness, often without hope of rapid backup units, although where possible, greater attention is given to providing back up to night shift officers, even during traffic stops. The police never know who or what awaits them around the next dark corner. The protective shroud of darkness given to the offenders makes the night shift officers more wary. After midnight, "graveyard" officers view alleys as theirs alone; anyone violating the peace of "their" alleys—especially one of the known "night people" or anyone wearing dark clothing or engaging in other suspicious activity—should be prepared to explain his/her actions and presence. Such persons may also be compelled to submit to a **stop-and-frisk** (pat down) **search**, which is not uncommon under such circumstances.

Once the alleys and buildings have been checked, the officers begin rechecking them, avoiding any routine pattern that burglars may discern. (Some burglars can tell which beats are "open," that is, wide open for burglarizing, by observing which patrol vehicles are parked at the station or at restaurants; therefore, officers need to vary their patrol routine each night.) At 2:00 or 3:00 in the morning, boredom can set in. Some officers welcome this change of pace while others loathe it and look for ways to fight the monotony of the "dog watch." For them, the occasional high-speed chase may be a welcome adrenaline rush, as are crimes in progress. Other means of staying alert include meeting and chatting with other officers who are also bored with patrol and coffee stops; however, these officers must be mentally prepared for action. They know that while this is normally a quiet shift after the initial activity, when something does occur on the night shift, it is often a major incident or crime.

COMMUNITY POLICING AND PROBLEM SOLVING

Given its spread across the nation as well as around the world and the frequent reference made to it in the following chapters, it is necessary to discuss the **community-oriented policing and problem solving (COPPS)** strategy and women's role in it. Because many books and articles about COPPS have been written and are available, here we present only a brief sketch of this contemporary approach to addressing crime and disorder.

A "Sweep" of the Nation

COPPS is indeed sweeping the nation. State and local police agencies now have about 113,000 community policing officers, compared to about 21,000 in 1997. Nearly two-thirds (64 percent) of local police departments serving 86 percent of all U.S. residents have full-time officers engaged in community policing activities.[17]

COPPS represents a dramatic shift from the traditional methods of policing. During policing's professional era (roughly from the 1930s to the 1980s), officers were often evaluated on their ability to go from call to call ("get in and get out"); they might even be chastised for leaving their patrol vehicles and interacting with citizens. The emphases were on law, technology, and crime fighting. Several quantitative measures were used to determine officer effectiveness, including response time; number of arrests, calls for service, citations, and crime clearance rates; and even the numbers of miles driven during a shift. Officers were reactive and accomplished little in the way of long-term problem solving. Meanwhile, crime rates were spiraling upward. Obviously, a different approach was needed.

What exactly is COPPS? Following is a definition that captures the essence of this concept:

> Community oriented policing and problem solving (COPPS) is a proactive philosophy that promotes solving problems that are criminal, affect our quality of life, or increase our fear of crime, as well as other community issues. COPPS involves identifying, analyzing, and addressing community problems at their source.[18]

Two principal and interrelated components emerge from this definition: community engagement (partnerships) and problem solving. The partnership between police departments and the communities they serve is essential. Problems are handled in a far different manner and involve listening to concerns of citizens and developing a better understanding of the community's problems and using other government resources.

The SARA Problem-Solving Process

The COPPS strategy involves solving problems through the use of a four-step process called SARA (Figure 1–4). An example of COPPS and the use of the SARA process is provided in Appendix I.

Scanning: Problem Identification Scanning means problem identification. Officers conduct a preliminary inquiry to determine if a problem really exists and whether further analysis is needed. They may look at calls-for-service data, especially repeat calls, crime analysis information, police reports, and officers' own experiences. Scanning helps the officer to determine whether a problem really exists before moving on to more in-depth analysis.

Analysis: Determining the Extent of the Problem Analysis is the most difficult and important step in the process. Here, officers gather as much information as possible from a variety of sources. Officers identify the seriousness of the problem, all persons affected, and the underlying causes. Mapping and geographic information systems **(GIS)** can identify patterns of crime and "hot spots." Police offense reports can also be analyzed for suspect characteristics, victim characteristics, and information about high-crime areas and addresses. Computer-aided dispatch (CAD) is also helpful, as it collects data on all incidents and specific locations from which an unusual number of incidents require a police response.

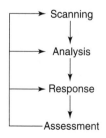

FIGURE 1–4   Problem-Solving Process
Source: John E. Eck and William Spelman, *Problem-Solving; Problem-Oriented Policing in Newport News* (Washington, DC: U.S. Department of Justice, National Institute of Justice, 1987), p. 43.

Response: Formulating Tailor-Made Strategies Once a problem has been clearly defined, officers seek the most effective responses. Responses to problems, however, rarely involve a single agency or tactic or quick fix. More appropriate responses often involve the police and public and other appropriate entities, including businesses, private and social service organizations, and other government agencies.

Assessment: Evaluating Overall Effectiveness The final stage of the SARA process is assessment. Here, officers evaluate the effectiveness of their responses and may use the results to revise their responses, collect more data, or even redefine the problem.

CONSTITUTIONAL LIMITATIONS

As stated at the beginning of this chapter, knowledge is power. Certainly it behooves women to be as knowledgeable as possible about how a career may alter their lives. In that vein, we next examine several areas in which police officers, by virtue of their position, are compelled to give up certain constitutional rights, at least compared to civilians.

Free Speech

Although the right of freedom of speech is one of the most fundamental and cherished of all American rights, the Supreme Court has indicated that "the State has interests as an employer in regulating the speech of its employees that differ significantly from those it possesses in connection with regulation of the speech of the citizenry in general.[19] Thus the state may impose restrictions on its employees that it would not be able to impose on the citizenry at large. However, these restrictions must be reasonable. For example, a department may not prohibit "any activity, conversation, deliberation, or discussion which is derogatory to the Department," as such a rule obviously prohibits all criticism of the agency by its officers, even in private conversation.[20]

Personal appearance is another area of restriction related to the First Amendment. The Supreme Court has upheld the enforcement of several grooming standards (regarding hairstyle and so on) and policies for the wearing of the uniform for police officers based on the necessity of making them readily recognizable to the public and to maintain the **esprit de corps** within the department.[21]

Searches and Seizures

The Fourth Amendment to the U.S. Constitution protects "the right of the people to be secure in their persons, houses, papers, and effects, against unreasonable searches and seizures." The Fourth Amendment usually applies to police officers when they are at home or are off duty in the same manner as it applies to all citizens. However, because of the nature of their work, police officers can be compelled to cooperate with investigations of their behavior when ordinary citizens would not. Examples would include equipment and lockers provided by the department to the officers. In these instances, officers have no expectation of privacy that affords or merits protection.[22]

However, lower courts have established limitations where searches of employees themselves are concerned. The right of prison authorities to search employees arose in a 1985 Iowa case, where employees were forced to sign a consent form as a condition of hire. The court disagreed with such a broad policy, ruling that the consent form did not constitute a **blanket waiver** of all Fourth Amendment rights.[23] Police officers may also be forced to appear in a lineup, which is a clear "seizure" of his or her person.

Self-Incrimination

The Supreme Court has also addressed questions concerning the Fifth Amendment as it applies to police officers who are under investigation. In *Garrity v. New Jersey*,[24] a police officer was ordered by the attorney general to answer questions or be discharged. The officer testified that information obtained as a result of his answers was later used to convict him of criminal charges. The Supreme Court held that the information obtained from the officer could not be used against him at his criminal trial because the Fifth Amendment forbids the use of coerced confessions. It is proper, however, to fire a police officer who refuses to answer questions that are related directly to the performance of his or her duties, provided that the officer has been informed that any answers may not be used later in a criminal proceeding.[25]

Religious Practices

Police work requires that personnel are available and on duty 24 hours per day, seven days a week. Although it is not always convenient or pleasant, such shift configurations require that many officers work weekends, nights, and holidays. It is generally assumed that one who takes such a position agrees to work such hours and abide by other such conditions, and it is usually the personnel with the least seniority on the job who must work the most undesirable shifts. However, there are occasions when one's religious beliefs are in direct conflict with the requirements of the job, such as the carrying of firearms, attendance at religious services, or periods of religious observance that occur during one's shift assignments. In these situations, the employee may be forced to choose between his or her job and religion. Title VII of the Civil Rights Act of 1964 prohibits religious discrimination in employment. Thus, Title VII requires reasonable accommodation of religious beliefs, but not to the extent that the employee has complete freedom of religious expression.[26]

Sexual Misconduct

To be blunt, there is ample opportunity for police officers to become engaged in adulterous or extramarital affairs. It is likely that no other occupation or profession offers the opportunities for **sexual misconduct** that policing does. It has been long established that **police "groupies"**—people who are sexually attracted to the uniform, weapons, or power of the police officer—may seek to participate in sexual activities with officers. Police officers frequently work alone, usually without direct supervision, in activities that involve frequent contact with citizens, usually in relative isolation. The problem seems to be pervasive in police departments from the smallest to the largest. Unfortunately, it is also an area of police behavior that is not easily quantified or understood.[27] In a related vein, several federal courts have recently considered whether police agencies have a legitimate interest in the sexual activities of their officers where such activities do not affect job performance. In one such case[28] the court held that the dismissal of a married police officer for living with another person's spouse was a violation of the officer's privacy and associational rights.

Residency Requirements

Many government agencies specify that all or certain members in their employment must live within the geographical limits of their employing jurisdiction. In other words, employees must reside within the county or city of employment. Such **residency requirements** have been justified on the grounds that officers should become familiar with and be visible in the jurisdiction of employment or that they should reside where they are paid by the taxpayers to work. Perhaps the strongest rationale given by employing agencies is that criminal justice employees must live within a certain proximity to their work in order to respond quickly in the event of an emergency.

Moonlighting

Moonlighting is holding a second job in addition to one's normal, full-time occupation. The courts have traditionally supported police agencies placing limitations on the amount and kinds of outside work their employees can perform. For example, police restrictions on moonlighting range from a complete ban on outside employment to permission to engage in certain forms of work, such as investments, private security, teaching police science courses, and so on. The rationale for agency limitations is that "outside employment seriously interferes with keeping the [police and fire] departments fit and ready for action at all times."[29]

Misuse of Firearms

Police agencies typically attempt to restrain the use of firearms through written policies and frequent training of a "**shoot/don't shoot**" nature. Still, a broad range of potential and actual problems remains with respect to the use and possible misuse of firearms. Police agencies generally have policies regulating the use of handguns and other firearms by their officers, both on and off duty. The courts have held that such regulations need only be reasonable and that the burden rests with the disciplined police officer to show that the regulation was arbitrary and unreasonable.[30]

Police firearms regulations tend to address three basic issues: (1) requirements for the safeguarding of the weapon, (2) guidelines for carrying the weapon while off duty, and (3) limitations on when the weapon may be fired.[31] Courts and juries are increasingly becoming more harsh in dealing with police officers who misuse their firearms. The current tendency is to "look behind" police shootings in order to determine if the officer acted negligently or the employing agency negligently trained and supervised the officer/ employee.

U.S. law enforcement officers are frequently exposed to places that are "brutish" and dangerous.

OCCUPATIONAL STRESS

There is a side of policing that we would prefer to ignore, but which must be acknowledged: the stress that is induced by the job. Stress is a force that is external in nature, causing strain upon the body, both physical and emotional. The job of enforcing the laws and helping people when they are at their worst has never been easy, but today it has been made worse by the war on drugs and by violent criminals.

There are several potential sources of stress for police officers, including those that originate within one's agency as well as outside. Stressors can include poor supervision, an inadequate reward system (perks similar to those in the private sector not available to government workers), policies and guidelines that officers may find offensive, large amounts of paperwork, verbal and physical abuse by some citizens, adverse work scheduling (often working nights, weekends, and holidays), fear and danger, and people pain (for example, the emotional and physical suffering endured by crime victims).

Eventually, if officers do not relieve their stress, they may suffer any of a variety of physical and/or emotional problems. It is therefore imperative that officers learn to manage their stress before it causes such harm by engaging in hobbies or activities that provide relaxation and practicing proper lifestyle choices such as exercise and proper nutrition, not smoking, and using alcohol with moderation.

SUMMARY

This chapter has provided the reader with a fundamental view of the often obscure world of law enforcement by discussing federal, state, and local law enforcement agencies, including their organizational structure, and the individual officer's role, community policing and problem solving, and officers' restricted constitutional rights. The chapter also revealed that law enforcement is one of the most rapidly changing, challenging, and rewarding occupations in America. As noted earlier, a more expansive look at fundamental aspects of law enforcement is taken in later chapters, particularly in Chapter 6 on the hiring process and Chapters 7 and 8, which specifically discuss or interview women who are actively engaged in law enforcement.

READER LEARNING OUTCOMES

Having examined this chapter, the reader should understand:

- the basic jurisdictional and functional responsibilities of federal, state, and local law enforcement agencies
- the organizational structure of a typical police agency
- the four basic duties of police officers
- the 11 elements of the police role as outlined by the American Bar Association
- the limitations placed on law enforcement officers regarding free speech, search and seizure, self-incrimination, religious practices, and other aspects of life
- the four primary tasks of the police
- the use of discretionary authority as a major part of policing
- how patrol work varies in terms of the shift to which an officer is assigned
- the community policing strategy and its four-step problem-solving process
- how stress in law enforcement must be recognized and managed

NOTES

1. U.S. Department of Homeland Security, Bureau of Immigration and Customs Enforcement, "Immigration and Customs Enforcement Statement," http://uscis.gov/graphics/publicaffairs/statements/032003_ICE.htm (accessed January 4, 2004).
2. Personal communication. Edward Duffer, September 23, 2003.
3. U.S. Department of the Treasury, Bureau of Alcohol, Tobacco, and Firearms, *Ready Reference 1994* (Washington, DC: U.S. Government Printing Office, 1994), p. 3.
4. U.S. Department of the Treasury, Bureau of Alcohol, Tobacco, and Firearms, *1993 Explosives Incidents Reports* (Washington, DC: Author, 1994), p. 65.
5. "DEA Mission Statement," http://www.usdoj.gov.dea/agency/mission.htm (accessed January 6, 2004).
6. Central Intelligence Agency, "CIA Vision, Mission, and Values," http://www.cia.gov/cia/information/mission.html (accessed January 4, 2005).

7. "About the CIA," http://www.cia.gov/cia/information/info.html (accessed January 5, 2005).

8. U.S. Department of Justice, Bureau of Justice Statistics Bulletin, *Federal Law Enforcement Officers, 1996* (Washington, DC: Author, December 1997), p. 3.

9. United States Department of Justice, Bureau of Justice Statistics Bulletin, *Census of State and Local Law Enforcement Agencies, 2000* (Washington, DC: Author, October 2002), p. 1.

10. Ibid.

11. Ibid., p. 2.

12. United States Department of Justice, Bureau of Justice Statistics Executive Summary, *Sheriff's Departments, 1997* (October 1999), pp. 1–3.

13. Kenneth J. Peak, *Policing America: Methods, Issues, Challenges*, 4th ed. (Upper Saddle River, NJ: Prentice Hall, 2003), pp. 57–58.

14. American Bar Association, *Standards Relating to the Urban Police Function* (Chicago: Author, 1973), p. 7.

15. Peak, *Policing America*, pp. 134–135.

16. Ibid., pp. 124–125.

17. M. J. Hickman and Brian A. Reaves, *Community policing in local police departments, 1997 and 1999*. Washington, DC: U.S. Department of Justice, Bureau of Justice Statistics Special Report (February 2001), pp. 1–3.

18. Kenneth J. Peak and Ronald W. Glensor, *Community Policing and Problem Solving: Strategies and Practices,* 4th ed. (Upper Saddle River, NJ: Prentice Hall, 2005), p. 80.

19. *Pickering v. Board of Education*, 391 U.S. 563 (1968), at p. 568.

20. *Muller v. Conlisk*, 429 F.2d 901 (7th Cir. 1970).

21. *Kelley v. Johnston*, 425 U.S. 238 (1976).

22. See *People v. Tidwell*, 266 N E.2d 787 (III. 1971).

23. *McDonell v. Hunter*, 611 F. Supp. 1122 (SD Iowa, 1985), affd. as mod., 809 F.2d 1302 (8th Cir. 1987).

24. *Garrity v. New Jersey*, 385 U.S. 483 (1967).

25. See *Gabrilowitz v. Newman*, 582 F.2d 100 (1st Cir. 1978).

26. *United States v. City of Albuquerque*, 12 EPD 11, 244 (10th Cir.); also see *Trans World Airlines v. Hardison*, 97 S.Ct. 2264 (1977).

27. Allen D. Sapp, *Police Officer Sexual Misconduct: A Field Research Study*, in Paul F. Cromwell and Roger G. Dunham (eds.), *Crime and Justice in America: Present Realities and Future Prospects* (Upper Saddle River, NJ: Prentice Hall, 1997), pp. 139–151.

28. See *Briggs v. North Muskegon Police Department*, 563 F. Supp 585 (W. D. Mich. 1983), aff'd 746 F.2d 1475 (6th Cir. 1984).

29. Richard N. Williams, *Legal Aspects of Discipline by Police Administrators*, Traffic Institute Publication 2705 (Evanston, IL: Northwestern University, 1975), p. 4.

30. See *Lally v. Department of Police*, 306 So.2d 65 (La. 1974).

31. Charles R. Swanson, Leonard Territo, and Robert W. Taylor, *Police Administration*, 5th ed. (Upper Saddle River, NJ: 2001), pp. 469–473.

Chapter 2

Women Enter Law Enforcement: A Historical Overview

--- ❖ ---

Key Chapter Terms

Administrative positions

Car 47

Competitive examinations

Crime Commission

Crime prevention

Desk sergeant

Discrimination

Diversity

Gender-based units

Great Depression

Operatives

Policewoman

Predelinquents

Prison matrons

Social work

Uniformed patrol duties

Women divisions

Women are no longer indentured to the kitchens, baby carriages, or bedrooms of America. There will be no turning back to the days when women found it necessary to justify their existence by producing babies or cleaning houses. Women have chosen to desert those kitchens and plunge exuberantly into the formerly all-male quarters of the working world.

—Freda Adler, *Sisters in Crime*[1]

Introduction

As will be seen in Chapter 4, today approximately 14.5 percent of all law enforcement officers in the United States are women. This figure may seem remarkably high to some; others, however, may view this figure as woefully low, given that nearly a century has passed since a woman first entered the full-time, sworn ranks of law enforcement.

This chapter presents an overview of how women came into this field. First, it examines the general movement in which the need for women to protect and care for women and children victims and offenders was recognized. Following that, the chapter describes the period from 1916 to 1971, in which females made slow progress. Finally, the so-called "modern period," from 1972 to the present, is considered.

IN THE BEGINNING: PRIOR TO 1920

Women's groups such as the National League of Women Voters, National Young Women's Christian Association, and the National Women's Christian Temperance Union and private volunteer civic associations (including juvenile and women's "protective associations") first sponsored the movement for women police in the United States. During the last half of the 1800s, such organizations worked to secure the appointment of women for the direct supervision of females and girls who were incarcerated in jails, detention houses, and hospitals for the insane.[2]

These efforts were rewarded in 1845, with the appointment of six female matrons in New York City, two at the city jail (The Tombs) and four on Blackwell's Island. These were the first **prison matrons** in the country. Soon, many other cities employed police matrons, marking the official recognition of the principle that women prisoners should be cared for by women. The initial purposes of employing matrons were the "moral rescue" of women who were involved in prostitution and alcohol abuse and the deterrence of sexual attacks against incarcerated women by male correctional officers and inmates. Coinciding with the

EFFICIENCY OF FEMALE POLICE IN WHAT IS VULGARLY CALLED A JOLLY ROW.

A cartoon in the *Illustrated London News* of 1852 was intended to show that the idea of women police was preposterous, as they are depicted as ineffectually ignoring an unruly mob nearby.
Source: Illustrated London News, 1852.

In the late-1800s, police matrons such as Amelia Boyle of NYPD were hired to tend to female arrestees—not only prostitutes and thieves but also servants caught stealing from households.
Source: Courtesy NYPD Photo Unit.

increasing professionalization of the field of **social work**, these matrons often applied social work skills to their tasks, which increased the pressure in most large cities to have trained women working with women and juvenile victims and offenders. By 1888, Massachusetts and New York had enacted laws mandating the appointment of police matrons to care for women held in custody in all cities with over 20,000 citizens.[3]

It would not be until 1905, however, that a woman would receive police powers to deal with social conditions threatening the moral safety of young girls and women. Prior to the Lewis and Clark Exposition in Portland, Oregon, it was feared that "lumbermen, miners, and laborers" would be attracted to come and go "on a spree."[4] Lola Baldwin was given police powers and the authority to supervise volunteers whose responsibilities were to protect visiting females. Her work was so successful that Portland implemented a "Department of Public Safety for the Protection of Young Girls and Women" with Baldwin as director. Female employees were not identified as police officers, but rather "**operatives**."[5]

In September 1910, Alice Stebbins Wells was appointed the first "policewoman" in the United States. Wells, a social worker in Los Angeles with an educational background in theology, thought that professionals working with women and children would be more effective if they possessed police powers. Obtaining the signatures of 100 influential citizens on a petition, Wells convinced the mayor to appoint her as a police officer. Her duties included the enforcement of laws surrounding dance halls, skating rinks, penny arcades, and movie theaters. Wells also created a general information bureau to advise women on police-related matters and to search for missing persons.[6]

The benefits of women serving in the police ranks were beginning to be noticed abroad as well. In 1914, women were appointed to the Metropolitan Police of London. As with their American counterparts, they were charged with "social services" kinds of tasks: the return of runaway girls to their homes and the suppression of dance hall evils, petty gambling in stores frequented by children, and the sale of liquor to minors.[7]

Owing to Wells's success, by 1915 in the United States women were serving in 25 police agencies in 20 states. Although their role continued to be primarily social service, there

Alice Stebbins Wells
Source: Los Angeles Police Historical
Society.

were exceptions. For example, in 1912 the New York City Police Department promoted Isabella Goodwin from police matron to detective after her undercover work led to the arrest of a group of armed robbers. Then, in 1914 Dolly Spencer became the police chief in Milford, Ohio. A community of about 1,500 inhabitants, Milford experienced widespread gambling, so the mayor appointed Spencer as chief, who at the time was termed the city's "general adjustor" of all kinds of social problems in the community. Spencer took the boys from the gambling houses to her home and summoned their parents. She led the fight against illicit gambling for two years until her service was terminated by a newly elected mayor.[8]

Meanwhile, Alice Wells became evangelistic in her efforts to arouse a national movement for women in policing. By 1914, Wells had spoken in over 100 cities in the United States and Canada, including Dallas, Los Angeles, New York City, and Toronto. In 1915, she founded and served as president of the International Association of Policewomen,[9] whose objectives were "to fix standards for the service of policewomen, to secure the appointment of qualified policewomen, to encourage the establishment of Women's Bureaus in Police Departments and to promote such service internationally."[10]

Although Dolly Spencer's service as police chief in Milford, Ohio, certainly did not foment a surge of such chief-executive-level appointments, some police agencies did appoint women to **administrative positions** to oversee functions concerning women and children. Ellen O' Grady's appointment in 1918 as Fifth Deputy Police Commissioner of the NYPD probably stands as the nation's highest-ranking female appointment in a major department prior to recent times. O'Grady's position was created as a temporary World War I emergency measure to do general welfare work with women and children. Ten more women were added the following year. Their services proved so successful that by an act of the state legislature in 1920, they were incorporated into the police department as "patrolwomen," without pension benefits.[11]

A SURGE OF REFORM: THE 1920s

The 1920s witnessed a number of seminal events that would greatly facilitate the entry of women into law enforcement. In 1921, two publications appeared concerning two giants in policing and greatly bolstered the standing of women in the field. First, the *San Francisco Chronicle* reported that August Vollmer was a "firm believer in the employment of women in police work."[12] Vollmer's influence over the development of modern policing and police professionalism in general cannot be overstated. He became Berkeley, California's town marshal in 1905, and soon Berkeley was recognized as one of the most progressive departments in the country.[13] Vollmer would later become a nationally known author and consultant in the field and remained steadfast in his appreciation and endorsement of women serving in a police uniform. Indeed, in 1918, Vollmer trained the first woman **desk sergeant** of any police department. Mrs. Barbara Pearson was "given charge of the patrolmen of a night detail. Her work was highly successful."[14] By that time, Vollmer had had a number of women in his criminology classes at Berkeley and had trained many women in the various branches of police work, including those who later performed expert services in fingerprint analysis, police psychology, and IQ testing in adult probation.[15] Vollmer's other pioneering efforts for women are discussed further later in this chapter.

Raymond Fosdick,[16] another highly respected police writer, believed that the police should be more proactive and devote more attention to **crime prevention**, a role that he felt was ideal for women:

> The development of women police, although still in a vague and uncertain stage, is a factor of supreme significance. The possibilities of their work with women and girls along preventive lines are almost immeasurable. In too many departments women police have been installed with no clear idea as to what functions they were to perform. Thus, in some cities they have been used merely as police matrons; in others they have been uniformed and assigned to ordinary patrol duty. In one large city, the women police who had recently been appointed had been taught to shoot and were then given pistols and blackjacks and assigned to precinct stations! Gradually, however, the peculiar value of women police officers as preventive agents in working with women and girls has come to be recognized. In some cities the women police have proved particularly successful as detectives in certain types of cases.[17]

The views of Vollmer and Fosdick doubtlessly influenced the views of many people in favor of women's service, the nature of which was gradually being expanded. Although still primarily responsible for women and juvenile offenders, many female officers began receiving formal education in police functions and related areas of social work. They counseled and referred offenders to the appropriate social agency.

The importance of special training for women police officers was becoming increasingly clear, and in 1918 the University of California offered a course entitled "Women Police and their Work" in the criminology department. This course, organized by Alice Wells, had a number of important guest speakers, including police chiefs and directors of city police academies. By 1923, some academic programs, like the New York School of Social Work, began offering a program of police instruction for interested women.[18]

In 1924, August Vollmer, ever one to experiment, initiated a crime prevention bureau in the Berkeley Police Department and selected a **policewoman**, Elizabeth Lossing, a highly trained social worker, to be at its helm. Vollmer informed her that policewomen across the nation had been spending too much time working with the end product of bad social conditions. He urged Lossing not to concentrate on prostitutes and other habitual law violators, but rather to spend her time with young, moldable **predelinquents**. Lossing enthusiastically attempted to lead juveniles away from careers of crime, and by 1928, 500 juvenile offenders, boys up to age 12 and girls up to age 21, had been brought to the Berkeley Police Department. Some were too far advanced in their delinquencies to be given much help, but others could be assisted.[19]

Lossing thus kept many youths from entering the juvenile detention home and acquiring a police record. The children reported weekly to the "Children's Room" in city hall, which displayed scooters, toys, soap boxes, bicycles, dolls and carriages, and an assortment of small pets that the children brought in. Lossing had to deal with a variety of situations; she might be surprised by a white rat crawling out of a boy's sleeve, or have to listen to yodeling, a harp, a 10-cent store violin, or a three-stringed ukulele. Always there was scuffling, squealing, and friendly squabbling.[20] Lossing became a respected author on the subjects of juvenile work and the role of policewomen, writing "The Functions of a Policewoman" in the *City Manager Yearbook* in 1931.[21]

THE "DEPRESSION STAGE": 1930–1949

While the 1920s gave cause for optimism to women seeking greater opportunities in policing, this optimism and their entrance into the field could not withstand the **Great Depression**. Frances Heidensohn labels 1930 to 1945 as the "latency and depression" stage of women's entrance into law enforcement.[22] The organizational limits of separate women's bureaus and the ideological limits of the social work orientation placed women in such a restrictive role that they were soon reduced in numbers and assigned temporary positions. They were often reassigned whenever and wherever a woman might be needed to search or interview a female suspect. Female officers once again became generally isolated and restricted, not only because of the physical separation of a woman's unit but also because the social work movement became obsolete as crime fighting increased in popularity. The tide of change could not be totally stopped during this long dry spell, as women began working for state police agencies, first in Massachusetts in 1930 and in Connecticut in 1943. Still, however, they were assigned the limited responsibility of dealing with women and children.

Although the movement suffered during the Depression, the Wickersham Commission, a major presidential commission studying criminal justice in the United States, joined the prowomen ranks in 1931. This body, directed by August Vollmer, surveyed police officials of 575 cities of more than 10,000 population. The Commission felt the need to follow the lead of Raymond Fosdick (mentioned earlier) and stake out a strong position for greater police efforts in crime prevention. The police were urged to become more proactive and apply crime prevention efforts to *persons* as well as property. The role women could play in this effort was not overlooked in the Commission's final report:

> The newer crime prevention units . . . have the school, church, welfare societies, associated charities clearinghouse, police commissioner, and probation officer represented. Women police are found more effective in handling cases of delinquent girls and women, and in supervising dance halls and other recreational establishments.[23]

Aside from the crime prevention role, the *general* benefits of having policewomen in the field did not go unnoticed:

> The important contribution which women police have to offer . . . is being recognized in increasing proportions. In 1930 there were 509 policewomen in 200 police organizations of this country.[24] Actual street patrol by women police has been found to provide a better perspective of the [juvenile] problem by furnishing practical examples upon which effective techniques must hinge.[25]

The Commission also pointed to Elizabeth Lossing's successes in Berkeley and recommended that great care be taken in recruiting and training policewomen for this type of work: "Two years of training in a recognized school of social work or its equivalent is possibly not too much to ask of this type of worker."[26]

The 1940 census reported 1,775 women in police agencies. Although there had been an increase in the number of women officers, there was little change in their role.[27] But women did not abandon hope of police careers entirely: In 1938, in the middle of the Depression, more than 5,000 women had applied for the 29 policewomen vacancies in New York City. They wanted the job and income, and although well educated, they were not the previous upper-class reformers who had begun the movement, but rather contemporary career-minded women.[28] World War II also brought a sharp spike in the hiring of women in order to compensate for the loss of men to the military. Still, however, women served primarily as social workers for women and children and in the area of crime prevention.

1950–1970: SLOW GROWTH, GREATER DIVERSITY IN ASSIGNMENTS

For many proponents of policewomen, the 1950s served only to continue the slow, quantitative increase of women in the field, with most departments certainly appearing indifferent, if not totally resistant, to their entry.

The range of proportionate employment of women within selected agencies was difficult to understand. In 1956, while there were more than 523 female officers in London, there were as few as two policewomen in Denver. NYPD's women comprised approximately 1 percent of the total force, and those in Los Angeles, Detroit, and Cleveland barely exceeded 2 percent.[29]

The 1950s are, however, perhaps most notable for ushering in an era of greater promotability and **diversity** in terms of women police officers' assignments. Some exceptions to the general lethargy were Cleveland and Washington, D.C., where women could compete for ranks up to captain in the same manner as the men. Detroit had 12 superior-ranking women officers, and women could compete for the six sergeant's and five lieutenant's positions. In Los Angeles, there were 11 women sergeants, as a result of **competitive examinations**, and a lieutenant known as City Mother was appointed. Portland had three female sergeants and one captain who commanded 14 policewomen, while Philadelphia and Chicago each had two female sergeants and a lieutenant in command of considerably larger numbers. Although most of these females of rank served in the women's or juvenile bureaus, in several cities they were assigned to other commands.[30]

The dissemination of New York's policewomen among various commands gave rise to the question, "Where, other than the Women's Bureau, could a female sergeant be assigned?"

Clearly, although many police administrators still felt it would be inappropriate to assign a policewoman to a precinct to supervise uniformed male officers, the NYPD broke new ground by assigning female sergeants to positions in the juvenile aid bureau, planning and training, statistics and records, liaison with courts, social agencies, educational institutions, missing persons bureau, bureau of special services, and pickpocket and confidence squad.[31] For the first time on a major scale, women demonstrated that they could perform police functions beyond that of matron's duties and the care of lost children. Seeing this trend, in 1959 NYPD Officer Felicia Shpritzer wrote, "Perhaps the time is not too distant when women sergeants will be accepted." She further opined nearly a half century ago:

> Prejudice dies hard in police circles. Now and again a "diehard" gives a convulsive shudder when the subject of women police comes to be raised. The convulsions grow more and more feeble; a few more years will see prejudice not only stone dead but decently buried.[32]

Shpritzer bemoaned the lack of "full career service" opportunities for policewomen and observed that this lack had been deplored in *The New York Police Survey* of 1952, popularly known as the "Bruce Smith Report." Smith is another renowned police author who, like Vollmer and Fosdick, looms large in the annals of police history and helped to change conventions. Smith wrote *Police Systems in the United States* in 1960, arguing that the vast majority of American police agencies continued to function according to patterns laid down several generations before and that the administrative structure had not kept pace with the growth of the departments and the creation of specialized units. He recommended that the principles of organization commonly found in the industrial and military fields be applied to the structure of police forces:

> Experience has shown that women armed with the general authority of police can often patrol and regulate such establishments [amusement parks, dance halls] more effectively than most men. Hence some of the larger forces include women police on their regular rosters, not only for work of this specific type, but also for the entire range of police activities involving women or children in any respect—women criminals, prostitutes, and wayward minors to child vagrants, runaways, and peddlers.[33]

In 1960, there were 5,617 female police officers and detectives in the United States, all but 400 of those women serving in urban areas. But doors still remained closed.[34] Notwithstanding their progress in several larger cities, even in the late 1960s most policewomen served primarily as clerical staff, in communications, or as matrons. A few women had plainclothes positions as decoys and undercover or remained in crime prevention or juvenile positions. There was less emphasis on separate **women divisions**, so many were teamed with male officers.[35]

Several important events helped set the stage for change in the 1970s. The Johnson Administration, with its commitment to the War on Poverty, helped to fuel the public's new concern for social justice. Women began postponing marriage and children until after they had established careers. The media and such influential leaders as Betty Friedan supported the women's movement. In policing, the newly reorganized International Association of Women Police provided women with a professional association. In addition, two New York City female officers sued to force their department to open promotional exams to women. In 1963, New York's Appellate Court decided that women officers should be allowed to take promotional exams (in *Shpritzer v. Lang*,[36] discussed in Chapter 3). Felicia Shpritzer

Bruce Smith argued in the 1950s that women should be assigned to patrol duties, instead of merely serving as matrons and dispatchers.
Source: Courtesy St. Louis PD.

and another female officer, Gertrude Schimmel, took the exams and were appointed to sergeant. This decision was a major factor in ending the relegation of women to separate, **gender-based units** and began their acceptance into general police work.[37]

Furthermore, in 1965, as a harbinger of the changes coming to America's social climate, the role of policewomen in Berkeley, California, became markedly different from that of Elizabeth Lossing's term of duty. There, and in many other cities, the role of women officers was rapidly expanding, even into increasingly potentially dangerous assignments. Juvenile bureau officers were often called into junior and senior high schools and nearby parks to address problems involving drug use and trafficking, assaults, loitering, and gambling and were especially besieged with problems involving runaway girls. Such officers were particularly exasperated by girls who were described as the "typical beatnik type, unwashed, long hair, dirty jeans, no shoes" who sometimes lived in houses that were "filthy . . . [with] garbage strewn all over the rooms." Runaway girls proved a very "discouraging business" for policewomen, who were ill-equipped to deal with Berkeley's delinquents.[38]

Then, in 1968, the Indianapolis, Indiana, police department became the first agency to assign women to patrol cars. Two women working in the juvenile division, Betty Blankenship and Elizabeth Coffal, had sought a patrol assignment for years and mentioned their hopes to Winston Churchill, a training academy sergeant. When Churchill became the city's police chief in 1968, he appointed the two women to patrol in "**Car 47.**" Even though the experiment was not well planned (the women receiving no training and were given only one day's notice of their new assignment), after some initial growing pains they were generally accepted by other officers and the public. (By 1972, eight women officers had been assigned to Car 47, in three cars, seven days per week, on the day and evening shifts.)[39]

Still, progress remained unhurried and measured. In 1967 the President's Commission on Law Enforcement and Administration of Justice (popularly known as the **Crime Commission**), observed:

> The role of policewoman today is essentially what it always has been. Female officers serve in juvenile divisions, where they perform investigative and social service activities for women, teenaged females, preteen youngsters, and infants. In addition, some larger forces (including New York, Detroit, and Los Angeles) routinely assign female officers to other operational commands.[40]

The Crime Commission went on to note:

> Policewomen can be an invaluable asset to modern law enforcement, and their present role should be broadened. Qualified women should be utilized in such important staff service units as planning and research, training, intelligence, inspection, public information, community relations, and as legal advisors. Women could also serve in such units as computer programming and laboratory analyses and communications. Their value should not be limited to staff functions or police work with juveniles. Women should also serve regularly in patrol, vice, and investigative divisions. Finally, as more and more qualified women enter the service, they could assume administrative responsibilities.

At about the same time, Samuel G. Chapman, a former understudy of Vollmer's at the University of California, Berkeley, county police chief of Multomah County, Portland, Oregon, and consultant to the Crime Commission, was noting:

> Increasingly, and happily, [there have been] female inroads in the police service. Their numbers have increased from one in Los Angeles in 1910 to approximately six thousand in 1970. But the nation has not yet seen a major breakthrough for women in police service. True, in limited numbers they serve in protective and preventive roles, working with women, girls, and other young people. They also work lovingly with senile and mentally ill persons. And a few are invited to perform some investigative, usually undercover, work. However, general duty patrol assignments and traffic enforcement have been elusive; they just have not been asked yet to routinely perform in these capacities in the United States.[41]

Chapman added that many reasons had been given for not assigning women to **uniformed patrol duties**. Most were the obvious ones: hazard, physical limitations, it "just isn't done," and so forth. But perhaps the most intriguing reason that Chapman could identify for not having women serving as patrol officers was that women fought too fiercely! Anthropologist Margaret Mead so noted when the issue of women in combat military roles was proposed at a conference. She felt that men have such "nice" rules, like not fighting on Christmas; a dedicated woman would not necessarily be swayed by such fancy. Chapman thought that Mead may have based her "fierce female" warrior notion on historical antecedents, such as Boadicea, an Anglican queen of the first century A.D. who sacked three enemy cities before the Romans crushed her army; and Joan of Arc, who led French soldiers to success in five battles. Chapman concluded: "Qualified women must progress steadily toward being made a full-fledged member, not a tolerated auxiliary, of America's law enforcement team. This implies that women assume regular patrol and detective roles. It also implies that there be more female supervisory and command personnel, including executives."[42]

THE 1970s AND 1980s

Many related aspects of this chapter's historical overview of women in policing, such as court decisions and legislative enactments of the 1980s and 1990s, are covered in Chapter 3 and thus omitted here.

As of 1970, dozens of American police forces had women serving in intermediate command positions. But almost without exception, they were still working in specialized positions focusing on women and children. What might be termed the Modern Era for women in policing may well have begun in 1972, a landmark year for several reasons. A Ford Foundation-supported study found that although having women officers could benefit the community and the police department, a large amount of **discrimination** existed against policewomen, who represented only 1 percent of all police officers in the nation.

Why this reticence to admit women into the field? Freda Adler believed that this antagonism toward policewomen was possibly related to the kinds of women who were attracted to police work. Like their male counterparts, they often shared many of the aggressive, action-oriented, risk-taking characteristics of the criminals they pursued. In this regard, Adler argued, these women would seem to be more like policemen than policemen's wives. Why, then, would the wives object so strenuously? Precisely, it is suggested, because of the similarity—it threatened to obliterate the sexual differences—not because of the women's weakness, inability, or lack of effectiveness.[43] In light of these obstacles, Adler felt it remarkable that women drew enthusiastic praise from police administrators. After female officers in New York City began patrolling the precincts in one-person cars, one lieutenant

By the 1970s, the deployment of women officers was more established than ever before.

told her, "The women have worked out to a degree that many people just didn't expect. In the first place, they have proven themselves very capable of handling the variety of situations they come in contact with. They also seem to be a bit better at calming down family disputes; even situations involving violence, their mere presence has had a calming effect."[44] In Washington, D.C., one of the first cities to embrace female officers, a male lieutenant reported that women worked out "fantastically," saying, "As a matter of fact, we have many women who are more qualified to be riding around in patrol cars than a lot of the men. The girls are quick, bright, and physically capable of doing their job. They've proven that."[45]

The Ford Foundation study resulted in many changes, including the hiring of the first women as special agents in the Federal Bureau of Investigation and the Secret Service. Concurrently, the Pennsylvania State Police became the first such agency to employ women for duties identical to those of the men. The Metropolitan Police Department of Washington, D.C., the St. Louis County Police Department, and the NYPD placed uniformed female officers in field patrol assignments, and other cities soon followed.[46]

Exhibit 2–1

OVERCOMING THE ODDS

A Female, Single-Parent, Casino Dealer's Successful Career in Law Enforcement

It is probably fair to state that the decade of the 1970s, when women began entering law enforcement in greater numbers, was when at least the concrete foundations were poured for the bridge that connected the old "there's no place for women in law enforcement" and the new "women can do the job as well as men" notions about women in law enforcement. During the 1970s, women certainly confronted many obstacles in attempting to enter what had been a totally male-dominated occupation.

A good case study is that of Gladys Brister. Gladys was born in Texas, but at a very early age, she and her family moved to Bakersfield, California. At the time, her four brothers were involved in federal and local law enforcement, following their father's example (he had previously served with the Texas Rangers, as did his father before him). None of the males in her immediate family encouraged Gladys to enter law enforcement. In fact, they advised her against it, fearing that she would be hurt. In 1952, as a single mom, she moved to Reno, Nevada, and learned how to deal "21" at the Golden Hotel and Casino, which paid $3 per hour plus tips. She also dealt "21" at Lake Tahoe at Harvey's Wagon Wheel and Harrahs. After 16 years at Lake Tahoe, she moved to Stockton, California, making a career of dispatching rental cars. Living in Stockton for six years and marrying and divorcing twice, she moved to Carson City. In 1972, while attending her daughter's wedding in Virginia City, Nevada, she was encouraged to apply for a dispatcher's vacancy with the county sheriff's office in Carson City, Nevada. She was hired as a dispatcher, but because the salary was only $3 per hour, she took a second job dealing cards at Sharkey's Casino in Gardnerville, Nevada.

She dispatched for three years, but she really had her sights set on becoming a sworn deputy. She applied for every position that became available, but each time, her supervisor re-

moved her name from the list because he thought she would only make a fool of herself. After three failed attempts to be included in the testing process, the newly elected sheriff, who felt women should have at least the opportunity to take the examinations, made it possible for her to test. Once given the opportunity, Gladys passed the written and physical examinations, graduated from the POST Academy, and was sworn in as a deputy sheriff in December 1975.

Her initial assignment as a sworn deputy was as a jail dispatcher. In 1977 she began her "patrol duty," working with the school district teaching bicycle safety, drug prevention, and "stranger danger" programs. During her early months on patrol, the male officers would sometimes monitor her work, trying to catch her doing something wrong. But after about three months, the male officers soon realized that she was highly capable of doing the job, and she became fully accepted as a deputy sheriff by not only the male officers but the community as well. During her tenure with the Carson City Sheriff's Office, she worked every assignment within the department. One highlight of her duties was being selected as a "celebrity security guard" for John Wayne while he was in Carson City filming the movie *The Shootist* in 1976. Another cherished assignment was working at the Nevada Supreme Court for about 17 months. Although most young officers aspire to be detectives, Gladys preferred to be out in the community working with people.

Although Gladys was the first female sworn deputy in the Carson City Sheriff's Office, she certainly wasn't the last. The department has had female deputies since she paved the way. All together, Gladys gave 24 years to law enforcement, 20 as a "patrol deputy." Her home is adorned with awards, trophies, certificates, and news clippings attesting to her success as a mother, a single parent, a casino dealer, and a law enforcement officer. She accomplished this against all odds.

Source: Gladys Brister, personal communication, January 31, 2002.

By the close of the 1970s, women were more firmly established in policing than ever before (see Exhibit 2–2, a timeline of women in policing). Indeed, from 1960 to 1980, the percentage of women in police agencies doubled,[47] and during the early 1980s all-female classes of police recruits were attending and graduating in several states, including California's highway patrol. Furthermore, many agencies dropped the "policewoman" terminology. In 1985, Portland, Oregon was the first major city to hire the nation's first female police chief, Penny Harrington, and in 1994, in Atlanta, Beverly Harvard became the first African American woman to be named chief of police for a large city. These accomplishments are a testament to the perseverance of women—and the breaking of the traditional mold by the police and political administrations.

Exhibit 2–2

A TIMELINE OF WOMEN IN POLICING

- *1905:* the first policewoman, Lola Baldwin, was hired as a sworn officer in Portland, Oregon, Police Department.
- *1915:* the International Association of Policewomen was formed, with the help of Alice Stebbins Wells and others (Wells served as the IAP's first president).
- *1919:* Georgia Robinson, the first African American policewoman, was hired by the Los Angeles Police Department.
- *1932:* the International Association of Policewomen was disbanded, owing to the Depression and political forces working against the association.
- *1956:* the International Association of Policewomen was reestablished, turning away from a social work orientation toward integration of women into all police departments.
- *1964:* the Civil Rights Act was passed and expanded in 1972, making it illegal to discriminate in employment in *public* agencies, including police departments.
- *1968:* Betty Blankenship and Elizabeth Coffal became the first women to work as patrol officers, in Indianapolis, Indiana.
- *1985:* Penny Harrington became the first female police chief in a major city, in Portland, Oregon.
- *1994:* Beverly J. Harvard becomes the first female African American police chief in a major city, in Atlanta, Georgia.
- *2000:* a survey by the National Center for Women in Policing found that 13 percent of all sworn officers in the United States were women.

Source: Adapted from the National Center for Women in Policing, "Changing the Face of Policing: A History of Women in Policing in the United States," http://www.womenandpolicing.org/history/ (accessed September 9, 2003). Used with permission.

SUMMARY

To summarize, traditionally few women were hired by police departments, and those who were were assigned to the youth-aid division, as clerical workers, or to take "special" assignments dealing with the apprehension of male sex offenders. In keeping with their general status, female officers were paid less than their male counterparts and they were seldom, if ever, promoted. They were not allowed to wear uniforms. They were rarely allowed to do work on their own without male "protection." Male officers were often hostile toward females and questioned their value as equals, refusing to ride with female partners; threatening boycotts, resignations, and picket lines; and questioning women's right to carry guns.[48]

Changes in these attitudes and practices would probably not have come to pass without the social upheaval of the 1960s and 1970s. The impact of such legislation as the Civil Rights Act of 1964, and its subsequent amended versions, contributed immensely to the rights of women in all fields of endeavor. The social, legal, and economic changes of those decades were obviously important factors in bringing women into policing and, as noted, are discussed in later chapters.

READER LEARNING OUTCOMES

Having examined this chapter, the reader should understand:

- how and where women entered the field of law enforcement and paved the way for a greater female role in the field
- the importance of the events of the 1920s that facilitated the entry of women into the field of law enforcement
- the changes that took place in the field of police work as the numbers of women within the ranks increased
- the challenges faced by the first "policewomen" as they sought to improve their career and advancement opportunities
- the importance of early studies on the performance of women in policing
- the major court cases that effected changes in the field of law enforcement for women
- the major historical events of women in policing

NOTES

1. Freda Adler, *Sisters in Crime: The Rise of the New Female Criminal* (New York: McGraw-Hill, 1975), p. 12.
2. Chloe Owings, *Women Police: A Study of the Development and Status of the Women Police Movement* (Montclair, NJ: Patterson Smith, 1969), p. 97.
3. Ibid., p. 99.
4. Ibid., p.99
5. Ibid., p. 100.

6. Ibid., p. 102

7. Elmer D. Graper, *American Police Management* (New York: MacMillan, 1921), pp. 226–229.

8. Lois L. Higgins, "Historical background of policewomen's service," *The Journal of Criminal Law, Criminology, and Police Science* (41) (March–April 1951): 826.

9. Proceedings of the First Annual Meeting, International Association of Women Police, San Diego, California, May 22, 1956.

10. Owings, *Women Police,* p. 200. These objectives were set forth in the association's revised constitution, developed at its June 1924 annual meeting in Toronto, Canada.

11. Felicia Shpritzer, "A Case For the Promotion of Police Women in the City of New York," *Journal of Criminal Law, Criminology, and Police Science* 50 (4) (November–December 1959): 415.

12. Will March, "Super-Police Trail Thieves By Radio," *San Francisco Chronicle* (October 9, 1921), p. E1.

13. Nathan Douthit, "August Vollmer," in Carl B. Klockars (ed.), *Thinking about Police: Contemporary Readings* (New York: McGraw-Hill, 1983), p. 102.

14. Alfred E. Parker, *The Berkeley Police Story* (Springfield, IL: Charles C. Thomas, 1972), p. 88.

15. Ibid.

16. Raymond Fosdick, *American Police Systems* (New York: The Century Company), 1921.

17. Ibid., pp. 376–377.

18. Owings, *Women Police*, p. 274.

19. Parker, *The Berkeley Police Story*, pp. 88–90.

20. Ibid.

21. Elizabeth Lossing, "The Functions of a Policewoman," in *City Manager Yearbook,* Vol. 3 (Chicago, IL: Proceedings of the 17th–19th Annual Conventions of the International City Manager's Association, 1931–1933).

22. Frances Heidensohn, *Women in Control? The Role of Women in Law Enforcement* (Oxford: Clarendon Press, 1992), p. 41.

23. National Commission on Law Observance and Enforcement, *Report on Police* (Washington, DC: Government Printing Office, 1931), pp. 116–117.

24. Citing Lossing, *The Functions of a Policewoman,* p. 155.

25. National Commission on Law Observance and Enforcement, *Report on Police,* pp. 118–119.

26. Ibid., pp. 119–120.

27. Susan E. Martin, *Breaking and Entering* (Berkeley, CA: University of California Press, 1980), p. 24.

28. Ibid.

29. Shpritzer, "A Case For the Promotion of Police Women in the City of New York," p. 414.

30. Ibid.

31. Ibid., p. 418.

32. Quoting Lilian Wyles, one of the first five sergeants appointed to the London Metropolitan Police Force, in *A Woman at Scotland Yard* (London: Faber, 1952), p. 73.

33. Bruce Smith, *Police Systems in the United States,* 2nd ed. (New York: Harper and Brothers, 1960), pp. 208–220.

34. U.S. Bureau of the Census, *U.S. Census of Population 1960. Subject Reports: Occupational Characteristics—Final Report* (Washington, DC: U.S. Government Printing Office, 1963), Table 1, p. 9.

35. Heidensohn, *Women in Control?* p. 55.

36. 13 N.Y. 2d 744.

37. Peter Horne, *Women in Law Enforcement,* 2nd ed. (Springfield, IL: Charles C. Thomas, 1980), p. 34.

38. Parker, *The Berkeley Police Story,* pp. 98–102.

39. Catherine Milton, *Women in Policing* (Washington, DC: Police Foundation, 1972), pp. 64–65.

40. President's Commission on Law Enforcement and Administration of Justice, *Task Force Report: The Police* (Washington, DC: Government Printing Office, 1967), p. 125.

41. Samuel G. Chapman, *Police Patrol Readings,* 2nd ed. (Springfield, IL: Charles C. Thomas, 1970), p. 57.

42. Ibid.

43. Adler, *Sisters in Crime,* p. 49.

44. Ibid., p. 50.

45. Ibid., p. 51.

46. Horne, *Women in Law Enforcement,* p. 56.

47. National Center for Women & Policing, http://www.womenandpolicing.org/ history/historytext.htm (accessed October 11, 2002).

48. Adler, *Sisters in Crime,* p. 49.

Chapter 3

Help from on High: Legislative Enactments and Court Decisions

---------- ❖ ----------

Key Chapter Terms

Administrative code
Affirmative action
Bona Fide Occupational
    Qualification (BFOQ)
Comparable worth
Equality
Hostile work environment

Law Enforcement Assistance
    Administration
OSHA
Positive discrimination
Protected groups
Punitive damages
Quid pro quo

Reverse discrimination
Sexual harassment
Vicarious liability

It shall be an unlawful employment practice for an employer to fail or refuse to hire . . . or otherwise to discriminate against any individual . . . because of such individual's race, color, religion, sex, or national origin

—Section 703(a1) of Title VII, 42 U.S.C. 2000e

Introduction

Since the early 1960s, there have been a number of important court decisions and legislative enactments concerning women's rights in the workplace. These decisions and legislative acts expanded the opportunities for women to enter the male-dominated profession of law enforcement. This chapter reviews those decisions, beginning with the general entry of women into the workforce and job discrimination. Next we examine sex and race discrimination, with a focus on **sexual harassment**, and then discuss cases and legislation involving family care and comparable worth.

ENTERING THE INDUSTRIAL WORKFORCE

In the late 1800s and early 1900s, as industries began manufacturing some of the products that were previously made in the home, women initially entered the workforce as seamstresses, laundresses, waitresses, and later as factory workers. Working conditions for women were generally even more horrific than for men. Women worked longer hours under stricter work rules, and their workplace was often more unsafe and unhealthy than those of men. These conditions worsened until 1911, when a fire destroyed the Triangle Shirtwaist Company in New York City, killing 141 women who had been locked inside. New legislation limited the women's hours and conditions of work but also served to keep them in their place under the rationale of the state's paternal interest in the protection of women because of their childbearing role.[1]

Legislation such as the Fair Labor Standards Act of 1938 was passed to establish uniform hours and protection for men and women, but such legislation was suspended during World War II because of the labor shortage. During the war, women were an indispensable source of labor, so the War Manpower Commission passed guidelines to ensure equal pay and to prohibit sex discrimination. Once the war had ended, Congress reimposed the Fair Labor Standards Act on women, preventing them from working at certain jobs and restricting them to certain hours. It was in this environment that numerous court challenges and political efforts emerged to help women strive for **equality** in the workplace, addressing the issues of job discrimination, sexual harassment, and family care.[2]

COMBATING JOB DISCRIMINATION: LEGAL AND LEGISLATIVE DEVELOPMENTS

Civil rights, especially for people of color, have been debated since the writing of the Constitution, but the issue really had little impact on the workplace until the early 1960s. The following is an outline of legislation and court decisions that addressed workplace gender discrimination.

Sex and Race Discrimination

Some of the major changes in the law that were enacted by Congress and the federal courts to address discrimination on the basis of sex and race are the following.

Shpritzer v. Lang **13 N.Y. 2d 744 (1963)** After 20 years of service as a policewoman, Officer Felicia Shpritzer of the NYPD sought judicial review of a decision by the New York City Civil Service Commission that made women ineligible to take the promotional examination for sergeant. The NYPD segregated women into a separate division, and its **administrative code** required that "sergeants shall be selected from among patrolmen of the first grade."[3] The New York Court of Appeals found no reasonable ground upon which to deny women the opportunity to take examinations for promotions. Following the court's decision, in 1964, 126 female officers took the promotion exams. Two officers, Shpritzer and Gertrude Schimmel, earned the highest scores on the exam, and in 1965 were promoted to the rank of sergeant. (Both women later became lieutenants; Schimmel retired in 1978 as a deputy chief.)[4] This decision played a major role in ending the relegation of women officers to separate units and in their acceptance into general police work.[5]

Equal Pay Act of 1963 A precursor to the Civil Rights Act of 1964, the Equal Pay Act was only a very narrow interpretation of pay equity. Although it forbade "discrimination between employees on the basis of sex by paying wages to employees at a rate less than the rate at which the employer pays wages to employees of the opposite sex for equal work on jobs that require equal skill, effort and responsibility and which are performed under similar working conditions,"[6] it did not consider "comparable worth" (discussed later) or attempt to determine equal pay for jobs of comparable worth. Also, Congress provided employers four defenses against charges of sex discrimination: pay differences based on (1) a seniority system, (2) merit system, (3) a system that measures earnings by quantity or quality of production, or (4) any factor *other* than sex. For instance, most police agencies have pay scales that account for years of service. Unless female officers can demonstrate equal numbers of years of service, it is not considered discriminatory for male officers to be paid more for a particular job if they have more years of service.

Title VII of the Civil Rights Act of 1964 Although primarily enacted to address racial discrimination, this legislation prohibited private employers with 25 or more employees to discriminate against **protected groups** in any area of work, including recruitment, promotions, or work conditions. Protected groups were those based on race, color, sex, ethnicity, or national origin, although in its original form, the act did not include sexual discrimination. Its inclusion was actually a last-minute amendment proposed in an attempt to defeat the bill, one of a number of amendments opponents of the act proposed in hopes of weakening the bill to the point that it could be destroyed. Instead, the act that passed included the sexual discrimination amendment. Hastily drawn up, the amendment was poorly written. In fact, Congress had to take up the act again in order to add the word *sex* in several places where it had been omitted. This oversight raised doubts among enforcement agencies and courts about Congress's concern about sex discrimination, making it difficult for women to seek remedies under the new act.[7] Still, with Title VII, employers and other agencies covered by the act could not discriminate in the areas of hiring, termination, or terms of employment. Women finally had a legal basis to compete with men for jobs and promotions.

The Equal Employment Opportunity Act In 1972 the Equal Employment Opportunity Act was enacted to extend Title VII to state and local governments, including their police agencies. It also established the Equal Employment Opportunities Commission (EEOC). Women were given the right to compete with men for jobs and promotions and to receive the same compensation upon being hired. Later, in 1979, the enforcement of the Equal Pay Act was transferred to the EEOC, which issued new and more restrictive guidelines to employers, including **affirmative action**, which outlined the need for quantifiable goals for the hiring and promoting of protected race and gender groups.[8] Several subsequent court cases established that jobs need only to be substantially equal, not identical, in order to be compared.[9] For example, in *County of Washington v. Gunther,*[10] four female prison guards charged that they had been paid unequal wages for work equal to male prison guards because of sex discrimination. The state of Oregon required that women inmates be guarded by women officers, so the county attempted to argue that sex was a **bona fide occupational qualification (BFOQ)**. The court disagreed that sex was a BFOQ in this case, but instead felt that the officers could sue under Title VII because they were alleging that their wages were depressed due to sex discrimination.

Legislative enactments and federal court decisions of the 1960s and 1970s served to reduce or eliminate a number of discriminatory obstacles to women wishing to join the ranks of law enforcement.
Source: Courtesy NYPD Photo Unit.

Omnibus Crime Control and Safe Streets Act of 1968 Passed to create the **Law Enforcement Assistance Administration**, this act primarily improved educational and training standards for law enforcement. With its emphasis on gender and racial equality, not only men but also women and minorities were provided the means to obtain degrees in criminal justice and related fields. Many women became researchers, professors of criminal justice, and lawyers working in the courts. This act was amended in 1973 to prohibit discrimination against women by any agency receiving LEAA funds. Agencies were required to assess all their recruiting, promotion and training procedures to ensure job relevancy and equality and to establish an Equal Employment Opportunity (EEO) program to provide a vehicle for hearing discrimination grievances.

Griggs v. Duke Power Company **(1971)** Considered a landmark case, the decision in this case ruled that employment practices are discriminatory if they have disparate impact on members of protected groups. The U.S. Supreme Court held that tests or degrees as conditions for employment or transfer are prohibited if they disqualify protected groups at substantially higher rates than the majority and do not appear significant to the job. Once it is shown that a protected group is being disqualified at a substantially higher rate than the majority, the burden is on the employer to demonstrate that the specified job conditions are related to successful job performance (BFOQ). *Griggs* was first used in law enforcement to prohibit height and weight requirements that excluded women from employment in policing. Law enforcement administrators could not prove that the height/weight requirements were critical job functions, or BFOQ, which led to a number of police-specific cases striking down height/weight requirements.[11]

Rosenfeld v. Southern Pacific Company[12] **(1971)** The Ninth Circuit Court of Appeals ruled against an employer who argued that women in general were not suited for jobs requiring long hours and strenuous physical effort. As a BFOQ, the employer tried to characterize women as the "weaker sex"; however, the courts interpreted that Congress's intention in Title VII was to restrict stereotyping. Gender could only be considered a BFOQ if necessary to successfully perform a particular job, such as depicting a female in an acting role. Women could not be segregated or refused employment unless employers could prove gender was necessary for the operation of that specific business or agency, and gender must be shown to be a *bona fide* occupational qualification. Employers could not deny women employment based on assumptions of employment characteristics such as strength or preferences of customers or clients. If a job required specific physically strenuous work, a woman must be given the opportunity to demonstrate her ability to do the job.[13] The employer must have "a factual reason for believing that all or substantially all women would be unable to perform safely and efficiently the duties of the job involved."[14]

Sexual Harassment

There are two forms of sexual harassment: (1) **quid pro quo**, and (2) **hostile work environment**. Quid pro quo harassment occurs when "submission to or rejection of sexual conduct by an individual is used as the basis for employment decisions affecting such individual."[15] A sexual advance or proposition with which the woman either must comply or lose an employment benefit must have occurred. A hostile environment includes remarks about a woman's appearance or sexuality, touching, or any behavior that makes the woman's work environment unfriendly. The victim does not need to show concrete effects from the conduct, such as decreased performance, but rather that the conduct made it more difficult to do her job. To be considered a hostile environment, the conduct must be (1) unwelcome or unwanted, (2) sexual in nature, and (3) a pattern of persistent existing harassment that a reasonable person would find offensive.[16]

The EEOC guidelines also detail the employer's responsibilities. Sexual harassment by supervisors and other employees are the responsibility of the employer, even if the employer has specific guidelines against sexual harassment and regardless of whether the employer knew or should have known of the actions. The employer is required to take steps to prevent the harassment from occurring, and if incidents do occur, must take immediate and appropriate corrective action. Title VII gives employees the right to work in an environment free from intimidation, ridicule, and insult based on sex, race, religion, or national origin.[17]

The Civil Rights Act of 1964 does not mention sexual harassment. A number of lower court decisions found sexual harassment to be a form of sexual discrimination, and finally in 1986 the Supreme Court ruled on the issue. It was not until the Civil Rights Act of 1991 that Congress passed legislation forbidding sexual harassment.

The following cases are considered to be the landmark sexual harassment cases that established the standards for determining when sexual harassment exists.

Tomkins v. Public Service Electric and Gas Company[18] Tomkins was the first case involving sexual harassment. Adrienne Tomkins, a secretary with Public Service Electric and Gas, was invited by her supervisor to lunch. He discussed the possibility of a job promotion and indicated his desire to have sexual relations with her. When she attempted to leave the restaurant, he first threatened to fire her, then physically threatened her, and then physically restrained her. When she complained, she was demoted and placed in another department, where she continued to be subjected to a pattern of harassment by other employees. The federal district court stated that Tomkins' treatment was not sex discrimination, but rather a physical attack motivated by the supervisor's sexual desire. The Third Circuit Court of Appeals overruled, declaring that Title VII applies when supervisors' sexual demands are made a condition of an employee's job.[19] As noted earlier, the EEOC then developed guidelines that defined sexual harassment and the responsibility of the employer and gave employees the right to work in an environment free from intimidation, ridicule, and insult.[20]

***Meritor Savings Bank FSB v. Vinson* (1986)**[21] In this decision, the U.S. Supreme Court affirmed that both quid pro quo and hostile environment forms of sexual harassment are prohibited by Title VII. It also stated that the hostile environment cases do not necessarily need to include psychological instability or economic loss, but they do need to be severe enough to alter the victim's conditions of employment. The Court also noted that the voluntariness of the sexual relationship is not relevant as long as the plaintiff indicated by her conduct that the sexual advances were unwelcome. In this case, a female bank employee had been subjected to sexual harassment by her male supervisor, whose behavior towards her included public fondling and sexual demands. She waited until she was terminated for excessive use of sick leave before filing suit against the supervisor and bank. Despite the bank's defense that it could not have taken remedial action because it was not aware of the situation, the U.S. Court of Appeals and the U.S. Supreme Court found the supervisor's actions to be in violation of Title VII.

Faragher v. City of Boca Raton **(1998)** Here, the U.S. Supreme Court found that an employer is vicariously liable under Title VII of the Civil Rights Act when an employee is a victim of a sexually hostile environment created by a supervisor who has authority over the employee. The employer is not liable, however, if it can be shown that reasonable care was used to prevent or correct any sexually harassing behavior, and the victimized employee unreasonably failed to take advantage of the corrective opportunities provided. In *Faragher,* a female lifeguard sued her immediate supervisors for creating a sexually hostile atmosphere by the supervisor's repeated lewd remarks and "uninvited and offensive touching."[22] The federal district court concluded that the harassment was pervasive enough to infer knowledge on the part of the city. The court of appeals reversed the decision, but the U.S. Supreme Court reinstated the district court's decision, deeming that the employer was subject to **vicarious liability** for a sexually hostile environment. The city failed to disseminate its policy on sexual harassment, made no attempt to monitor the conduct of its supervisors, and was not able to describe any action that connoted reasonable care.

Family Care and Well-Being

Historically, when women became pregnant, they were forced to take maternity leave without pay and often lost their jobs. Only after the passage of two important legislative acts, the Pregnancy Discrimination and Family and Medical Leave acts, did they receive protection in the workplace.

The Pregnancy Discrimination Act of 1978[23] This act requires employers to treat pregnancy, childbirth, and related medical conditions like any other temporary disability. Therefore, employers must provide employment benefits for pregnancy if benefits are provided for other types of temporary disabilities. Employers cannot discriminate in hiring, promoting, suspending, or discharging based on any condition surrounding pregnancy. Nor can they require women to take leave at an arbitrarily set time in their pregnancy, fail to grant full reinstatement rights including credit for previous service and accrued retirement, fail to pay disability or sick leave, refuse to hire or promote a woman because she might become pregnant, or ask preemployment questions about her childbearing status.

United Autoworkers v. Johnson Controls[24] In 1991, the Seventh Circuit Court of Appeals found that an employer's fetus-protection policy discriminated because the policy required a female employee to prove that she was not capable of reproducing. The company had previously had a number of employees who became pregnant while manufacturing batteries and their blood-lead levels were in excess of the level found to be safe by the Occupational Safety and Health Administration (**OSHA**). The employer implemented a policy barring all women from working in jobs that involved exposure or potential exposure to lead at excessive levels *except* those who had documented proof of their inability to have children. Under the Pregnancy Discrimination Act of 1978, sex discrimination includes discrimination on the basis of pregnancy, so the employer's choice to treat all female employees as potentially pregnant was clearly sex discrimination. The U.S. Supreme Court stated that the policy could not fall under the BFOQ exception since fertile women could work in the manufacture of batteries as efficiently as anyone else. The Pregnancy Discrimination Act mandates that decisions about the welfare of future children be left to the parents who conceived and support them; concerns about the next generation are not part of the employer's business.

The Family and Medical Leave Act (FMLA) of 1993[25] Under FMLA, eligible employees may take 12 weeks of unpaid leave for the birth or adoption of a child. Employees are not required to use all their sick or vacation leave before they can apply for unpaid leave, nor can the employer count their sick or vacation benefits toward the 12 weeks of leave. Interestingly, this act states that its purpose is to balance the demands of the workplace with the needs of families. Although women may possibly make greater use of the leave, it is not restricted to mothers nor is it only limited to childcare. Family members, both male and female, are also permitted to request leave for serious family health conditions.

Comparable Worth

The concept of **comparable worth** attempts to establish equal pay for equal jobs; however, it is difficult to establish if the extent of pay disparity between men and women is based on differences in job characteristics or in the individuals who are employed. Considering the high percentage of women serving in *civilian* law enforcement positions, comparable worth is likely to become an important issue for law enforcement administrators. Title VII states,

> it shall be an unlawful employment practice under this title for any employer to differentiate upon the basis of sex in determining the amount of wages or compensation paid . . . if such differentiation is authorized by the provision of The Equal Pay Act of 1963.[26]

This language can be interpreted to mean that either Title VII is limited to the standards of the Equal Pay Act or the employer can raise the same defenses for unequal pay (merit, seniority, incentive, or anything other than sex) as written in the Equal Pay Act. If Title VII is limited to the Equal Pay Act, then comparable worth cases cannot be considered by the court at all.

Many states and local governments have implemented pay equity plans, often after negotiating with unions. In the past, unions supported men, not women, but recently labor has become more interested in organizing women employees. This is no wonder, given that the greatest union membership increase has been in female-dominated workplaces.[27]

Civil Rights Act of 1991[28]

The Civil Rights Act of 1991 provides the relief of both compensatory and **punitive damages**. Back pay, medical bills, and legal fees are considered compensatory damages. Punitive damages are limited to evidence of intentional discrimination. During the past few decades, the higher courts have generally supported protection from sexual harassment. Most employers have taken steps to reduce its occurrence in their workplaces. Sexual harassment does continue to transpire, however, especially in policing, so it is imperative that managers continue to be conscientious in this area.

Positive Discrimination

Positive discrimination, also termed **reverse discrimination**, was initiated in the 1970s.[29] Affirmative action does favor a particular group, but it does so in order to give the individuals in the group remedies for past wrongs and injustices. Some police agencies resisted pressures to hire more women and minorities. In some cases, the courts ordered police departments to hire more women, often requiring preferential treatment of female and minority applicants. By the end of the 1980s, many police agencies had adopted equal opportunity policies and had staff members who were promoting those policies and recruiting females and minorities. Of course, women also experienced a negative impact from affirmative action; they were perceived as having been hired without the proper qualifications. As noted by one author, "the goal is not, and should not be, statistical parity. The goal is equality of opportunity."[30]

SUMMARY

Legislative actions and court decisions have had a tremendous impact on women's career opportunities. They have affected such issues as job discrimination, sexual harassment, and family care. Historically, good intentions and protective laws kept women safe, but restricted them from many professions. The fortuitous inclusion of the word *sex* in the Civil Rights Act of 1964 broadened opportunities for women in the workforce. The next three decades saw slow expansion of those opportunities and provided the chance for women to enter the male-dominated profession of law enforcement. However, until legislation is passed that addresses comparable worth, women may have equal opportunities, but not equal pay with men.

Legislation protecting women's freedom to make decisions concerning pregnancy and family care continues to occupy the courts and legislators. Providing both men and women equal benefits within the family structure appears to truly strengthen the family.

READER LEARNING OUTCOMES

Having examined this chapter, the student should understand:

- the first court decisions that spurred changes in the treatment of women regarding work conditions, pay, and benefits
- the role that such major pieces of legislation as the Civil Rights Act played in regard to gender discrimination in the workplace
- the Equal Pay Act and the impact of the Equal Employment Opportunity Act
- how early hiring and promotional standards discriminated against women and the rationale the courts used in landmark cases that created change
- what constitutes sexual harassment in the workplace and how employers can be held accountable
- how government agencies attempt to address the issues of pregnancy and family care

NOTES

1. Ann Harriman, *Women/Men/Management,* 2nd ed. (Westport, CT: Praeger, 1996), p. 46.
2. Ibid., p. 48.
3. *Shpritzer v. Lang,* 13 N.Y. 2d 744 (1963).
4. Kathryn E. Scarborough and Pamela A. Collins, *Women in Public & Private Law Enforcement* (Boston: Butterworth Heineman, 2002), p. 24.
5. Peter Horne, *Women in Law Enforcement,* 2nd ed. (Springfield, IL: Charles C. Thomas, 1980), p. 34.
6. *Fair Labor Standards,* 29 U.S.C. § 206 (d) (2002).
7. Harriman, *Women/Men/Management,* p. 52.
8. Susan Martin and Nancy Jurik, *Doing Justice, Doing Gender: Women in Law and Criminal Justice Occupations* (Thousand Oaks, CA: Sage, 1996), p. 8.
9. Harriman, *Women/Men/Management*, p. 49.
10. *County of Washington v. Gunther,* 454 U.S. 161 (1981).
11. *Mieth v. Dothard,* 418 F. Supp. 1169 (1975).
12. *Rosenfeld v. Southern Pacific Company* 444 F.2nd 1219 (9th Circuit, 1971).
13. Martin and Jurik, *Doing Justice, Doing Gender,* p. 8.
14. *Weeks v. Southern Bell,* 277 F.Supp. 177 [S.D. Ga. 1976], as cited in Harriman, *Women/Men/Management,* p. 57.
15. *The Guidelines on Discrimination because of Sex*, 29 C.F.R. § 1604.11.
16. Harriman, *Women/Men/Management,* p. 62.
17. *Henson v. City of Dundee,* 682 f. 2d 897, (1982).
18. *Tomkins v. Public Service Electric and Gas Co.,* 568 F.2d 1044 (1977).
19. Harriman, *Women/Men/Management,* p. 61.
20. *Henson v. City of Dundee,* 682 F.2d 897 (1982).
21. *Meritor Savings Bank v. Vinson,* 477 U.S. 57 (1986).
22. *Faragher v. City of Boca Raton,* 525 U.S. 775 (1998).
23. *The Pregnancy Discrimination Act of 1978,* 42 U.S.C.Section 2000e–2.
24. *United Autoworkers v. Johnson Controls,* 111 S. Ct. 1196 (1991).
25. *Family and Medical Leave Act of 1993.*
26. *The Equal Opportunity Act of 1972,* 42 U.S.C. Section 2000e–2.
27. Harriman, *Women/Men/Management,* pp. 64–67.
28. *Civil Rights Act of 1991,* 5 USCS §7122.
29. Frances Heidensohn, *Women in Control? The Role of Women in Law Enforcement* (Oxford: Clarendon Press, 1992), p. 58.
30. Harriman, *Women/Men/Management,* p. 54.

Chapter 4

Women Who Serve Today:
A Profile

❖

Key Chapter Terms

Interpersonal communications   Managers   Supervisors
Leadership style   Mid-level personnel   Sworn personnel

Women will have to take power, because no one is giving it away.

—Congresswoman Shirley Chisholm

Introduction

Chapter 2 examined how women throughout history made their way into the traditionally male-dominated field of policing. Certainly, female officers demonstrated their tenacity and ability to perform the job and their potential for contributing to the field. Now, in a more contemporary vein, several questions have arisen: Are women well represented and succeeding in today's law enforcement ranks? Does it take a unique woman to become a police officer? What kinds of assignments do they currently have? Have minority women been as successful as white women in finding their niche in this arena? What kind of occupational backgrounds and family situations do policewomen tend to possess?

This chapter addresses those questions, providing a snapshot of progress. First, we review the representation of women in local, state, and federal law enforcement agencies, including the types of jobs to which they are currently assigned. There follows a discussion of their representation in a supervisory capacity and a review of their racial composition, educational level, backgrounds, and family responsibilities. Finally, we examine their representation as chief executive officers.

FEMALE REPRESENTATION IN LOCAL POLICE AGENCIES

Doing It All: Types of Assignments

The photographs of female officers throughout this book as well as interviews with them bear witness to the fact that today they are engaged in a wide variety of assignments. Indeed, the veteran women officers who were interviewed for the book had the following assignments to which they were either assigned part-time or full-time:

- *School resource officer:* working in middle and high schools to improve safety and interact with children in legal matters
- *DARE officer:* teaching Drug Abuse Resistance Education to public school children
- *Crime prevention officer:* educating individuals, communities, and businesses on crime prevention techniques
- *Drug task force member:* analyzing drug crime and planning and implementing drug enforcement operations
- *Street crimes team member:* providing backup for patrol officers on proactive and reactive enforcement action focusing on specific crimes
- *Violent crime task force member:* focusing patrol and investigative efforts on personal crimes
- *Homicide investigator:* investigating homicides and suspicious deaths
- *Domestic violence unit member:* responding to and investigating domestic violence crimes
- *Family services investigator:* following up on crimes with juvenile victims and offenders
- *Robbery unit investigator:* focusing on crimes of theft with force
- *Vice unit officer:* investigating and conducting operations on such crimes as prostitution, gambling, and drug offenses
- *Property crimes investigator:* investigating crimes involving burglary and automobile theft
- *Internal affairs investigator:* investigating complaints against officers
- *Training officer:* training officers in basic and in-service subjects
- *Recruiting officer:* helping recruit new officers and conducting background investigations, interviews, and physical assessments
- *Planning unit member:* conducting crime analyses, resource allocation studies, and research in any area that helps the agency operate more efficiently and effectively

Today's women officers have a variety of job assignments.
Source: Courtesy NYPD Photo Unit.

Representation by Agency Size

The number of women entering law enforcement has slowly been rising. Between 1990 and 2000, the percentage of sworn women in law enforcement in large cities grew from approximately 12 to 16 percent, an increase of 4 percent over 10 years. While this increase may appear impressive, during that same time, the U.S. population increased 10 percent, resulting in a 7 percent increase in sworn police officers. Therefore, the percentage of women officers has increased more slowly than the overall increase in sworn police officers.[1]

Large cities have a higher percentage of women officers. Agencies representing jurisdictions of over 250,000 population are composed of approximately 16 percent female officers. The exception to this composition is cities with populations between 350,000 and 500,000, which, inexplicably, have fewer female officers (approximately 14 percent). Between 1990 and 2000, the largest increase in female officers was in those cities with populations between 250,000 and 350,000 (see Figure 4–1).[2]

As shown in Figure 4–1, in most of the major cities the number of women officers increased, but a few cities actually had lower percentages in 2000 than in 1990. Table 4–1 provides a sample of cities in each of the population categories with some of the lowest to the highest percentages of women officers.[3] Note that Chicago, Nashville, Cincinnati, Omaha, and Buffalo had substantial increases in female officers. (Successful strategies used by several of these agencies and others to recruit female officers are discussed in Appendix II.)

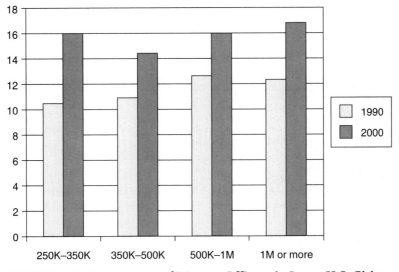

FIGURE 4–1   Percentage of Women Officers in Large U.S. Cities (Populations of 250,000 or More)
Source: Brian Reaves and Timothy Hart, *Police Departments in Large Cities, 1990–2000* (Washington, DC: Bureau of Justice Statistics, 2002), p. 3.

Since its inception in 1995, the National Center for Women & Policing (NCWP) has monitored and promoted greater inclusion of women in law enforcement. In 2000, the NCWP sponsored two surveys, one directed toward law enforcement agencies with 100 or more sworn officers[4] and the other directed toward small and rural law enforcement agencies (jurisdictions with fewer than 50,000 citizens).[5] The surveys were sent to 349 large agencies and approximately 12,000 small and rural agencies. The following is a discussion of the surveys' results.

Types of Agencies and Positions

Women represent 14.5 percent of the **sworn personnel** in municipal agencies and 13.5 percent in county agencies. These percentages decrease to 8.2 percent in the small agencies. Figure 4–2 shows that approximately 79 percent of the civilians in small departments and 67 percent in the large departments are women.[6] These positions generally pay less than the sworn positions and carry little chance of promotion.

State Police All states except Hawaii have police with state jurisdiction. There are more than 56,000 sworn state officers.[7] These state agencies as a whole have a much lower percentage of female officers than either local or federal law enforcement agencies. The NCWP study places the percentage of female state police officers at 6.8 percent.[8]

TABLE 4–1   Percentage of Women Officers in Selected Large Cities

Population Categories	Percentage of Women Officers	
	1990	2000
1,000,000 or more		
Las Vegas	10.2	10.9
Phoenix	8.1	15.0
New York	12.3	15.5
Los Angeles	12.5	18.4
Chicago	13.0	21.3
500,000 to 999,999		
Honolulu	8.3	10.3
Charlotte	15.5	13.9
Baltimore	10.9	15.7
Nashville	7.8	21.9
Detroit	20.0	25.3
350,000 to 499,999		
New Orleans	12.0	14.5
Minneapolis	10.5	15.7
Atlanta	12.9	16.6
Miami	12.1	17.6
Omaha	8.2	19.7
250,000 to 349,000		
St. Louis, MO	7.1	13.3
Arlington, TX	8.1	14.8
Cincinnati	10.1	19.6
Buffalo, NY	12.9	20.9
Pittsburgh	22.8	24.6

Source: Brian Reaves and Timothy Hart, *Police Departments in Large Cities, 1990–2000* (Washington, DC: Bureau of Justice Statistics, 2002), p. 11.

Federal Law Enforcement Table 4–2 lists the percentage of women officers in those federal agencies with more than 50 officers.[9] Although these large federal agencies employ on average a higher percentage of women than local agencies, federal agencies as a whole have an overall average of 14.4 percent women officers, which is similar to that of local agencies.

REPRESENTATION IN POSITIONS OF LEADERSHIP

The representation of women officers throughout law enforcement agencies is low, and this lack of representation is even more evident in the leadership ranks. In reviewing the following information, the reader may want to remember that top-level personnel are usually considered administrators, **mid-level personnel** are managers, and those who work directly with the rank-and-file officers are **supervisors**.[10]

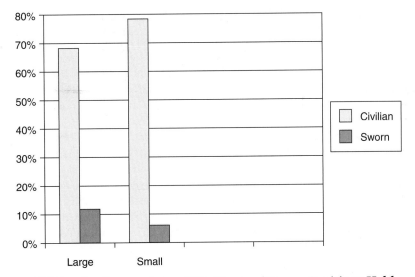

FIGURE 4–2   Comparison of Civilian and Sworn Positions Held by Women in Large and Small Law Enforcement Agencies
Source: Adapted from National Center for Women & Policing, *Equality Denied: The Status of Women in Policing* and *Equality Denied: The Status of Women in Small and Rural Police Agencies* (Washington, DC: Feminist Majority Foundation, 2001).

TABLE 4–2   Percentage of Female Agents in Federal Agencies

Department	Percent Female Officers Among Full-Time Federal Officers
Treasury	23.6
Defense	17.1
Health and Human Services	27.7
Housing	27.6
Social Security	23.7
Agriculture	31.3
Labor	25.2
Justice	16.0
Transportation	26.4
Veterans	23.4
Education	31.7
EPA	32.7
IRS	23.4
Customs	17.3
Forest Service	15.5

Source: Brian Reaves and Timothy Hart, *Federal Law Enforcement Officers 2000* (Washington, DC: Bureau of Justice Statistics, 2002).

Making It to the Top: Women Police Chiefs

Although they number only 1 percent of the police chiefs in the United States, the number of women serving as chief executive officers of law enforcement agencies has expanded considerably since Penny Harrington took over as chief in Portland in 1985, becoming the first woman chief in a large agency (see Chapter 7), and Elizabeth (Betsy) Watson assumed the helm in Houston in 1990, becoming the first in a city of more than one million population. A recent survey by Dorothy Moses Schulz[11] identified 157 women serving as chiefs of police and 25 who were sheriffs 96 of whom participated in a survey. Schulz intended to establish a demographic profile of the leaders, to learn what types of agencies they led, and to discover whether there were any discernible patterns in their career paths. Forty-eight (49 percent) of the chiefs were in charge of municipal police departments, and 40 (42 percent) led college and university police departments (see Table 4–3). Of the eight remaining respondents, two were county chiefs, two were airport authority chiefs, two were tribal chiefs, and two were state police chiefs.[12] Significantly, this 2003 survey was done prior to the appointments of female police chiefs in San Francisco, Boston, Detroit, and Milwaukee.

Even more varied than the types of agencies led were the sizes of their departments and their career paths to the top. The agency sizes represented by the respondents ranged from one sworn officer in addition to the chief herself, to 1,763 officers. Only six of the respondents led agencies with at least 100 sworn officers (five being municipal, one a campus police agency, and one a tribal agency). Conversely, 23 (25.8 percent) were in agencies with 10 or fewer officers. Others were fairly evenly dispersed within the range of 11 to 99 officers (see Table 4–4).

About one-third of the chiefs (33) led the departments in which they began their law enforcement careers. Of the remaining two-thirds who were no longer in the agencies in which they had entered policing, half had moved once, 19 had moved twice, eight had moved three times, three had moved four times, and one (a campus police chief) had moved five times during her career.[13] Wide variations in terms of their tenure in the chief's office were also noted, ranging from one municipal chief who was still in her first year to a university chief in her 25th year.[14]

These women CEOs typified the increasing levels of education achieved by today's chiefs, with three-fourths having either a bachelor's or a master's degree. Schulz was also interested in learning whether the women were influenced by having spouses who were also in law enforcement (as did both Harrington and Watson)—about a third had a partner who was also in policing.[15]

TABLE 4–3   Women Police Chiefs by Type of Agency Served

Type of Agency	Number
Municipal	48
College/university	40
State	2
County	2
Tribal	2
Airport authority	2
Total	96

Source: Police Quarterly, September 2003, p. 336.

In 1990, Houston's Elizabeth (Betsy) Watson became the first woman to serve as a chief of police in a city with a population of more than one million.

TABLE 4–4   Women Police Chiefs by Size of Agency Served

Number of Sworn Officers	Municipal	State	Campus	County	Airport	Tribal	Total
1–10	14		8			1	23
11–25	10		11				21
25–50	9		8	1	2		20
51–75	5		6				11
76–100	4		2				6
101–500	4		1			1	6
500–1,000							0
1,000 plus		2					2
Total	46	2	36	1	2	2	89

Source: Police Quarterly, September 2003, p. 337.

Women Officers' Ranks in Small and Large Agencies

As shown in Figure 4–3, fewer than 5 percent of the supervisory positions and fewer than 4 percent of *all* top administrative positions are held by women in small departments, compared with 10 percent of the supervisory and 7 percent of the top administrative positions held by women officers in large departments. Although there are higher numbers of females in leadership positions in large agencies, female supervisors in any size department do not represent their percentage in the general population, nor do they approach parity with men

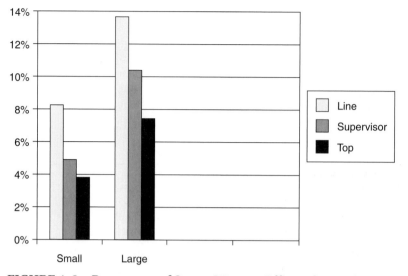

**FIGURE 4–3   Percentage of Sworn Women Officers by Rank
Comparing Small and Rural Agencies with Large Agencies**
Source: Adapted from National Center for Women & Policing, *Equality Denied: The
Status of Women in Policing* and *Equality Denied: The Status of Women in Small and
Rural Police Agencies* (Washington, DC: Feminist Majority Foundation, 2001).

in supervisory positions. Certainly, a large enough proportion of women have now been employed in policing long enough to be considered for promotion. A number of researchers question the commitment of police agencies and their male administrators to promoting women and have made recommendations for changing the evaluation and promotional process.[16]

An officer's initial assignment within an organization is important to her or his advancement by providing the new employee an opportunity to demonstrate competence and to prepare for later chances for promotion. If female employees are not offered the same access as male employees to challenging and demanding tasks, they are at a disadvantage in terms of credibility and ambition. Often, senior employees and supervisors, mainly men, will select people who look most like themselves for new responsibilities. These same supervisors are the most likely to mentor those whom they have selected.[17]

Researchers studying women in management positions have found few differences in the value and belief systems of female and male managers, but clear differences between women managers and women nonmanagers. In other words, gender does not appear to be a significant factor in one's ability to be an effective manager. Women managers, compared to women in nonmanagement roles, emphasize achievement and production more than their domestic roles. Women managers achieved their positions through aggressive career development and were in positions not considered to be traditionally feminine.[18]

Differences in Leadership Styles and Seeking Advancement

On the other hand, there are differences in leadership styles between the sexes. Women tend to encourage participation and input from their subordinates, probably because of their comfort and experience in using **interpersonal communications**. Men were comfortable using a more autocratic, task-directed style of management. Management literature encourages the democratic **leadership style** of women, advocating that it leads to acceptance from employees and improves their performance.[19]

Studies specifically examining women in law enforcement have discovered that women officers feel they have equal access to promotions, but they choose not to advance. As suggested by career development theorists, men and women have similar career aspirations, but have different backgrounds and role expectations. Police agencies, among other highly structured organizations, assume that their employees can separate their work and familial responsibilities. Women, especially single mothers, face parental duties and family relationships that hamper their ability to compete with males. If female officers have achieved a level of seniority, allowing them to shift to preferential or favorable assignments, they may feel the costs of promotion are not worth the effort. As a new supervisor, usually assigned to evening or night shifts, a new female sergeant would lose her opportunity to be with her children after school and/or at bedtime. There is little prospect for flexible or alternative career paths for women (or men) who have substantial family responsibilities.[20]

PERSONAL CHARACTERISTICS

One of the first studies examining women officers as a cohort involved 25 women who were hired by New York City Police Department (NYPD) in the early 1920s.[21] Different criteria were required for these women officers than for men officers during this era. Although male officers had no education or work experience requirements, women had to have a high school education; pass certain written, oral, and physical examinations; and possess work experience preferably in probation, education, or nursing. As will be seen, differences still exist between men and women officers.

Race

Those first 25 policewomen in New York City were white. During the same period, Detroit hired two African American females,[22] giving it a 15 percent minority representation among female officers, a figure higher than the current national average of minority women officers. The racial composition of women police officers has not significantly increased in 80 years. For instance, the NCWP reports that in police departments with 100 or more sworn officers, women of color hold only 4.9 percent of sworn positions.[23] Figure 4–4 displays the breakdown by gender of sworn and nonsworn positions in police agencies with 100 or more sworn officers. Women occupy about 67 percent of the nonsworn positions, and women of color occupy about 21 percent of that number.

Education

Better educated overall than male officers, 70 to 80 percent of women officers have some college or a completed degree. An additional 11 to 23 percent have completed postbaccalaureate work.[24] The educational levels of the veteran women officers interviewed are similar, with 79 percent having some college or a completed college degree. Although there is some controversy over the benefits of well-educated police officers, the courts have upheld educational requirements, stating, "Few professionals are so peculiarly charged with

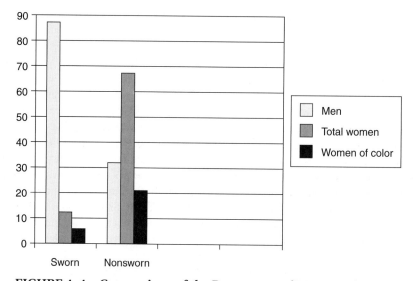

FIGURE 4–4   Comparison of the Percentage of Women of Color with the Total Percentage of Women and Men for Both Sworn and Nonsworn Positions
Source: National Center for Women & Policing, *Equality Denied: The Status of Women in Policing* (Washington, DC: Feminist Majority Foundation, 2001).

individual responsibilities as police officers. Mistakes of judgment could cause irreparable harm to citizens or even to the community. The educational requirement bears a manifest relationship to the position of police officer."[25]

Previous Work Experience

There does not appear to be one particular type of work background from which successful female officers emerge. As part of a larger Kuder Interest Inventory study,[26] approximately 350 women police officers were asked about the kinds of jobs in which they had been previously employed. Their prior occupations numbered more than 600, including cashier, waitress, security guard, factory worker, secretary, and teacher. More than half of these jobs required a high school degree, a third required some sort of additional training or education beyond high school, and 13 percent of the positions required a college degree.

The previous work experience of the veteran female officers who were interviewed for this book can generally be categorized primarily into three career paths: One group left low-paying blue-collar jobs for the higher pay of law enforcement; a second, smaller group entered law enforcement after completing a military tour; and a third group, higher in number, completed their criminal justice degree with the sole idea of entering law enforcement.

Family and Marital Background

As more women enter nontraditional professions, research focuses on differences between these women and those who entered the traditional female professions. Women with high career aspirations are more likely to consider nontraditional jobs. Although they seek relationships, they are often willing to postpone marriage to achieve their goals through their own efforts.[27]

Both of the parents of women in nontraditional careers provide emotional support and identification; however, it has been found that mothers who are dissatisfied with their roles and life in general were more likely to raise daughters who strive for nontraditional professions.[28] Women officers' birth families, often fairly neutral about the idea of their daughters working as police officers, react more positively once the women actually become officers. Almost half of the women have relatives in law enforcement.[29]

The 50 veteran, municipal officers interviewed speculated about what facets of their upbringing influenced their desire to enter law enforcement. Although fewer than half have family members in law enforcement or the military, many describe a background that encouraged independence and responsibility. As one officer stated, "My parents didn't take the bumps out of my road."[30] These backgrounds included caring for younger siblings while their single parents worked and working on family farms, requiring the completion of chores before and after school. Others spoke of living in high-crime areas, which exposed them to different types of people, and associations with alcoholic male family members, who often became so disruptive that the female members of the household called the police. These incidents often modeled a positive image of the police, in which the women viewed the officers as people who had the authority to defuse the potentially dangerous situation.

Additionally, some of the officers described themselves as "tomboys," growing up playing team sports with boys. The largest percentage of the officers were the youngest in their families—the child who is often given more freedom and fewer gender-role expectations than siblings. Chapter 7 provides further insight into the veteran female officers' backgrounds.

Women in law enforcement are slightly less likely to be married than women in other professions.[31] Between 39 and 58 percent of the female officers are single, between 28 and 33 percent are married, and between 9 and 24 percent are divorced.[32] Many (62 percent) do not have children, and less experienced officers were less likely to have children.[33] Female officers who are married seem to be more likely than males to be married to other officers. These women report a number of advantages to marrying another officer: helping each other maintain non-police-oriented relationships, helping one another prepare for promotional exams, dividing up household and child care responsibilities, and better understanding of the challenges of the job. (See Exhibit 4–1.)

When asked about the level of support they received from their significant others, 57 percent of both married and single women officers said that they received positive support, while 23 percent noted that it was negative. Many expressed the view that the men in their lives had difficulty accepting their profession and the authority that came with it.[34]

Responsibilities at Home

As later chapters will examine further, managing a family is hard for civilians, but it is even more difficult for women officers. Many of the women who have children are single mothers. Although men often find that marriage and family have positive effects on their career aspirations and performance, family life often seems to have the opposite effect on women.[35] Women often attempt to cope with their family responsibilities by requesting inside assignments on the day shift. Instead of providing an inspiration and support for professional achievement, the female officers' feelings of responsibility toward their families usually causes internal conflict for the officer. As noted earlier,

Exhibit 4–1

RAISING CHILDREN WHILE PURSUING AN FBI CAREER

Amelia Martinez, the FBI agent with whom the readers will become further acquainted in Chapter 8, is married to another FBI agent. She describes the experience of raising her sons:

> From the time of my sons' births, we have had someone come to the house to watch them; they were never in day care. We have been lucky in finding women who were flexible in their time. If we knew we had a late night or an early morning commitment, we would have the caretaker spend the night. We also had a backup we could call in the middle of the night if we were both called out. At no time during their childhood have we ever lived near family. Twice we had young mothers as our sons' caretakers, who did not want to put their own child in day care, so we allowed them to bring their children with them, and everyone was happy.
>
> Ever since preschool, we have hired teachers from their schools to care for them after school. The boys just go to the teacher's room after school and do their homework while the teacher finishes up. She takes them home to her house or runs them to practice or whatever. Also, because teachers usually need summer employment to meet their expenses, they were willing to continue our sons' supervision during the summer. Our first teacher was a grandmother type who has now retired, and the one we have now is a young married woman who wants to pay off student loans before starting a family.
>
> The FBI takes care of just about everything with a move—so the moves have not been very stressful. Both boys were born with some pretty serious medical problems that required five surgeries between them and about 15–20 hospitalizations. The FBI allowed me to work as little as 20 hours a week for a few years in order to be there for them during those times when they were the sickest. Between vacation and sick leave, I have managed to get time to be a part of their field trips and other school functions, as well as be home when the flu strikes. Of course, during trials or other major criminal justice concerns, I had to depend on friends to take the brunt of caring for the boys. They both seem pretty well adjusted, and they think all moms work long hours and carry guns.

Source: Amelia Martinez, personal communication, September 23, 2002.

women officers often decline to test for a promotion if it means working evening and night shifts, restricting time with their children.[36] Women officers were more likely to indicate that they would leave police work before retirement (19 percent of women versus only 3 percent of men). Female officers' reasons were primarily based on conflicts between job and family. Interestingly, these women were still likely to encourage their daughters and sons to enter policing.

SUMMARY

Although women now represent approximately 16 percent of the local sworn police officers and over 14 percent of the federal agents in the United States, they remain primarily in the lower ranks. Women of color are particularly underrepresented in sworn positions. These statements are also true concerning their representation in supervisory, mid-level management, and chief executive positions.

Even though they are now present in most areas of law enforcement, many female officers choose not to seek promotion and/or are not selected for supervisory positions. Those women officers who do remain in law enforcement and aspire to the upper ranks possess values and beliefs similar to those of male **managers**, although they manage their personnel more democratically than do male administrators.

Most women are socialized for their roles in the home and traditional professions by their families and society. Even so, female law enforcement officers come from all types of personal and professional backgrounds. Many believe that their family backgrounds taught them independence and gave them confidence to pursue the challenge of a policing career.

READER LEARNING OUTCOMES

Having examined this chapter, the reader should understand:

- the various assignments that women in policing currently have
- the number of women in the various federal, state, and local police agencies throughout the country
- the extent to which women hold leadership roles and the findings of several studies on the performance of women in these roles
- the backgrounds of women entering law enforcement and the differences between men and women in the field
- the demographic characterestics of women police chiefs

NOTES

1. National Center for Women & Policing, *Equality Denied: The Status of Women in Policing* (Washington, DC: Feminist Majority Foundation, 2001), p. 5.
2. Brian Reaves and Timothy Hart, *Police Departments in Large Cities, 1990–2000* (Washington, DC: Bureau of Justice Statistics, 2002), p. 3.
3. Ibid., p. 11.
4. National Center for Women & Policing, *Equality Denied,* p. 4.
5. Ibid.
6. Ibid., pp. 3, 5.
7. Reaves and Hart, *Police Departments in Large Cities,* p. 11.
8. National Center for Women & Policing, *Equality Denied,* p. 7.
9. Brian Reaves and Timothy Hart, *Federal Law Enforcement Officers, 2000* (Washington, DC: Bureau of Justice Statistics, 2002), p. 6.
10. Kenneth J. Peak, *Justice Administration: Police, Courts, and Corrections Management,* 4th ed. (Upper Saddle River, NJ: Prentice Hall, 2004), p. 5.

11. Dorothy Moses Schulz, "Women Police Chiefs: A Statistical Profile," *Police Quarterly* 6(3) (September 2003):330–345.

12. Ibid., p. 336.

13. Ibid., pp. 336–337.

14. Ibid., 341.

15. Ibid.

16. Peter Horne, "Special Report: Equality in Policing," *Law and Order* (November, 1999): 53–62.

17. Ann Harriman, *Women/Men/Management,* 2nd ed. (Westport, CT: Praeger, 1996), pp. 185–186.

18. Ibid., p. 157.

19. Ibid., pp. 159–168.

20. S. Whetstone and D. G. Wilson, "Dilemmas Confronting Female Police Officer Promotional Candidates: Glass Ceiling, Disenfranchisement, or Satisfaction?" *International Journal of Police Science & Management* 2 (1999):128–143.

21. Clarice Feinman, "Women in Law Enforcement," in Clarice Feinman (ed.), *Women in the Criminal Justice System,* 2nd ed. (New York: Praeger, 1986), pp. 79–103.

22. Chloe Owings, *Women Police: A Study of the Development and Status of the Women Police Movement* (Montclair, NJ: Patterson Smith, 1969), p. 263.

23. National Center for Women & Policing, *Equality Denied,* pp. 11–12.

24. Kathryn E. Scarborough and Pamela A. Collins, *Women in Public & Private Law Enforcement* (Boston: Butterworth Heineman, 2002), pp. 134–135; Samuel Janus, Cynthia Janus, Lesli Lord, and Thomas Power, "Women in Police Work—Annie Oakley or Little Orphan Annie?" *Police Studies* 11(3) (1988):124–127; Carole Garrison, Nancy Grant, and Kenneth McCormick, "Utilization of Police Women," *Police Chief* 55(9) (1988):72–73.

25. *Davis v. City of Dallas,* 777 F.2d 205 (5th Cir.1985).

26. Donald Zytowski and Kathleen Isgro, "Results of the Kuder Interest Survey," *Women Police* 22 (1988):9.

27. Harriman, *Women/Men/Management,* pp. 195–196.

28. Ibid., p. 196.

29. Janus et al., "Women in Police Work," pp. 124–127.

30. Veteran female officer interviewed on July 18, 2000.

31. Garrison et al., "Utilization of Police Women," pp. 72–73.

32. Ibid., pp. 72–73.

33. Janus et al., "Women in Police Work," pp. 124–127.

34. Sue Chance, "Partners in Life," *Police* 12(6) (1988):32–35.

35. Susan Martin, "Women Officers on the Move: An Update on Women in Policing," in Robert Dunham and Geoff Alpert (eds.), *Critical Issues in Policing: Contemporary Readings* (Prospect Heights, IL: Waveland Press, 2000), pp. 401–422.

36. Whetstone and Wilson, "Dilemmas Confronting Female Police Officer Promotional Candidates," pp. 140–141.

Chapter 5

Measuring Up: Performance and Perceptions of Female Officers

❖

Key Chapter Terms

Androgyny
Calls for service
Community policing
Cultural diversity
Decentralization of power
"Double marginality"
Feminist consciousness

"Group blame"
Job assignments
Mentoring group
Occupational self-concept
PoliceWOMEN
POLICEwomen
Quota

Racial justice
Sexuality and gender
Self-efficacy
Sex typing
Tokenism
"War stories"
"Work the streets"

There is no female mind. The brain is not an organ of sex. As well speak of a female liver.

—Charlotte Perkins Gilman, *Women and Economics*

Introduction

Previous chapters described the pioneering efforts of women as they strove to enter policing as well as their current status in the different types of police agencies. Several areas remain to be explored concerning their presence in this traditionally male-oriented occupation.

The chapter opens with a discussion about what early research revealed concerning the overall performance of women in their relatively new law enforcement positions. Then, in a contemporary vein, we examine the unique role of women officers in the **community policing** and problem-solving era. Next, we discuss what has been found to be the prevailing attitudes of women officers by their male counterparts as well as citizens' perceptions and the attitudes of the women themselves. Finally, after reviewing some means by which women cope and adapt to the role, we examine the unique challenges faced by women officers of color.

EARLY RESEARCH CONCERNING WOMEN OFFICERS' PERFORMANCE

Methods of Call Handling

Studies focusing on women officers in large municipal police agencies began appearing even as women were entering law enforcement. In 1972, one of the earliest studies of officers in the New York City Police Department (NYPD) found that civilian encounters were approached similarly by male and female officers, although male officers were more apt to become aggressive. Women were more likely to be cordial, so as a result, civilians behaved in a friendlier manner toward female officers. As the researchers followed the female officers to see how they adapted to the stressors of the job, they concluded that women encountered conflicting messages from family members, supervisors, and co-workers about their roles and performance as police officers. It was also observed that the majority of women officers chose to work with female partners in order to avoid pressure from male officers to act womanly.[1]

In 1973, another study matched 86 Washington, D.C., female recruits with 86 male recruits and evaluated them after one year of service. The study focused on the attitudes of male officers and community members toward female officers and the performance of both groups of officers. The female officers were found to perform favorably compared to the male officers. Women responded to similar calls and had similar results in handling violent citizens. Although women officers made fewer arrests and issued fewer traffic citations, they appeared to be more effective than men in diffusing potentially violent situations. Women officers also had a less aggressive style of policing and were less likely to be charged with improper conduct.[2]

A 1975 study of the St. Louis Police Department determined that female officers were equally as effective as men in performing patrol work; however, female officers' policing styles were observed to be different from that of the male officers. They were less aggressive, made fewer arrests, and engaged in fewer proactive activities, such as car and pedestrian stops. Citizen surveys indicated that women were more sensitive and responsive to their needs and handled service calls, especially domestic disturbances, better than men.[3]

Follow-up studies of NYPD officers were conducted in 1976, 1983, and 1988. The 1976 study, comparing 41 female and 41 male officers, supported the previous conclusions that female officers were as effective as male officers. The female officers performed similarly, used the same techniques to gain and keep control of offenders, and were equally as unlikely to use force or to display a weapon. Female officers were judged by civilians to be more competent, pleasant, and respectful than their male counterparts but were less likely to engage in coercive behavior or apt to assert themselves in patrol decision making. Compared to male officers, females were less often named as the arresting officer, were less likely to participate in strenuous physical activity, and used more sick time.

These disparities might have been connected to the professional environment at the time, which included a fiscal crisis in New York City in which female officers were more likely to be laid off. The women officers were often assigned traditionally female duties, such as searching female suspects and performing administrative duties. They were also unlikely to be assigned to the same partner each shift, thereby reducing their opportunities to acquire relevant information about their patrol area, to learn from their partner, or to negotiate over credit for arrests. This tendency to yield to their partners disappeared when they were assigned to female partners.[4]

Measuring Up with the Men

The 1983 study found that there were no longer significant differences between male and female officers' performances in terms of traffic stops, pedestrian checks, or other patrolling responsibilities. The only difference in performance between female and male officers seemed to be the more frequent dispatching of male officers to high-risk calls. A closer look at officer experience found that gender was not an issue—the more experienced officers were sent to such calls. The researchers also assessed whether women officers were over- or underutilized in particular categories of functions. They found that the female officers were not underutilized in any area and were overutilized in only a few areas, such as female searches.[5]

Another follow-up study of NYPD officers in 1988 found no basic differences in the methods used by males and females while working as a patrol team reacting to violent confrontations. Female police officers were more emotionally stable than their male counterparts, and with their less aggressive personalities, female officers were more likely to calm a potentially violent situation and less likely to cause physical injury.[6]

In summary, these early studies showed that women could perform as well as men on patrol; however, because the studies used different methodologies, it was difficult to establish whether they agreed with each other. The studies also used small samples and had few observations. This early research compared female officers with their male counterparts as women were first entering law enforcement and typically used measures that examined only the law enforcement aspects of policing, such as the use of weapons and physical exertion. Limiting the factors measured to these aspects ignores the fact that police officers are rarely called upon to enforce laws, but spend the majority of their time performing public service activities. In addition, considering the inability of police to prevent, deter, or solve crimes, the criteria used to assess the competency of female and male officers would not appear to be valid measures of achieving the goals of law enforcement.[7] These limitations do not disprove the studies, but rather it is surprising that women officers were shown in so positive a light.

A MORE CONTEMPORARY VIEW: WOMEN AND COMMUNITY POLICING

The advent of the current era of community policing and problem solving, discussed in Chapter 1, has brought new opportunities for female officers. A number of writers[8] have written about the general changes that community policing has brought, among them Susan Miller, who has described the *feminine* qualities of the ideal community policing approach.[9] The emphasis on involvement with the community to solve the problems of the neighborhoods has made an asset of the "feminine virtues" of interpersonal communication, conflict resolution, and mediation skills. Miller names four areas in which the roles and responsibilities of community police officers today are similar to those of policewomen in the late 19th and early 20th centuries:[10] (1) familiarity with community, (2) **decentralization of power**, (3) prevention, and (4) social work activities.

First, early policewomen were expected to be familiar with their assigned community, knowing its residents, the location of trouble spots, and neighborhood problems. Under today's community policing practices, officers are permanently assigned to one geographical area so that they will become familiar with the residents and help them work on their crime-related and quality-of-life problems.

Second, community policing emphasizes the importance of the decentralization of power. Most departments have implemented satellite offices, creating an informal "drop-in" environment for citizens to get to know their neighborhood officers. The early policewomen's units were separated from the main department to encourage women and children who needed help to drop in. As one author stated in 1924,

> In removing from the Women's Precinct all the earmarks of a regular police station, it at once became a center where a woman could seek information, advice or aid from her own sex without fear of the grim atmosphere of the average police desk. The red geraniums in the window boxes would attract a woman. The worried mother or weary, runaway girl could find the help, understanding and protection that only a motherly policewoman can give.[11]

Third, community policing emphasizes *prevention,* particularly activities directed at juveniles. Just as policewomen in 1936 in Philadelphia worked with children younger than 16, without male officer support, today's community police officers are finding means to keep juveniles interested in activities other than joining gangs. In addition, promoting better relations between young people and the police is a key factor of community policing.

Finally, the social work activities of early policewomen compare with activities under community policing today. In 1929, male police officers were often indifferent to identifying and correcting societal conditions influencing the crime rate among juveniles and adults, but these were the very conditions that concerned the policewomen. Today, as emphasized in Chapter 1, officers involved in community policing pay close attention to causes of disorder and crime.

Susan Martin states that, historically, women and people of color were the first willing to risk the community policing approach.[12] After it appeared that the community policing officers really were supported by the police administration and faring better with respect to promotions than regular officers, white males became involved with the strategy. Women were drawn to community policing for reasons other than promotion or career advancement. Women of color in particular were committed to **racial justice** and **cultural diversity** within the neighborhoods and the police agency. In Asian neighborhoods, where the residents have brought with them a fear of the police from their home country, female community police officers have bonded easily through their mutual interest in children. As the female officers gained more informal social control, they strengthened their role as confidantes, aiding them in their ability to carry out crime fighting.[13]

ATTITUDES TOWARD FEMALE OFFICERS

With the conclusion reached in the early 1980s that female officers performed as well as male officers, most of the research then turned to the attitudes of their male counterparts toward female officers. Female officers have had to contend with the opinions of male officers and the public regarding their competency on the job as well as their own sense of efficacy. Because attitudes are more vague than observable in nature, theoretical explanations for attitudes become important and will be discussed here.

Male Officers' Perceptions

In the early 1970s, many male officers preferred not to work with female officers, believing they were ineffective, incompetent, and too passive to physically handle the job.[14] They also assumed that their female counterparts were hired because of equal employment opportunity legislation, not due to merit, or that they received **job assignments** based on their **sexuality and gender**.[15]

By 1994, there had been little change in male officers' attitudes toward female officers. A survey of the perceptions of male officers concerning female officers in city, county, and the state police in four Northwestern states found that only one-quarter of the male officers accepted women officers. Minority male officers were more positive toward women officers; they indicated that women had the mental and emotional ability to do the job and sufficient aggressiveness and competency to apprehend and restrain a subject, execute a search warrant, and successfully engage in foot pursuits. These minority male officers did not feel that it was necessary for them to lead the way when their partner was a woman. On the negative side, the minority male officers like the white male officers declared that they would rather have a male officer backing them for a dangerous call and preferred a male sergeant and a male partner.[16]

Male officers' attitudes toward women officers seem to vary by locations and by what is being measured. For example, a 1995 study of a large Midwestern city found more acceptance of female officers than previous studies had.[17] This study measured officers' opinions based on professional conduct, not physically volatile situations. Both sexes scored female officers' written reports as more professional, and the actions taken by male officers as slightly more appropriate, but both sexes scored the same on knowledge of procedure.

Possible Explanations

There are a number of theories about male officers' attitudes toward female officers. The predominant theories center around the "**sex typing**" of professions, **tokenism**, and feminism.

Occupations are considered "sex typed" when a large majority of the people in them are of one sex, and there exists an associated belief that "this is as it should be." The belief presumes natural differences between men and women that should be considered in the workplace. Therefore, when the minority sex enters the occupation, the focus is on sex status instead of occupational status. As women enter the field of policing, long considered a masculine field, the response is to them as women first and as professionals second. A colleague, supervisor, or citizen may try to compensate for this attitude by being overly solicitous, courtly, underdemanding, or overdemanding.[18]

Policing, traditionally associated with crime, danger, and violence, in reality primarily consists of service or order-maintenance calls. Some researchers argue that women officers entering the profession threaten male officers' self-image and social status.[19] Some male police officers have created an image of policing as action-oriented, violent, and uncertain—"real police work"—involving physical abilities associated with masculinity. Women entering police work threaten this image: either physical prowess is not as necessary for police work as these male officers have depicted it, or working with women officers will be a disadvantage in a physical street confrontation.[20] Some researchers go further and argue that men have traditionally had the sole right to preserve law and order. The entrance of women shatters this tradition of male solidarity.[21]

Robert Merton uses the term *tokens* for those people who are identified through the characteristics ascribed to gender and race. These people are seen first as having the traits so ascribed to them and not as individuals, and assumptions are made about their culture, status, and behavior. Merton further introduced the idea of viewing organizations from an insider's versus an outsider's perspective. Insiders are powerful and privileged, and the distinctions between insiders and outsiders are based more on ascribed traits than acquired reputations based on performance. These ascribed traits are further supported by powerful network memberships—knowing the "right" people.[22]

Allowing normally excluded groups in as tokens is the way dominant groups promise entrance into the dominant class, but such upward mobility is severely restricted.[23]

Thus, it is not enough to increase the numbers of women in male-dominated jobs; gender-based attitudes concerning women's abilities also have to be changed. In fact, the more women who enter a male-dominant field, the greater the opposition to women. Males feel threatened when they realize women can adequately perform jobs previously available to males only.[24] There are four responses typical of male colleagues: (1) paternalistic actions that shield women from the primary functions of the job; (2) higher expectations for the females than for their male colleagues; (3) impediments to accessing the "good old boy" network, restricting critical information and contacts; and (4) sex-stereotyped job assignments.[25] Women are often pushed into roles similar to traditionally female roles, such as writing reports or working with children, and away from means of gaining the information and experience necessary for promotion. It has been suggested that tokenism is a possible explanation for barriers to female advancement in policing.[26] In some police agencies, the promotional processes are unequal and discriminatory, or they are equal and nondiscriminatory, but the effects of tokenism on female officers are sufficient to inhibit them from competing.

According to feminist theories, activities and professions in which men are involved are considered high status in comparison to women's activities and professions. Even "where economic activities are less differentiated, men's control of social, political, and religious activities ensures their social dominance."[27] Even in the female-dominated nursing profession, when men entered the field, the status of the nursing profession rose.[28] As women increasingly enter the field of criminal justice, according to feminist theory, they are faced with obstacles based on organizational and social processes that support women's subordination to men. Studies of police officers working with permanent partners have found that when two people work together, the individual believed to be more experienced and therefore more competent is given higher status and exercises greater influence. This ranking holds true in law enforcement with same-sex partners, but it is not the case when partners are of different sexes. The male officer is usually given higher status and greater influence. In fact, pressure is placed on both officers to keep the male partner at a higher status, no matter the experience level. If the male officer doesn't assume his expected leadership role, then he is teased. If the female officer does not comply, she becomes the target of hostility and sexual innuendos.[29]

Male and female police recruits undergo the same physical and psychological assessments before they are hired and the same training afterward. By exhibiting **androgyny**—both feminine and masculine traits—police officers are more adaptable to a variety of situations. Some situations require the use of those characteristics traditionally associated with men, such as aggression and competitiveness. Other situations are likely to need characteristics and behaviors more associated with women, such as compassion, sensitivity, and cooperativeness. The "new policewomen" possess androgynous attributes; they are self-confident, professional, competent, and attractive. Consequently, these new female officers are feared and respected because they have overturned the male ideology, winning for women a clearly defined slot, at least on the margins. They have learned to balance femininity with projecting a professional image, emphasize a team approach, use humor to develop support and ward off unwelcome advances, and gain sponsorship to enhance positive visibility. Other constructive behaviors include remaining on patrol, playing by the rules, treating the public well, building close ties with the community, and working hard.[30]

Exhibit 5–1

WOMEN MURDERED WHILE ON DUTY

[*Authors' note:* The number of officers murdered in the line of duty varies each year; 136 officers were killed in 2002, and 233 officers were murdered in 2001 (owing to the World Trade Center attacks). While most of these officers are male, the percentage of female officers killed is disproportionate to their overall numbers. The following information is not included to alarm readers; rather, it is to alert them to the fact that police killers do not select their victims based on gender.]

As of July 2004, 194 female officers were inscribed on the wall of the National Law Enforcement Officers Memorial in Washington, D.C. As their numbers have increased in policing, so too has the risk of injury and death. The very nature of the occupation, and not gender, ensures that women will be in harm's way. Overall, events leading to female officers being killed on duty are similar to those that take the lives of male officers. Injury and death is most likely to occur when on duty, in plainclothes, on undercover drug assignments, but also in uniform writing traffic tickets.

The first two documented female officers murdered were detention officers. Anna Hart, a 45-year-old deputy with the Hamilton County, Ohio, Sheriff's Office, was beaten to death by a prisoner wielding an iron bar. Mary T. Davis, working with the Wilmington, Delaware, jail on May 11, 1924, entered the cell of a female prisoner to investigate escaping water and was brutally attacked as the prisoner escaped.

In 1980, a female U.S. Secret Service agent was the first female federal officer murdered while on duty. While conducting surveillance during a Los Angeles investigation, the agent and her partner were forced from their vehicle, disarmed, and murdered with their own 12-gauge shotgun. Five years later, the first female FBI agent was killed in Phoenix, Arizona, while helping other agents arrest an armed robbery suspect.

Source: Samuel G. Chapman, *Murdered on Duty: The Killing of Police Officers in America,* 2nd ed. (Springfield, IL: Charles C. Thomas, 1998), pp. 42–43.

Citizens' Perceptions

A 1997 study concluded that citizens' perceptions of women in policing had become positive overall and that there had been a decrease in skeptical attitudes toward women officers' ability to handle violent encounters.[31] A majority of the public said that policing is appropriate work for women because they are able to handle violent encounters, make competent decisions in emergency situations, and are more respectful to citizens than their male counterparts. The citizens felt safe with female officers on patrol, although a majority had never been assisted or apprehended by a female officer. The researchers concluded that citizens' opinions were the product of a more general progressive view of women.

To measure more directly the relationship between citizens and female officers, complaints of misconduct filed against police officers in a large police agency were examined to assess any differences in the volume of serious complaints.[32] Complaints were categorized as those involving force; nonviolent complaints involving threatening behavior, harassment, and discourtesy; dereliction in the performance of duties; and miscellaneous complaints, ranging from allegations of inappropriate driving to conducting personal affairs while on duty. Only 5.7 percent of the alleged complaints were against female officers. Other researchers found similar results, in which only 1 percent of constitutional violations claims against officers between 1989 and 1993 were filed against female defendants.[33]

Although the attitudes of citizens toward female officers are positive, and the lack of complaints against female officers also attributes to the citizens' opinions, there is an interesting dimension to citizen offender–female officer interactions. Offender–officer interactions typically follow a script: The offenders' behavior is respectful, and slightly subservient, toward the officer. According to the masculine dominance stereotype, this script places women officers at a disadvantage. To gain credibility, female officers must avoid smiling or appearing friendly and demand deference. Citizens are usually reluctant to talk to an officer or to behave in inappropriate ways; however, when the officer is female, the citizen may seek to disrupt typical interaction by disavowing the officer's identity as a member of the police and refocus on gender to gain advantage. So citizens may "do gender to lower the status usually given officers."[34] For example, the citizen may make sexual gestures or comments to the female officers. Female officers usually ignore sexual comments or gestures made by male citizens that do not alter the outcome. Instead, female officers focus on gaining control through voice, appearance, facial expressions, and other nonverbal actions to indicate that they are to be taken seriously. When women officers are given deference, it is usually out of gender-blind respect or because compliance does not challenge the citizen's manhood.

Female Views on Being Accepted

Women officers, unlike men officers, must not only learn the job of policing, but also how they will adapt to the male-dominant culture of policing. Given their role as tokens, female officers are also aware that they represent their gender. Often, there is a self-generated pressure to perform well all of the time, since other women's futures depend on their performance. Female police officers must be better and appear more competent than men to be accepted and viewed as equals. If they object to being excluded from the male police culture and circumvented by the stereotyped roles to which they are often assigned by male offi-cers, women officers can be reminded that "they are sex objects, vulnerable to harassment, yet held responsible for the outcomes of the interaction."[35]

When asked to describe the types of calls to which they were assigned early in their careers, the female officers interviewed for this book generally felt they were more likely to be assigned domestic, sexual assault, and traffic calls, but perceived that men were more likely to be assigned to higher-risk calls such as perpetrators with a gun and assaults. Many female officers felt their skills were not being utilized and believed they were overeducated for the job. Women with more experience were even less optimistic; policing seemed to them to be a male occupation no matter how hard women tried.[36]

A recent study[37] of the perceptions of female officers working for a large police agency found that when questioned about their acceptance by others, females responded that they had some difficulties being accepted by civilian employees, the public, male offi-cers, and male supervisors, although in general other female officers and supervisors ac-cepted them. In comparing their job performance with male officers, most of the female officers felt they performed their job as well as men, and several felt they performed their job better than male officers. More than half of the female officers believed that they had to do a great deal more work to receive the same credit as male officers, while only one-third of the females believed they were given just as much credit for their work as male of-ficers. There are differences in women officers' attitudes across police agencies, as well as in what more current studies indicate. For instance, women from smaller departments were more likely to believe that they were seen as officers first. They noted that their ideas were accepted, and they were recognized for good performance.[38]

Female Officers' Self-Perceptions

A lack of support from male officers can have an impact on female officers' development as professionals. Self-perception as the reflection of others' attitudes toward the individual is one theory put forth as a predictor of development for many female officers. If self-perception is a product of social interactions with people in other social groups, then unfavorable atti-tudes held by the public and male officers would play an important role in the formation of female officers' **occupational self-concept**.[39] Consistent with this theory is the use of the concept of **self-efficacy** (perception of one's ability) to attempt to explain the underrepre-sentation of females in traditionally male-dominated occupations. In general, self-efficacy studies have found that males were confident in their abilities, whether in traditionally male or female occupations, while females' confidence in their abilities was lower than that of males for traditionally male jobs and higher than that of males for traditionally female jobs.[40]

One study examining female and male police officers' perceptions of each other found that female officers had mixed perceptions of male officers and their own compe-tency.[41] Female officers characterized male officers as more threatening, less kind and pa-tient, more assertive, less trusting and intelligent, and less acceptable professionally. These officers also considered male officers to be less effective overall in performing police work, especially in handling domestic disputes; however, male officers were judged to be more effective in handling violent offenders and youth problems. Female officers rated them-selves as less effective in performing such duties as handling violent offenders and riot sit-uations and viewed themselves as less strong, less competitive, less assertive, and less acceptable professionally. Male officers, conversely, had more favorable perceptions of their abilities than those of female officers and perceived female officers to be less assertive, strong, and effective in handling violent offenders and riot situations.

Therefore, female officers' less favorable perceptions of themselves reflect how they assume their male colleagues see them and influence their levels of self-confidence. Such influence is also supported by other studies, in which female officers were found to have lower expectations for promotions and lacked self-confidence to handle a variety of different policing incidents.[42]

COPING AND ADAPTING

In 1980, Susan Martin developed one of the first models of female officers' behavioral adaptations to the discriminatory and stressful situations they were facing in the police culture. She labeled the two extremes of a continuum of behaviors as **POLICEwomen** and **policeWOMEN**.[43] POLICEwomen seek to gain acceptance from male counterparts by becoming even more aggressive, loyal, and streetwise than the male officers. Martin said this extreme masculine behavior often gets them labeled as "bitch" or "dike" rather than gain them the acceptance they crave, but can never obtain. PoliceWOMEN, at the other extreme, are unable or unwilling to fully accept the patrol role. They are uncomfortable on patrol, fearful of injury, and reluctant to take control of situations. The women at this extreme enjoy the service aspects of policing and seek nonpatrol assignments and personal acceptance as women. Although many followers of Martin's model thought that she placed all women officers in one of these two categories, she believed, instead, that female officers ranged along the continuum, with few female officers at either extreme.

During the past two decades, as women have become more comfortable in the role of patrol officer and other, more specialized police roles, they have successfully combined attributes associated with both masculinity and femininity and have developed self-definitions perceived to be "feminine, trustworthy, and professionally competent."[44] As mentioned earlier, many women have achieved new status by striking a balance and projecting a professional image, encouraging a team approach, using humor to develop solidarity and frustrate unwelcome advances, and gaining a mentor to enhance their career potential. Their professional image is founded on their willingness to "prove" themselves first on patrol by demonstrating physical courage and working hard, but also in treating the public well and emphasizing close links with the community. In presenting themselves as professionals, they must appear rational, objective, and loyal to the organization, restricting any show of emotion or concerns over personal relationships. The use of humor is a very sensitive balancing act; in "giving it back," the female officer must avoid acting in a sexual or flirtatious way. Sexual harassment is handled informally by relying on support from a trusted friend or partner, silently regarding this treatment as a price one pays for taking this kind of job, seeking transfers away from tormenters, and resigning. Formal complaints cause retaliation, making the female officer's life miserable.[45]

Although Alice Stebbins Wells organized the first International Association of Policewomen in 1915 (as noted in Chapter 2), only recently have women begun to develop collective responses to work centered on their special interests. Many department-based associations have foundered because of lack of interest, fear of reprisals by male officers, or tensions among women from different ethnic groups. Along with formal associations, women have developed "**war stories**." Initially lacking the inside knowledge provided male officers, female officers began collecting their own stories, helping instruct new female officers on how to "**work the streets**."[46] The lack of female role models has compelled many to become field training officers and trainers. They have a sense of mission to train male and female recruits both so that they might see women can be good patrol officers and still be women.[47]

Chapter 1 discussed common stressors in law enforcement. When gender is taken into account, female officers particularly have stressors unique to them, but also related to the police organization. For example, verbal abuse, intimidation, sexual harassment, rumors about the female officers, and the negative attitudes of male officers, who also blatantly ignore female officers, are stressors impacting female officers.[48] Also "**group blame**"—that is, when one female officer makes a mistake, all female officers suffer—continually haunts female officers. Women in male-dominated environments often need to resolve the problems of their unequal status through role negotiation or by discovering the role that is acceptable to their work environment. Negotiating their roles may increase acceptance, but it is also increases role stress.[49] Female officers more than male officers find certain task-related stressors, such as dealing with tragedies or giving death notifications, especially stressful.[50] Families are another large source of stress for women officers, with over half of the women in one study indicating that their primary reason for leaving law enforcement was to spend more time with their families, raising their children.

Strategies for coping with stressors are similar for male and female officers, but differ psychologically. Women use escape more often than men, and women with higher levels of stress use escape the most often. Escape falls along the continuum of avoiding colleagues and supervisors to calling in sick.[51] Resigning is still too common a means of coping with the stress of policing. Although it may be appropriate for some officers, for women it has a particularly detrimental effect. It diminishes efforts to increase women's representation within the agency as a whole, as well as the likelihood of women increasing their representation in specialized assignments and supervisory positions.[52]

ISSUES CONCERNING FEMALE OFFICERS OF COLOR

After two decades of women actively pursuing law enforcement careers, studies are beginning to emerge concerning female officers of color. As noted in earlier chapters, the first such examinations suggest that the combination of race and gender exposes women of color to "**double marginality**," because of the combination of two token characteristics that can be double-counted for affirmative action purposes. Women of color often gain the hostility of both white women and men of color, who feel that the women of color have taken "their" places. Other researchers argue that the double-minority feature provides extra benefits arising from "the positive effects of a double negative especially for affirmative action."[53]

A situation that arose in Chicago in 1973 makes it easy to understand how double minority works against women of color. The Chicago Police Department's police sergeant's promotional examination was found to be discriminatory so a judge imposed **quotas**. African American women were initially selected from the promotion list as African American, but when white women realized that some African American women were being promoted to the rank of sergeant ahead of them, they filed a claim asserting

Women officers of color often face challenges beyond those of their white female or male peers.
Source: Courtesy NYPD Photo Unit.

that *all* females should be treated as a single minority group. Because the judge ruled that African American women could not be given double benefits, the Afro-American League's legal representative was asked whether it was acceptable to count the African American women as women, rather than as African American, for the purposes of the quota. Without consulting the women, the lawyer agreed. The women officers of color became the losers because the white women officers scored better on the promotional exam than they did.[54]

In departments with a large proportion of African American personnel or an African American chief of police, the effects of racism seem to diminish, but do tend to heighten black women's awareness of sex discrimination, especially in the selection of administrative staff. African American female officers always have to contend with one minority ranking or the other.[55] The black women's inferior social status has produced a distinct **feminist consciousness** that is different from that of white women. White women, who have more contact with white men, also have the potential for increased power through these associations. African American women, on the other hand, due to racism, have experienced less power.[56] Four stereotypes, or controlling images, of women of color have been identified: African American women as mammies (nurses for white families), matriarchs (strong family leaders), welfare recipients (mothers with multiple children living off welfare), and hot mommas (sexual objects). These images plague African American female officers.[57] As one veteran female officer of color who was interviewed stated, "I got tired of the surprised looks on all those white officers' faces when I said that I had no children, especially since they knew I had never been married."[58]

Although both white and black women officers are targets of male officers' hostility, African American women receive a different level of treatment from men. Historically, white women have been put on a pedestal and spared physical labor, while African American women had always assumed the beast of burden role, performing heavy physical labor in fields, factories, and the homes of white women. These roles transferred into policing. White women assigned to patrol, particularly those who were physically attractive, were more likely than African American women to be protected by white male officers. African American women also are told to remain as backup for their male partners, who do not expect them to perform as equals. When they defer and accept a passive role, it is claimed that they cannot be counted on and may instead be viewed as lazy.

Working with African American officers helps to reduce racial discrimination to some extent, but the relationship is often strained. The African American male officers sometimes ally with white male officers. As one African American female officer noted, "The only thing that I hate more than a white man trying to run over me is an African American man clearing the way."[59] Aware of the historical role of police as oppressors in the African American community, the female minority officer is reluctant to adopt the policing style that has been characteristic of white men, that is, aggressiveness.[60] This reluctance is also often mistaken as laziness or fear on their part.

Relations among women officers are usually poor. Women do not unite across the races; African American female officers have found white female officers to be as racist as white male officers. Both white and African American male officers use racism to control the women of their race, preventing the women officers from unifying to redress sex discrimination. Female officers often also feel uncomfortable uniting as a group, believing they will be better accepted as individuals. They are afraid that they will offend people, specifically, white males. They consider it best not to be deemed guilty by association.[61]

There is greater unity among African American female officers, although they are usually few in number and spread thinly throughout the police agency. Chicago police have a women officers' organization in which African American female officers have become more assertive and conscious of abuse.[62] The municipal agency in which the 50 veteran officers were interviewed has developed a **mentoring group** (discussed further in Chapter 9), and several of the women officers of color have become very active. Their goal is not only to support the few officers who are of color, but also to help gain support for women as a whole.

Even newer to the policing field are Latin American females. The potential for competition between African Americans and Latin Americans is ample. Compared to other professions requiring high school degrees, policing is considered prestigious and rewarding. For the same reason, competition between Latin American males and females is also quite strong. However, a major impediment for young ethnic minority males is prior felony convictions, increasing the opportunities for Latin American females.[63] One of the best predictors of Latin American success in becoming police officers is the proportion of Latin Americans in the population.[64] Large populations provide a larger, more viable pool of applicants, but possibly more important will be language (Spanish) requirements and the local political influence of a large Latin American population.

In general, Asian Americans are less attracted to governmental positions. New and first-generation Asian Americans have an inherent distrust of governmental officials arising from their experiences in their own countries.[65]

When minority female officers are promoted, they often stand up to harassment and challenge the systemic racial and gender discrimination they perceive. Having survived isolation and performance pressures as officers and now as sergeants, they seek to use their new authority as a means of solving the problems they endured. As a ranking female officer of color noted, "I would never let others know that the discrimination bothered me. That would be giving in to them; they would know they had gotten to me. I would rather get involved and try to make a difference."[66] In 1993, a popular magazine for Latin Americans publicized the promotion of Kansas City's first Mexican American female, Ramona Arroyo, to sergeant.[67] Sergeant Arroya was promoted after 13 years of service. She noted that in contrast to the stress she had felt from prejudice due to her gender and race, she now experienced pressure in her attempt to live up to her new responsibilities as a role model for Latin American women.

SUMMARY

In this chapter we have presented both the good and the bad, historically and contemporaneously, of women's entrance into policing. We showed that although today's female police officers perform as effectively as male officers, there are nevertheless issues concerning their acceptance, that is, mixed perceptions of their abilities by themselves, the public, and their male co-workers. The current era of community policing with its transition from an emphasis on physical prowess to creative problem solving and effective communication skills would seem tailor-made for women officers.

We also saw that women of color continue to struggle against their double minority status, but as they make rank, they seek to change minority women officers' status within law enforcement agencies.

In sum, although women have worked hard to be accepted in law enforcement, and will have to continue to do so, they have found the means to cope with their own perceptions, and the attitudes of others, in order to have satisfying careers.

READER LEARNING OUTCOMES

Having examined this chapter, the reader should understand:

- some of the early research concerning the performance of women in law enforcement
- findings regarding how women handle **calls for service**
- the early attitudes of male officers toward women and the theories advanced regarding the basis for those attitudes
- general citizen perceptions of women in policing
- the attitude and perceptions of women in law enforcement with regard to acceptance and self-perception
- major stressors that are unique to women in policing and strategies for coping and adapting to them

- issues concerning women of color
- the concept of community policing and how this strategy provides opportunities for women in the field

NOTES

1. J. Sichel, L. Friedman, J. Quint, and M. E. Smith, *Women on Patrol: A Pilot Study of Police Performance in New York City* (Washington, DC: National Institute of Law Enforcement and Criminal Justice, Law Enforcement Assistance Administration, 1978).

2. P. B. Lock and D. Anderson, *Policewomen on Patrol: Final Report* (Washington, DC: Police Foundation, 1974).

3. Lawrence Sherman, "Evaluation of Policewomen on Patrol in a Suburban Police Department," *Journal of Police Science and Administration* 3(4):434–438.

4. Sichel et al., *Women on Patrol,* p. 6.

5. John Snortum and John Beyers, "Patrol Activities of Male and Female Officers as a Function of Work Experience," *Police Studies* 6 (1983):36–42.

6. J. D. Bell, "Policewomen: Myths and Reality," *Journal of Police Science and Administration* 10(1) (1982):112–123.

7. Merry Morash and Jack Greene, Jack, "Evaluating Women on Patrol: A Critique of Contemporary Wisdom," *Evaluation Review* 10 (1988):230–255.

8. See, for example, Kenneth J. Peak and Ronald W. Glensor, *Community Policing and Problem Solving: Strategies and Practices,* 4th ed. (Upper Saddle River, NJ: Prentice Hall, 2004); Ronald W. Glensor, Mark E. Correia, and Kenneth J. Peak (eds.), *Policing Communities: Understanding Crime and Solving Problems* (Los Angeles: Roxbury, 2000), pp. 315–321; Willard M. Oliver, "The Third Generation of Community Policing: Moving Through Innovation, Diffusion, and Institutionalization," *Police Quarterly* 3 (December 2000):367–388.

9. Susan Miller, *Gender and Community Policing: Walking the Talk* (Boston: Northeastern University Press, 1999).

10. Ibid., pp. 88–95.

11. In Miller, *Gender and Community Policing,* p. 90.

12. Ibid., p. 120.

13. Ibid., p. 155.

14. Frances Heidensohn, *Women in Control? The Role of Women in Law Enforcement* (Oxford: Clarendon Press, 1992), p. 97.

15. Robin N. Haar, "Patterns of Interaction in a Police Patrol Bureau: Race and Gender Barriers to Integration," *Justice Quarterly* 16 (1997):303–336.

16. Mary Brown, "The Plight of Female Police: A Survey of NW Patrolmen," *The Police Chief* (September 1994):50–52.

17. Mary Cuadrado, "Female Police Officers: Gender Bias and Professionalism," *American Journal of Police* 14(2) (1995):149–165.

18. Cynthia Epstein, "Encountering the Male Establishment: Sex-Status Limits on Women's Careers in the Professions," in Ronald Pavalko (ed.), *Sociological Perspectives on Occupations* (Itasca, IL: F. E. Peacock, 1972), pp. 364–384.

19. Susan Martin and Nancy Jurik, *Doing Justice, Doing Gender: Women in Law and Criminal Justice Occupations* (Thousand Oaks, CA: Sage Publications, 1996), pp. 63–65; Jennifer Hunt, "The Logic of Sexism Among Police," *Women and Criminal Justice* 1 (1990):3–30.

20. Martin and Jurik, *Doing Justice, Doing Gender,* p. 64.

21. Heidensohn, *Women in Control?* p. 215.

22. Epstein, "Encountering the Male Establishment," p. 366.

23. Joanne Belknap, *The Invisible Woman: Gender, Crime, and Justice.* (Belmont, CA: Wadworth, 2001).

24. Ibid., p. 366; also see Rosabeth Kanter, "Some Effects of Proportions in Group Life: Skewed Sex Ratios and Responses to Token Women," *American Journal of Sociology* 82 (1977):965–990.

25. P. Baunach and N. Rafter, "Sex Role Operations: Strategies for Women Working in the Criminal Justice System," in Nichole Rafter and Phyllis Baunach (eds.), *Judge, Lawyer, Victim, Thief* (Stoughton, Mass.: Northeastern University Press, 1982), p. 344.

26. T. L. Wertsch, "Walking the Thin Blue Line: Policewomen and Tokenism Today," *Women and Criminal Justice* 9 (1998):23–61.

27. Harriet Bradley, *Men's Work, Women's Work: A Sociological History of the Sexual Division of Labour in Employment* (Minneapolis, MN: University of Minnesota Press, 1989), p. 18.

28. Ibid., p. 19.

29. Gwendolyn L. Gerber, *Women and Men Police Officers: Status, Gender, and Personality* (Westport, CI: Praeger, 2001).

30. Nancy Jurik, "Striking a Balance: Female Correctional Officers, Gender Role Stereotypes, and Male Prisons," *Sociological Inquiry* 58 (1988):291–305; Malcolm Young, *An Inside Job: Policing and Police Culture in Britain* (Oxford: Clarendon, 1991); Heidensohn, *Women in Control?*, p. 104.

31. K. Leger, "Public Perceptions of Female Police Officers on Patrol," *American Journal of Criminal Justice* 9 (1997):231–249.

32. K. Lersch, in Kathryn Scarborough and Pamela Collins, *Women in Public and Private Law Enforcement* (Boston: Butterworth Heinemann, 2002), pp. 65–66.

33. Kathryn E. Scarborough and Craig Hemmens, "Section 1983 Suits Against Law Enforcement in the Circuit Courts of Appeal," *Thomas Jefferson Law Review* 21(1) (1999):1–21.

34. Erving Goffman, *Encounters* (Indianapolis, IN: 1961), p. 88.

35. Martin, *Gender and Community Policing,* p. 85.

36. C. Garrison, N. Grant, and K. McCormick, "Utilization of Women Police," *The Police Chief* (1988):69–73.

37. James Daum and Cindy Johns, "Police Work from a Woman's Perspective," *The Police Chief* (September 1994):46–48.

38. Joanne Belknap and Jill Shelley, "The New Lone Ranger: Policewomen on Patrol," *American Journal of Police* 12 (1992):47–75.

39. M. S. Singer and K. Love, "Gender Differences in Self Perception of Occupational Efficacy: A Study of Law Enforcement Officers," *Journal of Social Behavior and Personality* 3(19):63–74.

40. Ibid., p. 64.

41. Ibid., p. 70.

42. Allen Worden, "The Attitudes of Women and Men in Policing: Testing Conventional and Contemporary Wisdom," *Criminology* 31 (1993):236.

43. Martin and Jurik, *Doing Justice, Doing Gender,* p. 97.

44. Ibid., p. 98.

45. Ibid., p. 99.

46. Heidensohn, *Women in Control?,* p. 163.

47. Ibid., p. 176.

48. J. Wexler and D. Logan, "Sources of Stress Among Women Police Officers," *Journal of Police Science and Administration* 13 (1983):100; Curt Bartol, George Bergen, Julie Volckens, and Kathleen Knoras, "Women in Small-Town Policing: Job Performance and Stress," *Criminal Justice and Behavior* 19 (1992):243.

49. Ibid., p. 244.

50. B. Seagram and C. Stark-Adamac, "Women in Canadian Urban Policing: Why Are They Leaving Us?" *The Police Chief* (1992):126.

51. Merry Morash and Robin Haar, "Gender, Workplace Problems, and Stress in Policing," *Justice Quarterly* 12 (1995):130.

52. Jerry Jacobs, *Revolving Doors: Sex Segregation and Women's Careers* (Stanford, CA: Stanford University Press, 1989).

53. Susan Martin, "Outsider Within the Station House: The Impact of Race and Gender on Black Women Police," *Social Problems* 41(3):384; George Felkenes and Jean Schroedel, "A Case Study of Minority Women in Policing," *Women & Criminal Justice,* 4 (1993):65.

54. Martin, "Outsider Within the Station House," pp. 388–389.

55. Ibid., p. 390.

56. Aileen Hurtado, "Relating to Privilege: Seduction and Rejection in the Subordination of White Women and Women of Color," *Signs* 14 (1989):845.

57. Patricia Collins, "Learning from the Outsider Within: The Sociological Significance of Black Feminist Thought," *Social Problems* 33 (1986):14–32.

58. Veteran female officer interviewed on July 12, 2000.

59. Martin, "Outsider Within the Station House," p. 393.

60. Helen Greene, "Black Females in Law Enforcement," *Journal of Contemporary Criminal Justice* 16 (2000):238.

61. Martin, "Outsider Within the Station House," p. 388.

62. Felkenes and Schroedel, "A Case Study of Minority Women in Policing," pp. 81–82.

63. Nicholas Alozie and Enrique Ramirez, "'A Piece of the Pie' and More Competition and Hispanic Employment on Urban Police Forces," *Urban Affairs Review* 34 (1999):459.

64. Ibid., p. 471.

65. Ibid., p. 470.

66. Vivian Lord, "The Professional Life of Women Law Enforcement Officers." Technical Report for Charlotte–Mecklenburg Police Department, September 2000, p. 9.

67. Glen Townes, "Showing Her Mettle," *Hispanic* 6 (1993):2–3.

Chapter 6
Gaining Entry: The Hiring Process

❖

Key Chapter Terms

Academy training
Background investigation
Cadet programs
Conditional job offer
Drug testing
Field training officer
Hiring process

Internships
Medical exam
Oral interview
Personal history statement
Physical abilities test
Polygraph examination
Psychological evaluation

Recruit
Résumé
Ride-alongs
Use of deadly force
Written examination

Some of us are becoming the men we wanted to marry.

—Gloria Steinem

Introduction

Earlier chapters described women's progression into policing, as well as their ability to become successful police officers. We also discussed some of the obstacles that they have had to overcome in order to achieve success. This chapter extends those earlier discussions by taking the reader through the preparation, application, examination, and training processes that are generally used by law enforcement agencies for transforming individuals into functioning members of the law enforcement community. What is described is often a daunting and rigorous "hurdle process" for gaining entry into this occupation.

Therefore, it is crucial that prospective police applicants objectively assess their own strengths and weaknesses with respect to each phase involved.

The chapter begins by providing some ideas for assessing one's own abilities and career options. Then it examines the kinds of preparatory measures that can be taken if considering a law enforcement career, as well as the kinds of background and experiences that agencies like to see in their applicants. Next is a discussion of the various kinds of examinations and interviews that might be conducted as part of the overall **hiring process**. This discussion is followed by a look at the academy and field training that is required after the **recruit** has obtained employment.

The underlying theme of this chapter is that there is much that a person can do to lay the groundwork for a successful law enforcement career, both during the preemployment phase and immediately after securing a position.

ASSESSING ONESELF

Needed: A Realistic View of the Police Role

As indicated, the first task in seriously considering a career in law enforcement is to take an honest look at oneself, and then to take another hard look at the career one is considering. The picture of law enforcement is particularly susceptible to romanticization because of inaccurate movie and television portrayals of officers and agents in action. Historically, many television programs (for example, *CSI* and *Law and Order* episodes) and countless movies have glamorized the work of policing. They have also depicted policing as nonstop action where the "good guys" always win and have portrayed their lead characters (like *Police Woman*'s Sergeant Pepper, played by Angie Dickinson, and Clint Eastwood's Dirty Harry) in a false light, inflicting on suspects the most grievous violations of their constitutional rights. At a minimum, potential police applicants are encouraged to read textbooks and other essays that accurately describe the work of policing—much of which is full of drudgery, paperwork, and danger. Women working in law enforcement also strongly advise preservice individuals to get to know the agency they are considering (some methods for doing so are discussed in this chapter).

In sum, a woman must first take a realistic look at the field, what she wants in a career, what she expects from her work, and how well suited she is to that discipline. It is also advisable to go to a counseling department, if in school, or to visit a private career counselor, who can administer professional interest inventories and aptitude tests for helping explore career options.

What Do I Want from a Career?

Many people enter policing with the goals of helping people, making a difference in their community, job security, or having an exciting career. In order to be satisfied with a career in law enforcement, one must go beyond these important but idealistic goals and ask some or all of the following preliminary questions:

What are my personal values?
What lifestyle am I used to leading and wish to enhance?

What work conditions are important to me?

What can I tolerate?

What conditions do I reject?

What short-term and long-term personal goals do I have?

Where do I want to be in five years? Ten years?

Are there specific family issues or goals with which I need to be concerned?

In looking at a career, one should first look at such general characteristics as service versus technical tasks, requirements for physical ability or cognitive skills or a balance, indoor or outdoor work and working with other people or alone. The latter may seem relatively unimportant, but it is essential that one decide at the outset whether she or he is cut out to work with people—and especially their entire spectrum of problems, as the police do—or predominantly with non-people tasks, such as in accounting or with computers.

PREPARATION: SOME PRELIMINARY CONSIDERATIONS

Mobility

It stands to reason that one's likelihood of acquiring a position of the sort that is being sought will be increased by his or her mobility, that is, the ability and willingness to relocate where there are more openings. For example, sometimes the willingness to relocate a relatively short distance to a larger city will afford tremendous opportunities, not only to be hired by a larger agency, but also to work in a broader variety of specialized assignments that are not normally found in smaller jurisdictions.

Age

People interested in gaining a position with a law enforcement agency should first find out (from the job posting, human resources office, or some other available means) the minimum age for being hired. Although most agencies require police officers to be at least 21 years of age, there are a number of avenues to consider before determining whether one is too young to apply. For example, many police agencies have reserve or **cadet programs**, which provide potential police recruits with safe experiences while both the individual and the agency assess the future job-fit. Cadets are given responsibilities, ranging from administrative duties and analyzing data to interacting with businesses and residents about ongoing problems. Federal agencies often have a narrower window of employability than local agencies. People who are hired by a federal law enforcement agency must be between 21 and 37 years of age. This outer age limit is based on the requirement of 20 years of service before mandatory retirement at age 57.

Related Experience

Most law enforcement agencies will seek applicants who have some type of prior work experience. Such experience can demonstrate such strengths as reliability, honesty, punctuality, and interpersonal skills, as well as any weaknesses in these areas. All past employers should be listed on the application form or **résumé**; it is likely that they will all be interviewed as part of the **background investigation** by the agency. Law enforcement agencies are also interested in an applicant's extracurricular activities, such as volunteer work, service activities, sports, and any offices held in organizations. Volunteering shows that applicants care about and truly want to contribute to their community.

People who are interested in a law enforcement career can also begin to acquire related experience as early as high school. Many law enforcement agencies have Explorer programs that teach students basic policing skills, such as first aid, defensive tactics, firearms, and investigative skills, as well as exposing them to different opportunities in the profession. Community colleges and universities usually offer **internships** in a variety of fields. Although gaining internships in federal law enforcement agencies is quite competitive, completing an internship with a local police agency can also be beneficial when applying to a variety of law enforcement agencies, not just the agency in which the internship was conducted. Engaging in **ride-alongs** with regular officers is also very illuminating in terms of the general nature of police work.

By spending time with sworn officers, potential applicants are much more knowledgeable about the occupation, are able to judge whether or not they want to assume a role in it, and can even participate (if in an internship or ride-along) in some of the daily activities of officers or agents. By virtue of their association with potential applicants, either through an internship or a ride-along or some other means, the agency is in a better position to judge (and assist) the individual who is seeking a regular position. Another benefit is the opportunity to secure letters of reference from agency employees, which can be very important for obtaining a position either with that agency or another.

Education

Although many police agencies do not require more than a high school diploma, they are usually able to pick from among a group of individuals who have a higher level of education. As of 2000, almost 40 percent of the large-city police agencies required some college education.[1] Furthermore, opportunities for advancement and pay increases are often linked to formal education. Federal agencies will not consider hiring someone with less than a college education and often require additional knowledge, skills, and abilities, such as accounting, law, computer skills, or fluency in a second language. Such skills can set an applicant apart from the other candidates.

Résumé Preparation

Most police agencies and their human resources offices use their own application forms (discussed later), but a well-prepared résumé and cover letter are major selling points. They provide the administrator with a snapshot of the applicant, including highlights of the applicant's background.

A résumé, normally limited to one page, emphasizes significant areas of the applicant's educational and professional life. There are several books available that explain careers in criminal justice, discuss the process that should be followed in applying for them, and detail the kinds of information to be included in a résumé.[2] There are also many books and workshops devoted to résumé preparation. Required information generally includes personal information, such as name, address, telephone numbers, and email address; educational and work experience; a brief description of professional goals; any awards or special accomplishments; community involvement; and interests and hobbies. References should also be included. After determining the materials to be included, the material should be presented in a readable, attractive, and professional manner, and then proofread thoroughly for spelling and punctuation errors. A sample résumé is provided in Appendix III.

"NEGOTIATING HURDLES": THE HIRING PROCESS

Often viewed as a series of hurdles to be negotiated, the hiring process generally takes three to six months to complete and usually involves the following sequence of activities and tests, although the order will vary from agency to agency:

> *Application filed*
> *Written exam*
> *Agility test*
> *Oral interview*
> *Conditional job offer*
> *Background investigation*
> *Psychological exam*
> *Polygraph exam*
> *Drug screening*
> *Medical examination*
> *Applicant hired*

We will discuss briefly these steps in the process.

Application Forms

Law enforcement applications are actually **personal history statements** because they often consist of ten or more pages of questions covering most areas of an applicant's life. Truthfulness, neatness, and completeness are essential. An applicant should carefully review the directions for the entire application and follow them explicitly. A background investigator will verify all information that is provided and naturally be suspicious about any gaps in one's work or educational background that are not adequately explained.

Most applications include the listing of all places and dates of residency, places of employment, educational institutions, financial history, criminal history (this includes arrests as well as convictions), and drug use. Again, all of this information will be verified, and the applicant is likely to be asked about it during a polygraph examination if such is required. Other requirements might include a notarized signature, proof of residency, a copy of a social security card, a valid driver's license, educational transcripts, and military discharge papers.

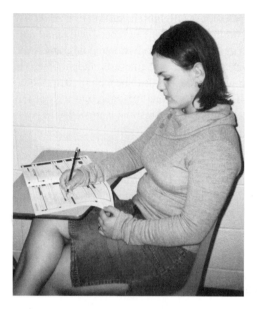

The written examination is a major part of the police hiring process.

Written Examination

The **written examinations** that are often used are cognitive tests measuring reading comprehension, mathematics skills, reasoning, and interests. The reading comprehension examination will usually include narratives consisting of a set of events with different characters and details. Assume, for example, that a "bulletin " reads as follows:

> A missing child has been reported; the parents of John Smith, age 8, have reported that he did not return home from school this afternoon. He was last seen at Pop Warner football practice at Owens Field, two blocks from his home at 89 Jasper Gulch, at approximately 5:30 P.M. He is approximately 4′2″, 68 pounds, with red hair and blue eyes. He was wearing a black and gold football uniform, and carrying a green tote bag. He may be in the company of his cousin, Judy Jones, age 10, who is about the same size and wearing a dark blue dress.

The reader must try to recall as many details as possible. In other test questions, the applicant will be required to understand the sequence of events, and the individuals involved leading up to, during, and following a hypothetical crime. After the applicants read the narrative, they will be expected to answer a set of questions related to the incident. As the applicants answer the questions, they will attempt to describe all the characters, how they relate to each other, and the action of the narrative. They are expected to write responses that answer who, what, where, when, why, and how as thoroughly as possible.

The applicant may also be required to write a simulated police field report, which will be scored on its accuracy, completeness, organization, sentence structure, spelling, grammar, and punctuation.[3] Although mathematical skills may not appear to be important in law enforcement, there are areas (for example, traffic accident investigation, crime trend analysis) in which the use of formulas, fractions, decimals, and percentages is necessary. (Indeed, the Federal Bureau of Investigation places considerable emphasis on mathematical skills in testing its applicants.) If an applicant has not attended school for an extended period of time, obtaining a mathematics workbook or tutor to help review some of the materials may be a good idea.

Spatial perception questions may be included in the initial written test or in the later psychological/intelligence testing. These questions usually take the form of a series of three-dimensional figures, oriented in space and/or folded in different ways. The applicant's success in selecting the matching figure helps test the ability to visualize and orient objects spatially.

Physical Fitness/Agility Testing

As explained in earlier chapters, law enforcement agencies must ensure that their entrance requirements do not discriminate against protected groups, including women. Prior to changes in the law, many agencies had minimum height and weight requirements that screened out a disproportionate number of women. Indeed, in 1956, 85 percent of all police agencies surveyed required that applicants be at least 5′ 8″ tall![4] Today, the **physical abilities tests** must be job-related and measure one's abilities to perform those activities actually required for the job.

Physical fitness is the ability to carry out daily tasks with vigor and alertness, without undue fatigue, and with ample energy to engage in leisure pursuits and to tolerate the above-average stresses encountered in emergency situations.[5] To determine the physical challenges, most state and many local agencies have conducted job task analyses in order to determine the tasks essential for their law enforcement positions; officers self-report what they actually do of a physical nature on the job. From these analyses, the agency can develop and administer a more job-related entrance-level physical fitness examination that is composed of exercises truly measuring the applicant's ability to perform tasks critical to the job. (It should be noted, however, that some authors[6] assert that job task analyses simply legitimate the status quo by collecting information about how a task is performed at a certain point in time and thus are limited as a means of defining what the police job *should* be.)

Usually, applicants may obtain a copy of the activities that are involved in the physical ability's test several weeks in advance of the actual test in order to prepare themselves accordingly. Many medical conditions (including surgeries) will not prohibit an applicant from becoming a law enforcement officer, but acceptance will depend on whether the medical or physical condition poses restrictions to carrying out the essential job functions. If an applicant has questions about the ability to meet the minimum qualifications or the impact of a prior medical history, the agency recruiter or website should be able to address them.

Although federal, state, and local agencies vary in their physical requirements, all are usually based on aerobic capacity, or cardiorespiratory endurance; strength, both lower and upper body; flexibility; and body fat composition. The assessment may include a battery of exercises such as a run or step-test that must be completed within a certain time; a specified number of sit-ups, push-ups, and pull-ups performed within a designated time; or a sit and reach test. Other tasks might include climbing through a standard window opening approximately 3 feet off the ground, crawling through a culvert, dragging a 150-pound dummy a specified distance, and pulling a double-action handgun trigger a specified number of times. Although women normally have less upper body strength than men, the required physical entrance testing should be passable by a majority of both sexes if they are physically fit. If applicants do not pass the physical fitness/agility test on their first attempt, they can then determine whether the agency allows applicants to retest. If so, they should continue their physical conditioning and try again.

The physical fitness testing is an area about which women seeking to enter law enforcement naturally have some trepidation—and many writers feel this concern is well founded. For example, Kimberly A. Lonsway[7] studied the negative effect that physical agility testing has on the number of women who are eventually sworn. Her survey (of 62 large police agencies) found that 88.7 percent of all agencies reported using a physical agility test, including 100 percent of state agencies, 94.7 percent of local agencies, and 76.2 percent of county agencies. Furthermore, the physical agility tests used by police agencies across the country were not consistent (there being a wide range of activities used), and evidence regarding their validity is almost completely lacking. Lonsway asserted that "there was a significant negative effect of physical agility on the representation of sworn women" and concluded that the difference amounted to almost 5 full percentage points:

> Agencies with no physical agility test reported having 15.8 percent sworn women, whereas those with such a test had 10.9 percent. In other words, agencies without a test have 45 percent more women than those with such a test.[8]

In light of this finding, Lonsway concluded that although the need for women in law enforcement has never been greater, and research has consistently documented that women perform the job of policing at least as successfully as their male colleagues, "eliminating the physical agility test as an entry-level screening device is therefore one option that police administrators should seriously consider."[9]

Given the widespread use (and, presumably, the popularity) of entry-level physical agility tests, and the fact that police agencies do not wish to hire individuals who cannot perform at a minimum level, the best advice for prospective women applicants is to be in good enough physical condition to achieve success in this part of the hiring process and later—for their own safety and well-being as much as for their agency's.

Oral Interview

Agencies will vary in their use of **oral interviews**. All applicants will be interviewed at least by one human resources officer or police agency recruiting officer to gather some initial information and to explain the application process. Although recruiting officers may screen for minimum standards, they may make no other employment decisions. Some agencies use oral boards consisting of supervisors of different ranks to interview applicants in the final phase of the hiring process.

Applicants who are to be interviewed by an oral board should attempt to prepare themselves by acquiring a thorough knowledge of both the agency and the entire jurisdiction (that is, the city, county, or state where application is being made) as well as their own personal history and attributes. With respect to the jurisdiction, the applicant should be familiar with its form of government and its officials, any highly publicized issues, and crime rates. Agency information includes the size of the organization and its mission and values. Many police agencies now have comprehensive Internet home pages that can be of assistance here.

Physical agility tests are typically a part of the hiring process.
Source: Courtesy Washoe County (Nevada) Sheriff's Office.

The primary purpose of the oral interview is for the agency administrators to get to know applicants personally as well as for applicants to get familiar with the organization and whether they would be happy working within it. The interviewers' roles are to listen to applicants, to observe their performance under stress and ability to analyze problems, to ask probing questions that will assist in determining character, and to ascertain communication

The oral interview is typically included in the hiring of law enforcement recruits and is one of the most critical phases of the process.

and interpersonal skills. They will also want to observe how candidates dress and groom themselves for the interview.

Following are examples of the kinds of questions that may be asked of applicants during the oral interview:

> *Why do you want to work for this particular agency?*
>
> *Why should we hire you?*
>
> *What are your strengths?*
>
> *What are your weaknesses, and what have you done to strengthen those areas?*
>
> *What do you feel is your greatest accomplishment?*
>
> *What have you done to prepare yourself for this position?*
>
> *How would you describe your work ethic?*
>
> *What are your career goals (or, where do you want to be, and what do you want to be doing five years from now)?*

Another primary purpose of the oral interview is to gain perspective on the applicants' values. Police agencies cannot afford to hire someone who is of low moral and ethical character, who is going to engage in corrupt behavior, and who will pose a serious risk in terms of liability. Accordingly, candidates may be asked the following kinds of hypothetical questions, focusing on ethical behaviors and use of force:

- You and another officer are dispatched to a burglary call at an office building. While searching the scene, you observe the other officer remove an expensive fountain pen from a desktop and then pocket it. How would you respond?

- You are in the locker room at the end of shift. You hear another officer talking about a male officer's anatomy. What response would you have?

Other kinds of questions may attempt to determine how an applicant might prioritize actions in different situations; note that some questions also emphasize officer survival:

- You are dispatched to a neighborhood park to check out a young man who is acting strangely. Upon arrival, you see the youth standing near a group of children playing on a merry-go-round. He is holding a .22 calibre rifle. What is your next action?
- You are dispatched to an apartment complex. Upon looking through the open front door, you observe a man with a knife standing over a woman who is lying on the floor, severely wounded and bleeding. There is an infant sitting in a high chair nearby. Your reactions?
- You are in a downtown area making an arrest. A crowd gathers and you begin to hear comments about "police harassment." Soon the crowd becomes angry. How do you react?

Although candidates are not expected to know departmental or legal procedures in depth, they are expected to give weight to ethical behavior, human rights, officer survival—and to possess common sense. The interviewers may be more interested in the problem-solving process that the applicant uses to respond to a problem than in the answer itself. The interviewers might also be interested in whether the applicant has considered under what conditions deadly force can be employed; applicants would be well advised to familiarize themselves with the U.S. Supreme Court's decision concerning the **use of deadly force**.[10]

At the conclusion of the formal interview, the interviewers usually ask whether or not the candidate would like to ask any questions. It is *not* a good idea to decline this offer, and the candidate should view it as an opportunity to indicate interest in the position, agency, and community by asking relevant questions to demonstrate interest and prior thought concerning these matters.[11] Furthermore, candidates should use this opportunity to make a brief closing statement that lets the board know that they are very interested in the position (if such is the case) and are confident in their ability to do a good job. It is also good to follow up the interview with a letter that expresses appreciation for the board's time and, again, interest in the position.

The Conditional Offer

The Americans with Disabilities Act (ADA) protects individuals with disabilities from discrimination.[12] In general, individuals cannot be asked questions about disabilities, but rather, whether they can perform the critical functions of the job. Because information about a disability might come out during the selection process, the process is divided into two steps: before and after a **conditional job offer**.

Before a conditional job offer is made, the agency's recruiting staff must restrict its assessment of a candidate to areas that clearly will not disclose a disability, but do help to ascertain the candidate's ability to perform the job. Included are written exams assessing the candidate's ability to read, write, and perform math functions (discussed earlier); physical performance; and drug use and carefully screened interviews.

Qualified candidates may then be offered a position on the condition that they can successfully complete the rest of the selection process, such as the psychological exam, background investigation, **medical exam**, and **polygraph examination**—any of which might disclose a disability. A disability still cannot disqualify the applicant as long as the applicant is capable of performing the job. If, for example, a female has a medical problem such as endometriosis (a condition in which the endometrium, the lining of the uterus, is found in locations outside the uterus), this condition should not affect her ability to perform the activities of a law enforcement officer. When she is conditionally offered a job, the condition might be documented during her medical exam; however, because she passed earlier tests that allowed her to be given a conditional offer, this discovery should not influence a job offer.

The Background Investigation

Done properly, the background investigation is probably the most expensive and time-consuming portion of the law enforcement agency's recruitment and hiring process. As with the oral interview, this step measures a major fact about the applicant: character. But it goes beyond merely asking questions of the applicant or having the applicant demonstrate specific skills. Rather, it involves conversations with people who are familiar with the applicant professionally, academically, or personally.[13] Background investigators, like polygraph examiners, do not expect people to be perfect; everyone has "skeletons buried in the closet." These investigators are trained to identify deceptive behavior through verbal and nonverbal clues, and it is not wise for applicants to attempt to deceive them.

The background investigation usually begins with the completion of a personal history statement by the applicant. The applicant will first be asked to sign a "release of information" form that authorizes the agency to delve into background information. The background investigator will then verify all information that the applicant provides in the application form(s): dates and places of employment and reasons for leaving, graduation dates and degrees completed, financial health, and so forth. The investigator will interview not only the references that applicants provide but also people with whom they have worked, neighbors, and recent classmates. Applicants should contact potential references and other people with whom a background investigator might talk to notify them of the possible interview. These individuals will normally be asked to comment on the applicant's work habits, any prior substance abuse, the ability to interact with others, financial responsibility, examples of work or anger under stress, problem-solving ability, maturity, and ethical behavior. They will probably be asked to divulge any reason why they believe the applicant should not be considered for a law enforcement position.

It is therefore critical that applicants be totally honest when responding to questions about their background. Giving false information on an application form or resume or during a polygraph examination or oral interview will cause them to be eliminated from consideration or terminated if false information is discovered after hiring. It is also important to know what is not acceptable to law enforcement agencies in terms of prior criminal offenses, drug use, traffic violations, and financial problems.

With regard to *criminal offenses,* it is important to remember that law enforcement agencies normally want to know about offenses for which the applicant was arrested at any age (not just convictions as an adult). The agency will take into account the applicant's age at the time of committing the offense, but all arrests must be accounted for; omissions will be considered lying. Even offenses that have been expunged should be revealed. Most law enforcement agencies will not hire an individual who has been arrested for a felony as an adult. Certain felonies, however, under certain circumstances might not be enough to eliminate an applicant if the crimes were committed while a juvenile.

One's *financial history and current credit status* are also very important to law enforcement agencies. People who have had problems managing their financial affairs and have amassed credit problems might be susceptible to accepting gratuities or bribes. Therefore, law enforcement agencies need to be sure that they are hiring individuals who have demonstrated the ability to live within their means. It is also advisable to obtain a current credit report before one is sent to the police agency. Often, credit reports are inaccurate, and it is critical to resolve discrepancies before the background investigator reviews the report.[14]

Although ideally this is not the case, because of the subjective nature of the background investigation, it can be a prime area for discrimination against women and minorities. Women struggling to raise children on their own, who were out of the job market while raising children, or who were past victims of domestic or sexual assaults may not appear to be viable candidates to the investigator. If a female who is interested in law enforcement knows that she has a history that might disqualify her, she should discuss it with her recruiter so that she can explain her resolution of those issues. For example, a female may have a poor credit history that began immediately after separating from her spouse. If she is able to demonstrate her constructive efforts to settle her financial situation, the agency might see her not only as a viable candidate but also as one who has valuable life experiences that could make her an effective community policing officer.

Finally, because the selection process often takes six months, it is expected that applicants will apply at more than one agency. Applicants should just inform the background investigator of the agencies to which they have applied.

Psychological Evaluation

Psychologists who evaluate the applicants' responses to a battery of psychological tests and possibly conduct a clinical interview should be not only licensed but also knowledgeable about law enforcement officers' jobs and experienced in conducting **psychological evaluations** for law enforcement agencies. It may be difficult for individuals to acquire information about the specific instruments used for the psychological evaluation; however, they all will attempt to screen out those individuals who have difficulty managing anger, coping with stressful jobs or life situations, or interacting with people who are different from them.

The battery of instruments will include at least one measure that identifies mental illness and one or more measures that assesses traits important to police work, including compatibility, self-confidence, diplomacy, independence, dependability, decisiveness, and integrity. Currently, emphasis is also placed on traits considered important for community-oriented policing and problem solving.[15] For example, the agency would likely test for such applicant abilities as taking the initiative to analyze and solve neighborhood problems and communicating with different types of people without bias. (These traits are discussed further in the section on training.) As in the other stages of selection, honest reporting by the applicant is essential. The psychological instruments contain questions designed to detect responses that attempt to mislead or make the applicant more desirable.

The psychological exam may also include questions concerning victimization by domestic violence or sexual assault. Responses to these questions should not be independent disqualifiers. If they were, agencies would screen out an enormous number of women who would make excellent police officers. As noted by the National Center for Women & Policing, one in every six women in the United States will become a victim of sexual assault, and half of all women will be victims of domestic violence within their lifetimes.[16] If the psychological evaluation is conducted before the conditional job offer, it cannot include measures of mental illness. Some agencies will conduct a preliminary psychological evaluation that measures traits important to law enforcement, such as anger and stress coping skills. Once a conditional job offer is made, then the applicant returns for a follow-up evaluation of mental illness.

The results of the psychological evaluation are not ranked or graded, but rather assessed as acceptable or not acceptable. Some psychologists will also use a "marginal" category. If applicants are asked to see a second psychologist, more than likely they have received a marginal rating. Applicants will also be told in the introduction to the test that the information belongs to the agency, not the applicant. The agency will keep the information confidential in the applicant's file, but the applicant will not normally receive a copy of the results.

It is difficult to prepare for a psychological assessment, but prior to the test an applicant can attempt to identify any problems or stressors and consider the means available for reducing them. This self-assessment should be conducted several weeks before the psychological exam, not only to improve the assessment results but also for general personal well-being. The day before taking the psychological assessment, the applicant should make plans to spend a relaxing evening. That may mean a quiet, uneventful evening with family or alone—anything that will be relaxing and that will reduce stress levels. Several good nights' sleep are also important, as well as allowing plenty of time to prepare and arrive at the test site.

Polygraph Examination

Although the polygraph examination, commonly called a "lie-detector" test, is not admissible in court for criminal cases, it is legal for law enforcement hiring purposes. The courts have ruled that it is in the public's interest to be able to ascertain the integrity and other characteristics of its future police officers, who will be carrying firearms and will possess the authority to use lethal force.[17] The primary purpose of the examination is to substantiate the information collected during the selection process, particularly the background investigation.

Most polygraph operators have been trained and certified by the American Polygraph Association.[18] The polygraph exam is based on the fact that when humans experience anxiety, their respiration, perspiration (Galvanic skin resistance), and blood pressure rates increase.

The polygraph examiner will connect the applicant to a machine that measures these physiological changes, a process that is completely painless. A baseline measure is taken at the outset so that any initial nervousness the applicant is exhibiting will be discerned. Often, the applicant is shown the list of polygraph questions before the test is administered, so if the applicant is concerned about any of the questions, the anxiety level will begin to be exhibited in anticipation of the question.

As with the other steps in the selection process, gender bias can exist with polygraph examinations even though all the questions must relate to the job and are asked of both male and female applicants. Questions about sexual acts cannot be designed to explore the applicant's sexual orientation. The applicant should not be asked questions about previous victimization by domestic violence or child abuse. Of course, questions in connection with criminal activity can be asked.[19]

As with the psychological examination, the polygraph test will not determine hiring decisions; rather it provides information about the applicant's truthfulness. The results are often categorized as truthful, inconclusive, or deceptive. If an applicant inadvertently tells a lie or omits information on the job application, it is important to notify the polygraph operator of that discrepancy before the examination begins.

Drug Testing

The requirements of law enforcement agencies differ with regard to experimental drug use. Few agencies, if any, will hire someone who has been arrested for a felony for drug use or drug trafficking. Some agencies will not even consider an applicant who has engaged in the casual use of marijuana during the previous five years. (However, as agencies now find their applicant pools shrinking dramatically, many are reevaluating and adjusting such requirements.) Again, if in doubt, it is best to obtain a listing of the agency's minimum qualifications (either from its website or human resources office).

Preemployment **drug testing** is considered legal for any position in which public safety is a concern.[20] As noted earlier, applicants for law enforcement positions may be tested for every form of controlled substance, including opiates, cocaine, marijuana, amphetamines, methamphetamines, barbiturates, and hallucinogenic drugs. A positive test for any of these drugs will disqualify an applicant for a law enforcement position. It goes without saying that anyone who is considering a career in law enforcement should *not* consider using a product that claims to provide a negative urine test for "dirty" applicants.

Medical Examination

There are a number of medical conditions that could be problematic for female police applicants, including breast, ovarian, or uterine cancer; menstrual problems; pregnancy or complications from pregnancy; and depression. As with all of the other decisions made in the selection process, the medical decision is based on the applicant's ability to perform the duties of an officer. Females who have survived cancer or recovered from depression or pregnancy complications should not be eliminated as candidates. Questions or information about abortions should not even be reported. As with the psychological assessment, medical findings are not rated on a scale, but rather are rated as acceptable or not acceptable for hire. Not-acceptable findings should be documented in detail so the agency is clear on what those factors were.

FORMAL ENTRY INTO POLICING: ACADEMY TRAINING

A Major Career Stage

Today, the concern over well-trained officers and civil liability has made **academy training** a vital part of the hiring process, or as Clinton Terry states, it is "merely another filter through which the candidate must successfully pass."[21] The recruit academy is a major

Firearms	Building Searches
PR 24/Side Handle Baton	Stress Awareness
Use of Force	Crimes against Persons
Emergency Vehicle Operation	Criminal Justice Process
Vehicle Stops	Crimes against Property
Defensive Tactics	Child Abuse
Mechanics of Arrest	Victims Rights
Officer Survival	Constitutional Authority
Physical Wellness	Effective Communications
Handgun Retention	Juvenile Procedures
Police Ethics	Emergency First Aid
Domestic Violence	Accident Investigation
Search and Seizure	Interviews and Interrogation
CPR	Miscellaneous Laws
Probable Cause	NCIC Procedures
Patrol Procedures	Coroner Law/Death Investigation
Traffic Law	Narcotics Law
DUI Investigation	History of Law Enforcement
Laws of Arrest	Crisis Intervention
Reporting	Handling the Mentally Ill
Principles of Investigation	Civil Liability
Classroom Notetaking	Fingerprinting
Courtroom Demeanor	Kubotan/Persuader Course
Collection of Evidence	

FIGURE 6–1   Basic Law Enforcement Academy Topics

stage in the career of the officer-to-be. For many police agencies, academy training provides the bulk of the formal training that the officer will receive during an entire career. The
length of academy training varies by state, with about 400 hours being the norm. The academy also plays a significant role in shaping the officer's attitudes and marks the beginning
of the occupational socialization of the officer. Figure 6–1 shows the kinds of knowledge,
skills, and abilities that are provided in a basic academy for local municipal officers and
sheriff's deputies.

   Some departments are authorized by some certifying body to train their own officers
in in-house academies; there are also state and regional academies, some of which are op-
erated by community colleges and universities using instructors from the area. A relatively

Among the many topics that are examined during academy training are arrests, searches and seizures, handling critical incidents, and officer survival.
Source: Courtesy Reno, Nevada, Police Department.

new development is civilian enrollment in police academies, which they do at their own expense in the hope of gaining employment as a "free agent" with a police agency after graduating and becoming formally certified. This "preservice" model is becoming more and more popular with police administrators, who realize tremendous savings by not paying salaries, registration fees, living expenses, and other costs normally accrued when employees attend academies. Many metropolitan police agencies, some federal organizations (such as the FBI), and many state agencies operate their own basic training academies. Several federal agencies send their personnel to the Federal Law Enforcement Training Center in Glynco, Georgia.

A uniform may be worn for the first time during academy training. This is typically an awe-inspiring experience for the new recruits. The uniform sets them apart from society at large and certainly conveys a sense of authority and responsibility to the recruits and to the public. "Image is everything," as a television ad for a brand-name camera used to put it, and the choice of agency uniform can go a long way toward setting the image and tone of the department. Police uniforms come in various colors, styles, and fabrics. Some agencies even have their officers wearing blue jeans or shorts and T-shirts (for beach patrol). The belt is one of the most important components of the patrol uniform and certainly one of the heaviest—it often weighs more than 20 pounds when laden with weapon, cuffs, baton, radio, flashlight, extra ammunition, Mace, and so on. The uniform hat comes in several styles and is probably the piece of equipment that most readily establishes the image of the officer and the department. Each type of hat makes a certain statement of authority to the public. The officer's badge also conveys a strong sense of authority.[22]

Some Challenges for Women

The attrition rate of women during academy training is much higher than that of men for a number of reasons, many or all of which could be resolved. Many traditional academies still follow the military model, and many lack female instructors in both the classroom and physical fitness training, signs that an agency may not be supportive of female officers. Academies that force recruits to stay overnight may also discourage women with children from applying. On the other hand, agencies that promote community-oriented policing (discussed in Chapter 1) and desire the retention of women will run academies that emphasize legal training, oral and written communication skills, and problem-solving and consensus-building skills. These academies provide a thorough discussion of the organization's values, rules, and policies so that the recruit understands the reasons for the organization's policies and procedures and the conduct expected. Physical fitness is also an important part of the training, but academies that are oriented toward community policing emphasize competence in controlling physical confrontations and carrying out the specific physical functions of the job. Women who are informed about the knowledge, skills, and abilities needed to become qualified law enforcement officers can assess the training required by the agencies they are considering and make an educated decision about the agencies' support of women and community policing. (As noted in Appendix II, many agencies have websites that prospective applicants can visit to learn about their mission, values, and overall practice of community policing and problem solving.)

Physical and weapons training can pose unique challenges for women. Physical training should increase students' confidence in their ability to control physical confrontations when necessary, as well as to perform any other physical components of the job. Instead of marching and other physical exercises that offend students and are irrelevant in law enforcement, an emphasis on physical fitness and developing a healthy life style through exercise and diet is more suitable. Because most females are less comfortable than males with physical confrontations, training in techniques and tools that span the entire continuum of force, including defensive tactics, chemicals, and impact weapons, is important. As much as possible, confidence-building exercises and other "hands-on" tactics should be part of the curriculum. Female instructors in both physical and defensive tactics can serve as role models for female recruits and demonstrate for the male recruits that women are capable officers.[23]

Women generally are not as familiar with firearms as men, but it is also true that as society becomes more urbanized, men as well are less likely to be comfortable with firearms. Academies should be prepared to focus individualized attention on each new recruit in firearms training. Even those students who are comfortable with firearms may use poor or unsafe techniques. Firearms instructors would rather work with a student who is willing, but totally unfamiliar with weapons, than a student who has developed bad habits. As more women are becoming users of firearms, instructors and firearm manufacturers are modifying their weapons and supplies to accommodate them. Females who previously were poor shots improved their scores dramatically when they were provided smaller grips and even different belts. The smaller hands of females cannot wrap around the large grips normally found

Academy training includes weapons training.
Source: Courtesy Washoe County (Nevada) Sheriff's Office.

on handguns, preventing the female shooter from grasping the weapon securely. Women need belts that fit lower around their hips so that they can pull their weapon out smoothly.

A female applicant should discuss with a veteran female officer the type of weapon carried by officers in the department and what her experiences have been carrying the weapon, firing, and qualifying on the shooting range with the weapon. If modifying the type of weapon that officers are required or allowed to carry on duty, the administration should have experienced female officers test the different weapons and consider the impact of any new grips, trigger pulls, and even styles of holsters and belts.[24]

THE FIELD TRAINING PHASE

Once the recruits leave the academy, their knowledge of and acceptance into the police subculture are not yet complete. Another very important part of the process is their assignment to one or more veteran officers, often known as a **field training officer**, or FTO, for initial field instruction and observation. This training program provides the recruits with an opportunity to make the transition from the academy to the streets while still under the protection of a veteran officer. Recruits are on probationary status during this time, normally ranging from six months to one year. They understand that they may be immediately terminated if their overall performance is unsatisfactory during the probationary period.

The veteran female officers interviewed for this book were the most animated when discussing their experiences with field training officers. For some of the women, their field training officers were very helpful and professional in teaching them how to bridge the gap between the classroom and the field. For these women, friendships with their field training officers continued beyond the actual field training. Other veteran female officers had field training officers who were hesitant to allow them to learn the job or clearly communicated that they did not want to train a female recruit. These women were forced to seek information and skill training from other officers. In a study of individuals who had resigned, Vivian Lord and Paul Friday[25] discovered that the resignations of a number of new officers were caused by the negative influence of field training officers who were unprofessional and/or racially biased.

In that light, we offer the following comments from veteran women officers:

> Don't goof off in the academy or during field training. It is during the training that initial evaluations and reputations are made.

Basic law enforcement training should be taken very seriously. First, the recruit will not become a law enforcement officer unless she performs well in basic training. More important, the training will teach the recruit skills essential to her responsibilities and possibly her professional and personal survival. Field training takes her to the next level. Her field training officer (FTO) is an experienced officer who will provide the recruit with additional skills to perform the job successfully. At the same time the FTO will be carefully assessing the recruit's ability to do the job, knowing that one day the recruit may be the FTO's backup. In both basic training and field training, the recruit is there to listen, observe, ask questions, and then, when appropriate, demonstrate what she has learned.

> It is important for new officers to stay in their place as recruits until they have proven themselves. The applicant's reputation is critical. She has to prove that she is trustworthy and a team player.

The best way to learn what is considered appropriate behavior is for recruits to observe what is going on around them. Law enforcement agencies are bureaucratic in nature, with the more experienced officers at the top and the least experienced officers generally at the bot-

The post-academy "field training" phase of policing is very important for the new officer's initial field instruction and observation.
Source: Courtesy Washoe County (Nevada) Sheriff's Office.

tom of the hierarchy. (And new recruits do not get to work day shift with weekends off, nor are they assigned to do detective work, be a DNA analyst, or be a criminal profiler, as is often portrayed in the movies!) Even though the new recruit may have just completed basic training academy and knows the latest techniques, it is best to keep one's eyes open and adopt an inquisitive, learning attitude.

> "Be willing to listen and learn. You don't know enough to put your "two-cents in."

Ask good questions and then be quiet and listen to the answer. Be sure the question is professional and positive. Don't ask personal questions or questions that sound like a criticism (for example, "Why didn't you stop that guy back there who was speeding?").

Another important area to understand is the politics of the department. Be careful when listening to negative information or gossip about another officer. Recruits should avoid offering personal opinions until they have gained some insights; recruits cannot be sure whose internal advice they should follow. Listen carefully, acknowledging the information. Never say anything that shouldn't be repeated, and don't repeat anything that was told in confidence.[26]

> Be careful what you complain about. If at all possible, take care of your own problems. You don't want to overreact to a situation, but you also don't want others to walk on you. Accept criticism positively. Listen to what you are being told carefully and politely thank the individual. Never argue. If in those rare cases you have been wrongfully criticized, discuss it calmly with the individual first before considering going up the chain of command.

> You will have to harden to the job without becoming hard. Have an outlet, a way to laugh and play.

It is easy to invest all of your energy and time into a new job, especially in a profession that is as challenging as police work, but it is important to find a balance. Keep your nonpolice friendships, activities, and hobbies. Stay fit by exercising, getting enough rest, and eating healthy.

SUMMARY

The law enforcement hiring process is long and arduous, but each step is critical if law enforcement agencies are to hire individuals who are truly committed to doing a difficult, largely unsupervised job. It is important to remember that the effort put into the application process will assist during the entire hiring process. This means that honest and complete responses will portray the applicant as possessing integrity and the ability to pay attention to detail, both critical characteristics for law enforcement. Approaching the selection process with the necessary knowledge about the agency and its requirements will also prepare the applicant for all steps in the process.

It is important to remember that not everyone obtains "the position of her dreams" upon applying the first time. But it is also important to remember that one can learn from the *experience* of having gone through the application and testing process, even if unsuccessful in obtaining employment. This knowledge can be invaluable in subsequent testing with other police agencies.

READER LEARNING OUTCOMES

Having examined this chapter, the reader should understand:

- the importance of conducting a thorough self-assessment before making a personal commitment to enter law enforcement
- strategies that may be used successfully to prepare for a career in police work
- the complicated process of testing and evaluation that candidates must pass in order to begin their careers
- some of the problems that may prevent a candidate from successfully completing the hiring process
- the importance of honesty with regard to the background investigation process
- the nature of several types of academy settings
- the challenges faced by women entering a police academy and some methods for meeting those challenges
- the field training officer concept and how to succeed during this phase of one's career

NOTES

1. Brian Reaves and Timothy Hart, *Police Departments in Large Cities, 1990–2000* (Washington, DC: Bureau of Justice Statistics, 2002), p. 3.
2. J. S. Harr and Kären M. Hess, *Seeking Employment in Criminal Justice and Related Fields* (Belmont, CA: Wadsworth Thomson Learning, 2003), pp. 195–212.
3. Larry R. Frerkes, *Becoming a Police Officer: A Guide to Successful Entry Level Testing* (Incline Village, NV: Copperhouse, 1998), pp. 39–47.
4. L. K. Gaines, S. Falkenberg, and J. A. Gambino, "Police Physical Agility Testing: An Historical and Legal Analysis," *American Journal of Police* 12(4) (1993):47–66.
5. Ibid., p. 54.
6. Kimberly A. Lonsway, "Tearing Down the Wall: Problems With Consistency, Validity, and Adverse Impact of Physical Agility Testing in Police Selection," *Police Quarterly* 6(3) (September 2003):237–277.
7. Ibid., pp. 238, 263.
8. Ibid., p. 262.
9. Ibid., pp. 240, 266–267.
10. *Tennessee v. Garner,* 471 U.S. 1, 105 S. ct. 1694, 85 L.Ed.2d 1 (1985).
11. Ibid., p. 72; also see Harr and Hess, *Seeking Employment in Criminal Justice and Related Fields,* p. 209.
12. Title 42. The Public Health and Welfare Act, Chapter 126, "Equal Opportunity for Individuals with Disabilities."
13. Kenneth J. Peak, *Policing America: Methods, Issues, Challenges,* 4th ed. (Upper Saddle River, NJ: Prentice Hall, 2002), p. 77.
14. Frerkes, *Becoming a Police Officer,* p. 108.

15. See, for example, Kenneth J. Peak and Ronald W. Glensor, *Community Policing and Problem Solving: Strategies and Practices,* 4th ed. (Upper Saddle River, NJ: Prentice Hall, 2005), pp. 152–153.

16. National Center for Women & Policing, *Recruiting & Retaining Women: A Self-Assessment Guide for Law Enforcement* (Los Angeles, CA, 2000), p. 75.

17. See *Woodland v. City of Houston,* 940 F.2d 134 (Fifth Circuit, 1991), and *Anderson v. The City of Philadelphia,* 845 F.2d 1216 (Third Circuit,1988).

18. Frerkes, *Becoming a Police Officer,* p. 97.

19. National Center for Women & Policing, *Recruiting & Retaining Women,* p. 79.

20. *National Treasury Employees Union v. Von Rabb,* 489 US 656 (1989).

21. W. Clinton Terry III, *Policing Society* (New York: John Wiley & Sons, 1985), p. 196.

22. Peak, *Policing America: Methods, Issues, Challenges,* p. 82.

23. National Center for Women & Policing, *Recruiting and Retaining Women,* p. 87.

24. Ibid.

25. Vivian B. Lord and Paul C. Friday, *Factors Influencing Resignation from Charlotte Mecklenburg Police Department* (Technical Report, 1999), pp. 7–8.

26. Harr and Hess, *Seeking Employment in Criminal Justice and Related Fields,* p. 218.

Chapter 7
Experiences of Female Veterans

---◆---

Key Chapter Terms

Ego defense   Selective omission   Sexualizing the workplace
Retrospective reasoning   Self-efficacy

If you want to be a police officer, go into it with your eyes open. Learn as much as you can, talk to officers, participate in ride-alongs.

—Veteran female police officer

A moment's insight is sometimes worth a life's experience.

—Oliver Wendell Holmes

Listen, where thou art sitting.

—John Milton

Introduction

Experience is a great teacher, so next we listen to the experiences of veteran women officers. They will convey to the reader why they decided to enter law enforcement and what it means to be there.

This chapter begins by discussing the kinds of factors that influenced women's decisions to seek employment in law enforcement. Included are the five general background characteristics that led to this career choice and the veterans' basic concerns about this occupation. Next we examine whether or not they felt accepted upon their entry, the impact of the police subculture, and whether or not they experienced discrimination or harassment on the job. After reviewing their general advice to new women officers, we conclude the chapter with the views of several high-ranking women law enforcement executives.

WOMEN OFFICERS SPEAK

To help the reader understand the career experiences of today, 50 veteran female police officers were interviewed for this book. All of these officers had a minimum of two years of law enforcement experience in their current agency, a large police agency that is known to have a progressive outlook overall, although not necessarily so with regard to the hiring of women. Although the agency is located in the Southeastern United States, studies show that, generally, there are no major differences between similar-sized agencies in different regions of the country.[1] The agency in which these female officers were employed had approximately 1,500 sworn officers, of whom 210 were women. The city they police has a population of 600,000 citizens. The women were selected from the patrol division (60 percent), different specialized and investigative units (16 percent), and administrative levels (22 percent). Sixty-four percent of the female officers were white; 32 percent were African American; and 4 percent were Hispanic American; therefore, their comments represent all groups of veteran female officers within this agency. Only two officers declined to be interviewed, so selection bias did not affect our results.

Most interviews lasted about two hours and were conducted privately in offices, patrol vehicles, and other locations such as public schools. Although a protocol of structured questions was used with all the officers, most of the respondents provided information beyond that requested on the questionnaire, and officers were encouraged to expand on their responses. The following are selected responses to the structured questions asked.

FACTORS INFLUENCING THE DECISION TO ENTER LAW ENFORCEMENT

Many of these 50 female officers knew from an early age that they wanted to be police officers, so they planned related experiences to help them prepare. Their preparation included education, internships, military experience, and security positions.

> I always knew I wanted to be a police officer and decided the best avenue to that goal would be to join the military. I joined the Navy and was able to work as a military police officer for two years. Then at the age of 21, I was ready to come and work with my current police agency. Probably because of my military experience, I was made squad leader for my basic law enforcement training class. I am still part of the police agency's honor guard.

> I planned to become a federal officer, but because there was a hiring freeze at the time, I applied with local departments. I was hired by my current agency fairly quickly. I am athletic so I did particularly well in the physical areas of the basic police training, even winning the physical fitness award.

While in high school, my best friend started getting in trouble. I saw what it did to his family. Ironically, he had been interested in law enforcement before the trouble. I became interested and interned with the Drug Enforcement Administration (DEA) during high school and am still interested in the drug enforcement side of policing. Most importantly, with my current agency I am able to also use problem-solving policing in attempting to alleviate the problems behind drugs.

Almost everybody in my family was in policing, but I still didn't have a good idea of what officers did. Each of my family members held different kinds of jobs in different types of departments. In college, I majored in psychology and minored in criminal justice. Once I finished four years of college, I knew that I had had enough with education and decided to carry on the family tradition of policing.

For other female officers, policing was their first interest, but their families were not supportive of their aspirations toward a police career. Family members influence a woman's career decision making more than they do a man's[2]; however, for the interviewees, the desire to become a police officer overcame their family's influence.

I have always had an interest in criminal justice, but my parents said teaching was right for females so I was pushed in that direction. I was a graduate student in education in California when I became disenchanted with the entire school system. After participating in a few "ride-alongs" with police officers, I realized how much I enjoyed the experience so I applied with the California Highway Patrol. I also applied to some agencies in the eastern part of the country, because I considered living in a new place. I did have some relatives in my current city, but knew nothing about the city itself. My current agency was the first agency to respond to my application so I flew in, took a battery of tests over two days, and was offered the job two weeks later.

I had wanted to be a police officer since I was eight years old, but my parents said no to my dream, so I didn't think any more about it. I went to work for the county pretrial release program. While there, I observed a female officer and thought, "If she can do it, so can I." So I applied.

I had been interested since the late teens in policing. Although my father is a fire fighter, and my sister was interested in emergency services, my father forbade me to apply to the police department. I took emergency medical training at night at the same academy in which the police training was taught, but I knew I was still interested in policing. So behind my father's back, I completed police training and became a police officer.

The concept of **self-efficacy** expectations, the beliefs that one can successfully perform a given role with its accompanying responsibilities,[3] is particularly relevant to the understanding of women's career development. Females in particular must gain successful experiences in a variety of domains outside the home; they must have available successful role models; they must receive encouragement and persuasion from others; and their level of anxiety, especially when considering an occupation perceived as dangerous, needs to be reduced.[4]

I was working part-time as a night auditor at a hotel where one of the security guards was an off-duty police officer. I kept asking him questions, so he finally told me that I should apply to the police agency. When I responded that I was not big enough, he brought three female officers to the hotel who were as petite as me.

Of course, as is true of many adults, many of the female officers began their working lives in an entirely different profession.

> I was a hair stylist, enjoying well enough what I was doing, but my best friend was a police officer. She knew I wanted more of a challenge in life, more diversity, so she suggested that I apply. She was right. I have since had a variety of assignments and opportunities to advance professionally and help people.

> I thought I might want to go into investigations, but instead found that I really like patrol work. I love to talk to different people. We are assigned to work one specific area so I can really get to know people and the businesses in my area. I plan community meetings and help citizens work through their problems and fears. My area has a large number of Asian people who have just arrived and know little English. It feels good to help them and see their fears decrease and their comfort with me increase.

> I graduated from college and jumped right into working in physical therapy; however, I was a big fan of the television series *Hill Street Blues* so I went back to school and received a criminal justice degree. I really wanted to be able to help people. I started out as a reserve officer for the college police, but moved to my current agency when I was offered a full-time job. I have recently become a field training officer so I can train new officers as they graduate from recruit school. This move is very important to the department and me. These new recruits are good going from call to call, but no good at documenting their calls. I really feel like I can make an improvement in the quality of the new officers.

> I took a job as a dispatcher with the department, because it paid pretty well. I found that I enjoyed my job and the environment. I talked to the officers and did some "ride-alongs" with them. I also worked a second job as a night auditor of a hotel that was in a high-crime area so officers worked as security on their off-duty hours. Then one night when I was dispatching, I received an emergency call from a little boy whose mother had overdosed. I wanted to be there at the scene helping him. When an officer told me that the police department had some openings, I applied immediately. After I finished basic training, I asked for a special assignment on the street crimes unit to get first-hand experience with drug dealers.

BACKGROUND CHARACTERISTICS LEADING TO THIS CAREER CHOICE: FIVE EMERGING THEMES

Five themes seem to emerge when the female officers considered the influence their backgrounds had on their desire to be a police officer: (1) coming from a law enforcement family, (2) coming from a military family, (3) being highly independent, (4) being involved in sports, and (5) being raised in a dysfunctional family.

A Law Enforcement Family

First, a number of the officers came from law enforcement families, thrilling at the war stories and hearing the pride in their family member's voice.

> My grandfather had been in the FBI, and my grandmother had been a store detective. They both had really great stories to tell us.

> My grandfather and his brother had been in law enforcement all of their lives. In fact, my grandfather's brother had died in the line of duty with the New York Police Department. Stories of their careers always came up at family gatherings.

> My father was a constable in the county, and I often went with him when he served civil papers. I also had several neighbors who had been police officers so they were always around telling their war stories.

A Military Family

Second, they were raised in a military family, which provided exposure to uniforms, a disciplined lifestyle, and interactions with people from different cultures.

> My father was in the military so we moved a great deal. I learned there were different types of people in the world, and I was also able to adjust to new places and new friends.

> My father was in the military, so my mother did most of the raising of us. I saw my mother as both the nurturer and disciplinarian. She was also able to do routine maintenance around the house.

Independence

A third theme is independence. Many of the female officers described a childhood in which circumstances thrust them early into adulthood or family members who embodied independence and expected them to follow suit.

> I was the oldest child and always expected to fend for myself. Both my mother and grandmother were very strong and were constantly telling me, "If you want to do something, then go out and do it."

> My father was in the army reserves for 32 years. He made sure that I knew how to change the oil and tires on the car and fight if necessary. He always told me that I could be whatever I wanted.

> My family had a farm, and we were all expected to carry our weight. My father taught me to change tires. Both my parents taught us not to depend on anybody but ourselves.

> I lived on a farm back in the country and was expected to do chores before and after school. My mother was very strict. She married a smalltown crook and was always terrified that the police would show up at our door.

> My mother was a single parent and worked, so I was expected to raise my little brothers. To make sure that they played sports, I played with them. We also grew up in the part of the city with all types of people so I learned how to interact with different types of people.

> My mother was a single parent who worked so I mothered my younger siblings, cooked for the family, handled money, and bought groceries.

> My mother had remarried so my father wasn't around. Then she died when I was 14, and after that I received little parenting. I became very independent and finished raising myself.

Before my mother's death when I was 12, I had been a "daddy's girl." But with her death, my father really flipped and stayed away from home all the time. I started working to make lunch money and had my own apartment by age 16. I really grew up fast.

My parents divorced when I was six, and my father raised all four of us. I was the tomboy of the family and was always selected first for neighborhood sports.

Participating in Sports

Engaging in sports activities, especially on teams and with boys, is a fourth common theme. Some of the women were particularly comfortable working with men after playing a male-dominated team sport during their early years.

I love to play all sorts of sports and even coached for the Police Athletic League (PAL). There I had a chance to see police officers helping the community and children in a really positive and fun way.

I was used to playing sports with boys. I even pitched on a boy's baseball team.

A Dysfunctional Family

Several of these women also grew up in dysfunctional families, in which either they observed police officers responding to disturbances occurring in their homes or their parents' alcoholism affected their interactions with others.

I had a huge extended family with strong women, but they would have to phone the police from time to time to come and straighten out the drunken menfolk.

My family was pretty dysfunctional. My father worked all the time, and my mother was an alcoholic. I was the middle child of five and was always trying to mediate among everybody.

I was the next to youngest of six children and the most independent, aggressive, and bossiest of all of them. I put my father in alcohol rehabilitation three times. I started working when I was 14.

PRIMARY CONCERNS ABOUT BECOMING A POLICE OFFICER

We caution readers that **retrospective reasoning** is not completely accurate and is often biased by the respondent's **ego-defense** system to reconstruct an image of the past by **selective omission**.[5] In other words, when individuals recall experiences, they often will omit information that is damaging to their own sense of self. For example, embarrassing situations are often repressed. Keeping this caution in mind, the following experiences are still representative of the officers' views.

The veteran women officers interviewed were primarily from backgrounds that included very little previous experience with police officers. Therefore they, like most of the public, believed that police work was too dangerous for women to handle,[6] a fear also shared by their families. In addition, although male officers are becoming more accepting of female officers, some male officers have a negative opinion of female officers with respect to their ability to handle the physical aspects of the job.[7] Carrying the double-minority weight of both gender and race, women of color have faced discriminatory practices in police departments as in other occupations.[8]

All these concerns were baggage with which the women had to wrestle before deciding to apply to the police agency. The concerns are divided into safety concerns, physical training, personal ability to be a police officer, treatment by male officers, family support, and race. As the reader will note, the veteran women officers handle their anxieties in a resourceful manner.

Safety

I was afraid for my safety, afraid that I might get injured or killed. So I talked to a female school resource officer at the local high school who mentioned that the good in wearing the uniform outweighs the fear. She acknowledged that the danger is always there, but she just had to put it away.

I worried about my safety so I participated in several ride-alongs with different police officers. During the rides, I observed how the officers looked out for each other.

I was worried about the danger of policing and working at night. My fear was initially alleviated with the training I received. My two field training officers were both family men who were very professional with no egos to bolster. They taught me a great deal, but also let me learn at my own pace.

Physical Training

Because I was concerned about the physical training, I obtained training requirements for the military and started training six months before the recruit class began. Once I got into the class, I was able to continue the conditioning.

I was not much of an athlete, so I was worried how I would make it through the physical training. I think my stubbornness and desire to succeed helped carry me.

Personal Abilities

I am very shy so I didn't know if I could be assertive enough to arrest or even shoot somebody. Basic training went okay, but then during field training I temporarily had a female field training officer who treated me like dirt. When my regular field training officer returned, I cried and told him I wanted to quit. He told me that I would need to dig deep inside myself and reject the negative comments people made to me. After that I started speaking up and becoming more assertive. I think I just needed the right role model who didn't necessarily have to be a female.

Anticipated Treatment as a Female Officer

Because I am petite, I worried about people on the street taking me seriously. I went through the police training academy with several other women, and we helped each other. With the help of other officers, male and female, I was internally fortified whenever I came up against people who didn't think a woman should be a police officer.

I was concerned about my height, because I am short. I had a female recruit officer who was very supportive and really mentored me through the selection process.

I worried that the male officers wouldn't want more female officers. I talked to several male officers who responded that female officers were needed as long as they were levelheaded and could handle the pressure.

I was worried about sexual harassment in such a male-dominated field. So I looked for a police agency in which there were a number of women who had already led the way. I also decided to begin as a reserve officer before jumping straight into policing as a full-time career.

Family Support

I was worried what shift work would do to my marriage, but my husband was supportive, and we learned to cope with my unusual work schedule.

I was worried that policing might put a strain on my marriage. As it turned out, my husband didn't support my career change, and we did divorce.

I was concerned about my daughter's safety. I thought she might be singled out, because of her mother's profession, but it was never an issue.

My parents were worried that the job was too dangerous, but it helped their anxiety when I first began as a crime scene technician. Once they saw that I was competent as a crime scene technician, they quit worrying about my desire to become a police officer, realizing that I could competently and safely handle police work.

My parents didn't think I should become a police officer, but I had several friends who were really supportive and that helped.

Racial Considerations

I had the double concerns of gender and race. I was worried that both might keep me from being accepted. I had a black female recruiter who really helped me through the hiring process.

FEELING ACCEPTED

According to John Crank,[9] bravery is an important part of the police culture. Fear is emotionally debilitating, yet officers do occasionally have to place themselves in danger. Training officers will test recruits by placing them in inherently dangerous situations to observe their ability to stand up under the pressure to back another officer. Any expression of personal fear is considered a sign of weakness, for the officer who expresses it might not be dependable in a dangerous situation. Because demonstration of bravery is a major area of acceptance, many of the female veterans noted that they were only accepted when they demonstrated their willingness to jump into the middle of physical confrontations, incidents that were usually quite memorable.

Acceptance by the community in which they worked as community-oriented police officers was also important to the female officers; however, approval by fellow officers was a by-product of their work, and they were proud of that recognition also.

Proof of Self

Acceptance came when I proved myself. I think this is true with every officer, male or female. When officers requested me to back them up, they wanted to see if I would support them and how reliable I actually was.

Overall the male officers seem apprehensive about female officers. I had been released from field training for only a month when I broke a guy's nose by punching him. He had just kicked a fellow officer in the groin. I was accepted then.

I faced my first fight when I was still in field training. I jumped right in and got my "butt whooped." I don't know how much help I actually was, but my willingness to get down in the dirt won the other officers' respect.

I had to work extra hard. I felt as if I had to show male officers that I didn't get the job because I slept around. Females have to prove themselves, while males only have to disprove themselves before they become unacceptable.

I first felt accepted when I was assigned to a drug task force. Other officers saw me fight and stand my ground.

I don't know if this is acceptance or harassment. As a new officer, I would walk by a male officer, and he would tackle me just to see what I would do. Since I was used to "rough-housing" with my brothers and male friends, I would just wrestle with the officer who tackled me. I guess it worked. I never felt that it was a sexual thing, but more to see if I was "one of the guys."

Female officers have to prove themselves physically, but they also have to be able to joke around without being weird. It is a tightrope act.

I have had to re-prove myself at every assignment. At first that bothered me; I didn't see male officers being put through that continual test of fire. I've gotten now that I don't even care.

Community-Policing Orientation

Females have to show their willingness to jump in and "handle their business," but at the same time, I don't want to go back time and again. Because I try to take time to help people with their problems, I have been accused of being a social worker. I think helping people is the reason community-oriented policing is so important.

I was a community coordinator for a housing project/high crime area. I met with officers in that area so they would know what I was trying to do. I built a reputation with both the officers and the citizens that I would help them if I could.

IMPACT OF THE POLICE SUBCULTURE

Crank discusses the shared thoughts, sentiments, and values developed among police officers.[10] He notes that the officers' authority to control the public with the backing of procedural law, the perception of being in a continuously unknown and unpredictable environment, and their constant presence in the public eye builds among officers a sense of occupational uniqueness. As women and minorities have joined the ranks, there is some sense that the culture is not quite as solid.

The veteran women officers were asked whether they considered the general as well as the specific agency police culture a support or a wall over which they had to climb. As will be seen, the women found themselves torn between the lure of joining the majority ranks and their uniqueness. Important to the veteran officers were other women police officers and especially to minorities, other women of color.

Agency Culture

I really like the sense of belonging. I feel like I can discuss issues and events with others going through the same thing. It is easier to hang around other officers, because I don't feel like I have to keep up my guard.

Overall the culture provides support, and I feel like part of a family; however, the subcultures within each district and shift can be detrimental. It was important for me to have other friends outside policing. New officers especially get showered with pessimism and cynicism.

I received a lot of support in learning the job from male and female officers. Officers would roll by when I had a call and make sure I was okay.

I enjoyed the closeness of my police family. I felt I could trust all my fellow officers and knew what to expect from them. I have to say it isn't the same now. Too many new recruits come in and see the department as a stepping stone. They are more out for themselves, whether they are male or female recruits.

I stuck with my police friends until marriage and subsequently buying a house, then nonpolice friends became important.

It's hard to get into "the family." The reputation of your training officer is important. If your field training officer is not respected, then it is hard for you as a new officer to get respect.

There is no brotherhood or tight-knit family in this department. The officers gossip about each other. If I was even seen talking or spending time with a male officer, other officers started gossiping that I was sleeping with him. I just don't talk to anybody now. Women officers are just as bad as the male officers.

Female Police Culture

I feel a sisterhood with other female officers. I can talk to them about the job and related issues. Much of this positive support starts with the higher-level women administrators and then is carried on by line women officers.

There were seven females in my basic training class so I never felt different.

On my shift, females were kept from backing male officers' calls. If a male officer who received the call heard that his backup was a female officer, he would say "disregard," which meant that he didn't need any backup. The female officers finally got together and backed each other's calls and that helped some, but it really hurt the overall morale of the shift. I finally complained to the supervisor, who officially mandated that calls could not be "disregarded."

There is a lot of competition among the women officers, and a lot of them aren't considered good officers. I want to be sure to be considered a good officer, so I mainly interact with male officers. There is one other female officer in my district who is accepted by the male officers, so she and I have become friends.

The Culture of Female Officers of Color

The comradeship among officers works both ways. It is obvious that I am not a part of it. For example, everybody is always very nice to me, but I am rarely asked to join other officers for meals or drinking after work. I am a black female, but I can't complain about discrimination just because I am politely shut out.

I felt completely isolated on the graveyard, or late-night shift. When I arrived, there was already a clique, and its members were not going to let me in. When I was transferred to evening shift, it was better because there were more black officers.

When I (black female officer) planned to go up for the sergeant's exam, I felt accepted by all other officers, except black male officers. I even had white male officers asking me why the black male officers were so negative toward me. When I approached some of the black male officers and asked them, they said that I would do anything to be promoted. I decided the promotion wasn't worth it and decided not to take the sergeant exam.

DEALING WITH DISCRIMINATION AND HARASSMENT

In the 1970s, Susan Martin[11] discussed the level of resistance that women faced when first on patrol. Male officers refused to teach new female officers the skills necessary to do the job, they would not assist female officers requesting backup, and supervisors would more rigorously enforce rules against the female officers and give them performance evaluations lower than that of male officers. Today, there is a growing proportion of male officers who are comfortable working with female officers, but even these men usually ignore other male officers' derogatory actions or comments toward female officers.

Discrimination and hostility are not openly tolerated now, but they continue to pervade some police organizations. Frequent comments or jokes draw attention to women's sexuality, making it clear to the female officers that they are still outsiders. "By **sexualizing the workplace**, men superimpose their supposed gender superiority on women's claims to work-based equality."[12]

The discrimination I encountered was a tough call for both my captain and me. Ironically it was caused by community policing. I had received the required training for bike patrol and was to be assigned to a specific neighborhood. The neighborhood association said that they wanted a white male, so a white male is who they got.

As a new supervisor, I was in charge of an older male officer who was insubordinate; he really had problems with taking orders from a female. I finally had to take disciplinary action against him. Only then did we come to a reluctant truce.

I had one inappropriate action made toward me by a sergeant. I confronted him about it, and we worked it out. Unfortunately another officer saw the action and reported it. Then we had to go through the entire review process, and the sergeant received days off. It's really better if you can learn to handle sexual harassment on your own. Female officers need to learn how to take it and dish it back.

Discrimination shows up in little subtle ways. I asked to go to Radar School. My traffic violations numbers were good, and I had seniority over many of the male officers who were chosen. I had to go to my supervisor and directly ask why these guys were sent rather than me before I was allowed to go.

I requested the specialized training given to all the members of the team I am on. I was denied because it would mean that I would need a separate hotel room. If they sent two male officers, they could share the room expense.

There are a certain number of women allotted to each district so I was moved to make room for another female. I complained, but it didn't matter.

There is a lot of language I don't find acceptable. I am not sure the male officers even realize that they are demeaning me when they talk about women in general, use vulgar language, or language with sexual connotations.

I had a sergeant making harassing comments towards me, and I think it bothered the male officers even more than me. They began running interference between the sergeant and me.

When I was a new officer, a captain kept trying to invite himself over to my house and assigned me to especially good secondary employment jobs. When I finally turned him down directly, the special jobs stopped, and he had me transferred out of his district.

I think that minority officers receive harsh discipline for actions that white officers are not even penalized for at all.

Over the years I have faced countless discriminatory and harassing situations. It's hard to point to race or gender. I just deal with things internally. I never reported them, because I didn't want anybody to know that it got to me. My solution was to get involved and change the professional environment. I have to admit if I had not had a small support group, I wouldn't have made it.

I think there is some reverse discrimination going on. The women who apply for certain assignments are qualified, but they often get positions before men who have been here longer.

I've noticed that women who become pregnant are really given a lot of grief. Supervisors get angry when a female officer needs time off because of a sick child. Supervisors may get angry with male officers also, but male officers don't have to ask as much as the female officers for time off with children.

GENERAL ADVICE TO NEW WOMEN OFFICERS

Although each female officer must tread her own path, these women provide "gold nuggets" of advice that are priceless when followed by new women officers. Listening carefully to these experienced women officers, who are still in the field, can save rookie female officers a great deal of stress. (Female officers also offer advice in Chapter 8.)

Don't date other officers, especially the first few years. You need to establish yourself as a professional first. Only after you have developed a reputation as a good officer and have actually developed friendships with other officers, do you dare consider a more intimate relationship. Consider some of the consequences: working the same shift and district as the officer you are dating; the possibility of him becoming protective of you rather than treating you as a fellow and equal officer; and the potential problems of breaking-up. Will those emotions affect how you will be able to back each other?

Know your limit when dealing with potential sexual harassment. If a man crosses your line, be quick to tell him that you don't appreciate his comment or action. He will respect you and back off. Waiting until you have to report it will be deadly to your own career.

Don't expect special treatment, but at the same time know your limitations. It is okay to ask for help, but make sure you volunteer for calls. Above all, don't have an "ATTITUDE."

Don't think you have to give up being a woman. Who you are as a female is an asset to policing. You don't have to act like a man or become "one of the boys."

Policing is very satisfying work, and I don't believe my gender has gotten in the way of advancement. My department, as well as many other police agencies, has made great strides and is no longer a "white man's club."

I really think most women can do police work; it doesn't take the exceptional woman. It's important to realize that police officers are notorious for complaining, but you can't let it jade you. You will have lots of opportunities to grow and make the job what you want. It is important to get past the two-year "new period."

If you want to be a police officer, go into it with your eyes open. Learn as much as you can, talk to officers, and participate in ride-alongs.

The experiences of these veteran women officers reflect many of the backgrounds and concerns of women everywhere. Their messages support the fact that it does not take an extraordinary woman to be a police officer, but it does take preparation, courage, and self-confidence. As the reader will continue to see from words of female police leaders, the need for women to support each other is critical.

COUNSEL FROM WOMEN LAW ENFORCEMENT EXECUTIVES

Any woman who remains in law enforcement, is accepted by other officers, and serves the public is successful; moreover, a handful of women now hold top-ranking positions in policing. Following are the biographical sketches and words contributed from women whose success in law enforcement is measured through promotions to high rank within a police agency or sheriff's office.

Penny Harrington, Founder, National Center for Women & Policing, and Past Police Chief of Portland, Oregon

It is not difficult to understand why Harvard Law School named Penny Harrington as one of the "10 Most Influential Women in Law" or *Working Woman Magazine* categorized her as one of "350 Women Who Changed the World from 1976–1996." In 1985, after 21 years in the Portland Police Department progressing through the ranks, Penny Harrington became Chief Harrington, one of the first women in the United States to become the top administrator of a police agency in a major city. During her administration, she reduced citizen complaints against police by 30 percent in one year and increased narcotic arrests by 33 percent. She initiated the plan to implement community-oriented policing, as well as a management system that emphasized community involvement and teamwork.

If there is one unique characteristic about Penny Harrington, it is courage. When she began her career in policing, women were not allowed to work in the patrol division. In fact, they were assigned to the women's protective division and not allowed to transfer. Penny Harrington challenged the system in different areas. She became her agency's first detective and then, a year later, its first sergeant. She eliminated the height requirement that had

Penny Harrington

prohibited numerous women from entering the Portland Police Bureau. She then organized the women in her agency, and together they brought a class action suit for sex discrimination. As a result of this legal action, every area of the agency was opened to females.

In 1995, Chief Harrington became Director Harrington by founding The National Center for Women & Policing, a division of the Feminist Majority Foundation. By 1998, she had built it into a major national vehicle for women in law enforcement. She has been consulted by the U.S. Department of Justice, testified before the U.S. Civil Rights Commission, participated in discussions with President Bill Clinton, appointed by Attorney General Janet Reno to a panel of police experts who were to study police brutality and the need to increase diversity in police agencies, and recently added published author to her professional accomplishments.

Director Harrington provided the following advice to women considering policing:

> One of the biggest mistakes that women make when entering the field of law enforcement is to try to be just like their male co-workers. Some women are successful at this strategy, but most are not. It is important to be yourself. Men and women have different styles of policing. Women tend to spend more time talking and trying to mediate and de-escalate violence. Women do not tend to take insults from angry citizens personally. And, we seldom resort to excessive force. Some men also have these traits and are excellent police officers. We must remember that we are usually dealing with people in their time of extreme distress. Whether we are responding to the scene of a traffic accident, a family disturbance, a bank robbery or issuing a traffic ticket, chances are that the person who

is receiving our services is experiencing an extremely high level of stress. And when people are under stress, they seldom are acting in a calm, rational manner. Therefore, we have to maintain a calm, soothing, rational attitude. Our actions have a tremendous impact on the people involved. The rewards of a career in law enforcement are worth the stresses of the job. It is one of the few jobs where you never know what you will be doing from one day to the next. You may be taking reports all day long, or you may be involved in a highly dangerous situation. The variety of the work is a definite asset. The most satisfying part of the job is the knowledge that you have helped other people. In addition, you will be in an organization with a clearly defined career path, equal pay, generous benefits, job security, and a retirement plan. The experience and training you gain as a law enforcement officer will increase your self-confidence and your ability to handle anything that life may throw at you. The downside of a career in law enforcement is the shift work, being on call, working outside in all kinds of bad weather and being subjected to sexual harassment and gender discrimination. Yes, women in law enforcement still face issues of discrimination and harassment. They are often held to a higher standard than their male co-workers. The solution to this problem is to greatly increase the numbers of women in these law enforcement agencies. By entering this career, you will be a pioneer. You will be paving the way for generations of women who will follow you. You will be part of setting a standard of excellence in policing. And, you will be serving your community. Law enforcement in many communities is in crisis due to police brutality, insensitivity, and corruption. It is up to those of you entering policing to help fix it. You can do this by always maintaining high ethical standards and always remembering that you are there to help your community, and not as a military force to impose rigid orders. The possibilities of success are endless. Many women who were the real pioneers are retiring after long and rewarding careers. Many of them were responsible for the advances made in investigating sexual assaults, child abuse, domestic violence, and other serious crimes. Some of them made inroads as canine officers, school officers, and crime prevention specialists. And, some of them were even on SWAT teams, rode motorcycles, and worked undercover assignments. They opened the doors for women like you to enter. They fought many of the battles for equality. Because of their work, you will have more opportunities. If you want a career helping your community and that is personally challenging and rewarding, I urge you to choose law enforcement. You can make a difference in the lives of many people.

Barbara A. Pickens, Sheriff of Lincoln County, North Carolina

In 1994, Sheriff Pickens became the first elected female sheriff in North Carolina history. She is presently serving her third term as sheriff as she enters her 30th year in law enforcement. Sheriff Pickens also serves the state of North Carolina as a member of the Sheriff's Legislative Committee, the Sheriff's Training and Standards Commission, and the DARE Foundation Board. She is currently listed in *International Who's Who of Professional Management, Who's Who of American Women,* and *Who's Who in Executives and Professionals.*

Barbara Pickens

From Sheriff Pickens:

Law enforcement officers are very special individuals who perform a unique service. It is the most rewarding and honorable profession anyone could choose. Any female who is interested in the criminal justice field should investigate the opportunities and prepare herself. She should have a good education and understand that all of this job is based on "good common sense." There is an abundance of diversity and challenges facing us in the 21st century. The way has been paved for new females to meet the challenges and carry forward what we have started.

Colonel Deborah Campbell, Highest-Ranking Female in the New York State Police

Colonel Campbell began her policing career as a trooper with the New York State Police stationed in the Poughkeepsie area. She also earned a master's degree in criminal justice. She was promoted to sergeant in 1989, and five years later to uniform lieutenant, supervising the New York State Thruway District.

Her responsibilities in recruiting and employee relations began in 1994 when she was appointed director of the Office of Human Resources for the New York State Police. During her tenure as assistant deputy superintendent of human resources, Deborah Campbell was responsible for the research that led to the report entitled, "Improving the Recruitment of Women in Policing: An Investigation of Women's Attitudes and Job Preferences." The report was instrumental in significantly increasing the number of females applying to the New York State Police. Colonel Campbell has received the National Center for Women & Policing "Breaking the Glass Ceiling" Award and New York State's 100 Women of Excellence Award.

Deborah Campbell

Colonel Campbell gives the following personal advice:

I believe that the greatest challenge I have faced since becoming a police officer is having people accept and respect me for the person I am, regardless of my gender. There can be a natural tendency among some people to judge you based upon their misperceptions and to attribute your accomplishments to preferential treatment you may have received based upon your gender. Not only is this hurtful, but, if you are not careful, you may find yourself "buying" into it, and it may affect your confidence in your own abilities. I have tried to remember never to doubt myself and to focus on the belief that I have earned what I've received. While I may have gotten here "sooner" because of a need in the organization linked to my gender, I have tried to concentrate on demonstrating that I deserve to be where I am and can do the job. I have found that slowly, but surely, I could win people over if I demonstrated competence and a positive attitude. People began to recognize me for my abilities. Find someone you respect, and who has a work ethic you support. Learn as much as you can from her or him. Ask that person to be your mentor and explain why (she or he will be flattered). Seek advice and guidance. Then, *BE* a mentor. Identify young officers who have promise or need direction and offer them the value of your experience. Provide encouragement and try to open doors for your protégés, which will help enhance their career. A fit body and a keen mind not only are essential tools for a police officer but also will help you to maximize your effectiveness in every aspect of your life. Challenge yourself mentally by identifying educational opportunities, which will benefit you personally and make you more marketable. Find a physical activity you enjoy—running, basketball, tennis, or biking—and stick with it. Resist the "need" to turn in your uniform for a larger size. It's easier to stay in shape than to get back in shape. Looking good makes you feel good about yourself and gives you the extra confidence to do your job to the best of your ability. We don't always control our work, but we ALWAYS control the attitude we bring to work. People are drawn to those with positive, "can-do" attitudes. Exhibit a confident, positive attitude. Avoid being sucked into the "complaint trap" where one negative aspect of the job corrupts everything else. You can and will be recognized for your good work ethic and positive attitude. That will set you apart from the rest and get you noticed. Many female officers are so focused on just trying to "fit in" that they forget who they are. Individuality can be a good thing, and you should be proud of the fact that you are a woman in policing. WE do the same job, we just may do it differently. You don't need to shy away from "associating" with other female officers. On the contrary, you can derive great strength from the understanding that you share common concerns, fears, aspirations, and goals.

Mary G. Bounds, First Female Police Chief of the City of Cleveland, Ohio

As an example of an African American woman who has been successful in law enforcement, Commander Bounds has served the City of Cleveland Division of Police for over 22 years, beginning in patrol and moving through investigations to supervisory and administrative positions. She is currently the commander of recruitment and retention for Cleveland after serving as Cleveland's first female police chief. Education played an important role in her development, having achieved a master's of business administration and graduated from the FBI National Academy. She has been honored as the 1999 Black Professional Woman of the Year and the recipient of the 2001 Business and Professional Women Achievement Award.

Commander Bounds sees women in law enforcement as change agents: "Impacting change, one promotion, one academy class at a time. Our responsibility is to guide and groom others."

Shirley A. Gifford, Chief of Soldotna, Alaska

Chief Gifford began her career in law enforcement in 1974 by typing Meridian police reports. When a position came open in patrol, the police administrator didn't believe women should be allowed on patrol and denied her request to be considered. She talked the supervisor of the township into allowing her to attend basic law enforcement training, thereby becoming the first female deputy for Meridian Township Police in Michigan. In 1977, she decided to join the Anchorage, Alaska, Police Department. Although women still had to prove themselves, Anchorage recognized and accepted women officers. Chief Gifford knew she had been accepted when she was told, "You're a good man."

In 1997, she was hired as the police chief of Soldotna, Alaska. Although she was met with open arms by the community, there was some internal skepticism (typified by some comments like "We'll all have to wear skirts"). Once word got around of her 21 years of experience in management and action-oriented areas, such as traffic, special response teams, and all kinds of investigations including homicide, she was accepted.

According to Chief Gifford, police work in Alaska and especially in a tourist town is different from that in the "lower 48." Alaska truly is the last frontier, and some people come to get away from authority, although overall the police are respected. Winters can be hard; domestic violence and alcohol-related crimes increase during that long season. Soldotna has a population of 3,900 citizens. Known as one of the best fishing areas in Alaska, during the summer, an additional 60,000 tourists, mainly responsible, well-established owners of motor homes, travel to and through Soldotna.

Women would find Alaska a state that accepts women into policing. Chief Gifford has done her part to help welcome women. She has hired one woman (thereby putting her above the national average for a department of her size) and is the founding member and past president of the Women Police of Alaska, a chapter of the International Association of Women Police.

Chief Gifford suggests:

> Take one day at a time, work very hard, and do the right thing for people. Women and men alike get into law enforcement to help people, serve people. If they are not in it for that reason, it's probably the wrong reason. Train everyday. Write the best report you can; conduct the best investigation. Alaska provides such an adventure. It is the most beautiful country you could experience. The people are very close. Alaska has only 627,000 citizens and 1,129 commissioned law enforcement officers. Many of the officers know each other and are able to get together annually for training and socializing. They all work cooperatively toward the common goal of crime-free communities.

Janice S. Strauss, Police Chief of Mesa, Arizona

Chief Strauss's career has followed the path that one would expect an ambitious individual to take to become chief. The major difference is that she is a woman, one of the few who have become police chiefs in the United States.

She began policing in 1970 with the Phoenix, Arizona, Police Department before the Equal Opportunity Act of 1972 opened the doors to equal opportunities for women in policing. She progressed from patrol officer through the ranks of the Mesa Police Department until she became chief in 1998. She had also returned to school while working full-time, obtaining a graduate degree in public administration. Chief Strauss has been active in the Arizona Association of Chiefs of Police and the Arizona United States Attorney Law Enforcement Coordinating Committee. As chief, she implemented the Mesa Police Department's first Citizen Police Academy and the Mesa Police Center Against Family Violence.

The following is Chief Strauss's professional story and advice for new officers:

> The concept of women in law enforcement has evolved greatly in the 30 years since I first began my career. When I began as a police officer in 1970, I was one of the first women to be hired. We were instructed to wear a white blouse with a black crisscross tie, a tight black skirt, and two-inch black heels. My badge hung precariously from the soft cotton material of the shirt. I carried my gun in an ugly black purse with a built-in holster and handcuff case. The department for which I worked was a large one, and yet all women were assigned to desk jobs, includ-

Janice Strauss

ing the front desk and the jail. By the time 1973 rolled around, my department decided to take a huge risk and put a woman in a patrol car! I was again one of the first. The most immediate concern for the department was the uniforms. They had by then decided that the females should wear the same uniform as the men, but the uniform stores had not yet figured out that women are not built like men. I spent most of my salary each month getting men's uniforms tailored to fit me.

Roll forward 30 years—today in Arizona I know of two female police chiefs, three female assistant chiefs, and a whole handful of female commanders, lieutenants, and sergeants. This, however, has not been an easy 30 years. I tolerated every dirty joke imaginable in the early years and dealt with outrageous flirting. I put up with citizens who, when I responded to their calls, told me they would wait for a male officer. I had suspects call me "honey," "Barbie doll," and "sweetheart." Nonetheless, every female officer I know has earned her badge of honor and the respect of her male counterparts. I truly believe that a woman has to prove herself twice over what a man does in the law enforcement field.

Is it all worth it? You bet. I have never regretted my decision. Law enforcement is an exciting and energized field where a person can literally change jobs about every two years if she continues to move about in her organization. I have been a street cop, a field training officer, a sex crime detective, a robbery detective, a detective sergeant, a hiring sergeant, a training lieutenant, a street sergeant, a street lieutenant, a training lieutenant, a patrol commander, and finally, an assistant chief and chief. I believe women bring a unique perspective to law enforcement. Women are typically wonderful communicators, and they are naturally nurturing with excellent people skills, skills many police chiefs now consider to be the most important in performing the function of police officers.

The concept that a person has to be able to leap tall buildings and be able to lift that same building is ridiculous. We encourage even our most robust officers not to perform these tasks so they will not get hurt. Some level of physical fitness, however, is paramount because of the rigors of the job. An officer may be sitting in his/her car for hours and then suddenly have to perform superman/woman-like physical activity to catch a fleeing suspect or to save a life. Most police academies still stress physical fitness for this reason, and I support that concept. I do not believe there is any law enforcement job that a female cannot do as well as a male. We have had female motorcycle officers and female SWAT officers, two of the most macho assignments.

My best advice is this. If you want to be a police officer, be prepared to be mentally tough, physically fit, and emotionally stable. This job is a difficult one. You see and hear things you may never have thought imaginable. You will experience great joy and great sadness, sometimes in the same day. You will make a difference every single day that you work. Remember that this is a difficult job if you want to raise a family; however, it can be done. I raised two girls and a boy, and none of them has reported me to Child Protective Services, and none of them is in jail. My oldest daughter received academic scholarships and my second daughter is presently on the dean's list at her university and has plans to teach junior high school math. My son is still in high school and is a well-adjusted seventeen-year-old boy. Additionally, I have virtually raised these three wonderful kids on my own. I was divorced seven years ago, but even before that, I was really the only parent. If you are a woman who wants to make a difference in her community and is willing to work hard, but enjoy a fulfilling life, law enforcement is the profession that you will want to consider.

Nina Wright, Deputy Chief of Charlotte-Mecklenburg Police Department, North Carolina

As the first female deputy chief of Charlotte-Mecklenburg Police Department (CMPD), Nina Wright, another successful African American woman in policing, takes her place among the other outstanding women in policing. Beginning as a patrol officer for CMPD in 1986, she has progressed through the ranks in a variety of different areas, working in crime prevention, internal affairs, investigations, and administration. She models community-oriented policing by actively volunteering with youth and police–community activities.

Deputy Chief Wright also understands and represents the importance of continuous mental and physical enrichment. After completing her undergraduate degree in criminal justice, she is currently working on her master's in public administration. Physically, she has been awarded the agency's Physical Fitness Excellence Award and two gold medals from the North Carolina Police Olympics.

Wright has taken a leadership role in actively recruiting and supporting women and minority officers. Some of her involvement includes active participation in the agency's Minority Recruitment Committee, the Women's Recruitment Subcommittee, and the Women's Network.

Deputy Chief Wright gives the following advice:

To all women: If you believe in a higher power, seek guidance before making this career choice so that you KNOW it is meant for you. That will give you the

Nina Wright

perseverance to face whatever challenges come your way. Be physically fit. You don't need to be a body builder, but you should be prepared for a challenging fitness program. It is important to know that you do not have to become "one of the guys." You can maintain your womanhood and be an excellent officer. Set career goals, and set yourself a plan of action to reach those goals.

To the women already in a policing career: As other women join the ranks of policing in your agency, reach out to them. Whether formally or informally, don't let them flounder. Think back to your experiences as a recruit and a rookie. Let that be your motivation to help others. The hand you reach out to them might be the only thing that keeps them from walking away from policing. Our goal should be to create an environment where women feel welcome and are appreciated for the talents we bring to the law enforcement career field. Ultimately, if we all do our part, this will one day not be viewed as a "nontraditional" career field for women.

To women of color: Being a woman in policing places you in the minority, but being a woman of color in policing can be a lonely trek if you try to walk it alone. A mentor is a MUST. If one doesn't seek you out, then you seek one out. Choose carefully. Studies have shown that the talents of minority employees are more likely to go unnoticed until well into their career, which helps to explain why it is so common for us to make it to middle management and no further. Having one or more mentors can be a true asset to your growth, understanding, and readiness to deal with the realities that lie ahead. Your mentor(s) also serve as advocates. They can be the difference in someone noticing your abilities and work record over that of an equally or lesser-qualified individual. Having at least one strong mentor gives you somewhere to go when you need to vent frustrations or ask the hard questions. This mentor can give you advice or help you work through difficult issues.

Diane Nicholson, Undersheriff of Washoe County, Nevada, Sheriff's Office

Undersheriff Nicholson is second in command of the sheriff's office, answering only to the sheriff. The sheriff's office is responsible for a variety of duties, including the jail that houses 1,000 inmates, enforcement of the laws in the county, court security, and civil process. As undersheriff, Nicholson is responsible first for the supervision of the two assistant sheriffs, who share the responsibilities of operations and detention; the internal affairs unit; and the crime lab unit. In addition, her duties include the budget, policy development and implementation, payroll and personnel, purchasing, and records.

     Undersheriff Nicholson knew that she wanted to go into law enforcement early in her life and decided that the best route would be through the military. She enlisted in the Army and served in the military police for three years. Her responsibilities included enforcement of the military code, United States military installation security, and canine handler. After she completed her tour of duty, she returned to California and worked for Immigrations before deciding that she wanted to work as a road deputy with the Alameda County Sheriff's Office. During her years as deputy, she often vacationed in the neighboring state of Nevada. Noticing a recruitment announcement for positions with the local police and sheriff's of-

Diane Nicholson

fice, she decided to apply to the sheriff's office. She was hired immediately. Although the agency had a number of female deputies, they were mainly assigned to detention, the jail. She too was expected to work in detention, and it was only after several years and persistent requests to be transferred to the road that she was allowed on patrol as a road deputy. After several years on patrol, she sought promotion and succeeded. Nicholson was first assigned to the jail as sergeant, then back to patrol as the first female sergeant in the county, and then to the narcotics unit.

Although she had worked with other agencies when on patrol, the narcotics unit worked across agencies encompassing local, state, and federal law enforcement agencies. She was promoted to lieutenant and again assigned first to detention and then to internal affairs. Nicholson found internal affairs particularly challenging because she was responsible for investigating complaints against other deputies and sheriff personnel. Although it was fulfilling to clear an officer of an unjustified complaint, she found it difficult when officers were determined to have committed an act against departmental policy or the law. She was promoted to undersheriff from captain when a new sheriff was first appointed to complete the previous sheriff's term. When the sheriff was elected, he kept Nicholson as undersheriff.

Undersheriff Nicholson gives the following advice: "Be competent in what you do and gain as much experience as possible. Experience and reputation will make you a better leader. Work hard and don't take shortcuts."

SUMMARY

This chapter has offered insights from a number of female law enforcement officers and top female administrators. Collectively, they provide valuable advice, as well as enthusiasm for their lives in law enforcement.

The chapter shows that with determination and tenacity, women can confront and overcome the concerns and problems they encounter and still maintain their identity. It also shows that women must learn as much as possible about the agency in which they want to become employed; must work hard to develop a reputation as a competent, dependable officer; and, once seasoned, should support other female officers.

Clearly, even today women entering policing face considerable challenges. It would seem, however, that veteran women officers and administrators feel the rewards are well worth the effort. These women have experienced professional lives that are diverse, fulfilling, and exciting.

READER LEARNING OUTCOMES

Having examined this chapter, the reader should understand:

- factors that influence women in their decision to become police officers
- the basis for concerns that women have when entering policing
- the impact the police culture has had on women who entered the field and examples of coping with such issues as sexual harassment and discrimination
- the experiences of several law enforcement women in leadership positions

NOTES

1. Kenneth J. Peak, *Justice Administration: Police, Courts, and Corrections Management,* 4th ed. (Upper Saddle River, NJ: Prentice Hall, 2004), p. 68.

2. A. Bandura, "Self-Efficacy: Toward a Unifying Theory of Behavioral Change,"*Psychological Review* 84 (1977):191–215; Vivian B. Lord and Paul Friday, "Choosing a Career in Police Work: A Research Study of Applicants for Employment with Charlotte-Mecklenburg Police and Charlotte-Mecklenburg Public High School Students" (Technical Report for Charlotte-Mecklenburg Police Department, 1999):13.

3. G. Hackett and N. E. Betz, "A Self-Efficacy Approach to the Career Development of Women," *Journal of Vocational Behavior* 18 (1981):326–329.

4. Lord and Friday, "Choosing a Career in Police Work," p. 11.

5. R. Gorden, *Basic Interviewing Skills* (Prospect Heights, IL: Waveland, 1998), p. 24.

6. D. J. Bell, "Policewomen: Myths and Reality," *Journal and Police Science and Administration* 12 (1982):47–75.

7. Robin N. Haar, "Patterns of Interaction in a Police Patrol Bureau: Race and Gender Barriers to Integration," *Justice Quarterly* 14 (1997):53–85.

8. George Felkenes and J. R. Schroedel, "A Case Study of Minority Women in Policing," *Women & Criminal Justice* 4 (1993):65–89.

9. John Crank, *Understanding Police Culture,* 2nd ed. (Cincinnati, OH: Anderson, 2004), pp. 232–235.

10. Ibid., p.8.

11. Susan Martin, *Doing Justice, Doing Gender* (Thousand Oaks, CA: Sage, 1996), pp. 67–68.

12. Ibid., p. 68.

Chapter 8

Selected Case Studies:
Those Who Wear the Badge
and Do the Work

---❖---

We hold these truths to be self-evident, that all men and women are created equal.

—Elizabeth Cady Stanton at the First Woman's Rights Convention, 1848

Introduction

As we saw in Chapter 2, after the law enforcement profession opened to women in the mid-1970s, female officers struggled to break into the rich variety of job opportunities. It was not enough to be "allowed" to work patrol or in family investigative areas. Women wanted to enter law enforcement at the state and federal levels as well as at the local level. This chapter will show that women are now functioning in every area of law enforcement; no area is considered off-limits to them. To give the reader an idea of what positions are available, we present here a sample of the kinds of positions women officers currently hold so that as the reader begins her own exploration of law enforcement, she can appreciate the diversity of experiences available. The women who were interviewed belong to different agencies across the nation. This chapter begins with opportunities at the local level and concludes at the federal level. The women discuss their lives prior to entering policing, their preparation for a law enforcement career, and their current responsibilities. The women also counsel readers about sustaining their careers.

LOCAL AND STATE LAW ENFORCEMENT OFFICERS

Officer Teresa Young, Patrol Officer
and School Resource Officer, Alaska

RESPONSIBILITIES   After working first as a patrol officer with the Savannah, Georgia, Police Department and then as a road deputy with the Liberty County, Georgia, Sheriff's Office, Officer Teresa Young now resides in one of the coldest locations in the United States. Young has responsibilities as a school resource officer (SRO) during the school year. As a SRO, she is available to both students and teachers, taking whatever cases come up in the schools, and also teaches Drug Abuse Resistance Education (DARE). She finds teaching DARE to be fulfilling; the students interact easily with her and trust her. Young has an open-door policy for all students, and they often come and see her about their problems. When students express an interest in law enforcement, she encourages them to ride with police officers during school breaks. When not busy in the public schools, Young's responsibilities include general patrol, securing businesses, and assisting tourists. Unlike local officers in other states, her jurisdiction is the entire state, which authorizes Young and other sworn police officers to enforce laws in all areas of Alaska.

Originally from Washington State, Young was not only used to a cooler climate but wanted to move back to such a climate. And it does get cold in Alaska: At 60 degrees below zero, it can become very difficult to breathe. The North Pole Police Department has four garage bays for the patrol cars, so the officers are able to park their vehicles out of the cold and prevent the engines and other mechanical parts from freezing. The main police problems in the North Pole are drunk drivers, domestic violence complaints, and shoplifting. The North Pole is not plagued with major crime problems, but the long winter nights often lead to violent behavior.

Native Alaskans are different culturally, and officers unfamiliar with their culture must learn how to interact with them. For example, native Alaskans are uncomfortable making direct eye contact and usually give short answers. Alaskans regard their privacy highly and see the police as intruders. Officer Young has learned to relate to their need for privacy, often noting, "Privacy is also one reason I moved to Alaska, but we were called to your house because of this situation. Once we can deal with it, then we will leave."

Being female, Young finds that she gets into fewer altercations than male officers and can usually talk those offenders she is arresting into handcuffs. She believes that women officers come off as less threatening to males, so they are less likely to fight female officers. Women also seem to handle problems differently from male officers, allowing for a variety of solutions.

BACKGROUND   Officer Young is an only child and was very much a tomboy. She married immediately after graduating from high school and soon became a mother. Officer Young knew she needed something more in her life, a challenge that included helping people, so she decided to go into law enforcement. She had been interested in law enforcement since high school and even tested for the military police. When her interest in law enforcement re-emerged, she applied at several places and accepted a position with the Savannah Police Department, where she was assigned to the River Street area. River Street has a number of housing projects that suffer high crime rates, so she experienced a variety of complaints and crimes. After two years, Officer Young went to work for the Liberty County Sheriff's Office as its first female road deputy.

When she first began working as a deputy sheriff, some male deputies tried to "gross her out" and do stupid things, but she never reacted to their stunts. Some deputies tried to protect her, not wanting her to get hurt, but she confronted them about it so they stopped. Early in her deputy career, she was serving civil commitment papers on a mental patient when he stabbed her 18 times in the head and face with a small screwdriver. He then jumped on top of her, and they both were wrestling with her weapon. Officer Young kept thinking, "The Sheriff is going to fire me." After the incident, many males in the agency told her she should get out. Officer Young just went back to work.

During her remaining time at the sheriff's office, she worked with the Major Drug Task Force, served search warrants, and made drug buys. The multiple agency drug task unit invited her to join, so again she took a position where she was the only female. She found the task force to be really enjoyable. It was cohesive, and she was automatically treated as part of the group.

COUNSEL   Officer Young believes training and equipment are better now than when she began. She believes prospective women officers should acquire as much education and training as possible.

> It will help your ability to make good decisions and to keep the survival edge. If things don't scare you, then you are in the wrong job. Learn not to take hostilities personally. It is not you who isn't liked, but what the uniform represents to some citizens.

Officer Celestine Ratcliff, DARE Officer, Large Police Agency, Southeastern State

RESPONSIBILITIES   For the past six years, Officer Ratcliff has been responsible for teaching kindergarten through fifth-grade students techniques to resist drugs and violence through DARE, a 17-week curriculum. She also has school resource officer responsibilities at her assigned elementary schools. These responsibilities include taking care of any enforcement problems or victim referrals for such offenses as child abuse or neglect. Officer Ratcliff, who is African American, finds her job fulfilling: " . . . watching the light bulb come on in a child's face, seeing a child thinking about what I said, and maybe changing his/her attitude." She believes being a DARE officer is the most rewarding interaction with kids an officer can have. It gives officers a chance to prevent children from becoming a criminal.

Kids are exposed to drugs constantly. Officer Ratcliff has talked to children who know how to make crack and have seen their parents abuse drugs. It can sometimes be overwhelming. She makes home visits to children who seem to need an extra boost. At school, she shows she cares by eating lunch with them or playing with them on the playground. Officer Ratcliff sees her job as a provider of information, not the punisher; however, she does tell her students, "I am your DARE officer. I love you and care about you. I want you to get all the information you can, but if you are involved in criminal activity or you are being abused, I have to act."

She believes that being a female has mainly helped her. She is able to talk to people in a motherly way. This approach allows her to deal with serious situations and heated verbal arguments without physical restraints. Other officers might choose to "put their hands on the citizen," but citizens see her as a mother or sister. When she was a patrol officer, there were a few negative aspects to being a female officer. Sometimes she would be the primary officer on a call but still be countermanded by male officers. While she didn't like it, she realized that the male officers thought they were protecting her. She never confronted the other officers during a call; it was not worth hurting "her own" to make a point. At times, after the call was completed, Officer Ratcliff would discuss this overprotectiveness with the male officers.

Officer Ratcliff spent several years as a patrol officer before becoming one of her department's original community coordinators as it moved into community-oriented policing. She really wanted to focus on the children in her area. She saw it as a way to prevent crime. So Officer Ratcliff worked with children who were truant. They called her "auntie" as she held "youth rallies" and youth counsels in an attempt to break down barriers between youth and police.

BACKGROUND   Officer Ratcliff has two older brothers, one younger brother, and one younger sister. When growing up, her brothers were told by their parents to protect their sisters but also to safeguard each other. The word in the neighborhood was "hurt one, another bigger will be there to hurt you." From these early experiences, Officer Ratcliff learned to protect those who were weaker, who needed a voice. Also her father didn't allow racial prejudice to be spoken in their home. He expected them to treat people the way they should be treated.

Ratcliff is from the city she polices and began college locally because her friends did. Even though she had a high GPA and made the dean's list, she didn't know what she wanted to do. Officer Ratcliff married, and she and her husband moved to Fort Bragg. They moved back after three years, and Officer Ratcliff worked first in service and then banking, finding all the jobs tedious. She wanted to make a difference. She decided that she would go into law enforcement, although nobody else in her family had ever been in that profession. All her contacts with police had been positive. Officer Ratcliff remembers when she was young that she was attracted to a huge police officer's sidearm. As she started to touch it, he placed his hand over hers and said, "Don't do that." He made an impression on her—he was strong and was there to protect her. Now when children ask her about her weapons, she pulls out her pen and tells them. "This is my most important weapon."

Officer Ratcliff's first criminal justice position was as a sworn deputy for the county, requiring her to complete basic law enforcement and jail training. Her job was primarily detention in the jail. Soon her family commented on the fact that she didn't smile much. After talking to a number of people, she decided to join the city police department. Ratcliff wanted to return to college no matter what the hardships. So when her daughter went to kindergarten, she enrolled in the local community college. Soon she found herself working midnight shift, going to school in the morning, sleeping a couple of hours, and then getting up to play with her daughter. Officer Ratcliff first earned her associate degree in police science and then her bachelor's in criminal justice (with honors).

COUNSEL   You have to be committed; you have to believe in yourself and the police profession. If you want to help people, there are plenty of different ways. Police work goes beyond helping people, and it sometimes requires your sacrifice of time with your family and your health. Women of color are needed badly, and there are so very few. If female African American female officers go on calls involving black subjects, they will be treated as their mother and sister. They can walk into a volatile situation and calm it down. Rarely do they want to fight a female African American officer. As a woman of color if you feel police officers are your enemy, you need to be part of the police culture in order to change it. If you believe police are there to repress or control you, then you definitely need to be involved in the change. Police work is a wonderful job. It is a way to touch people in a positive way.

Cassie Kirkendoll, Police Officer I, Midsize University Campus Police Agency, Western State

RESPONSIBILITIES   Officer Kirkendoll is responsible for a campus community, including students, faculty, and other university personnel. Although responsible for enforcing laws and preventing crime, as a campus police officer her role is primarily a helping position, and she finds that aspect rewarding. A large percentage of the student population is female, so it is very important to have female officers. Most of the citizens she encounters are young adults who are trying to get ahead but perhaps have used poor judgment. Reminding them that the consequences of their actions might be the loss of their scholarships or damage to their future usually helps them rethink their behavior.

Campus police are given additional tools unavailable to municipal officers. For instance, students and campus staff are required to abide by the campus code that goes beyond laws and ordinances. If students violate the campus code, they are required to face Student Judicial Affairs. If students disobey a criminal law, they face criminal court as well as Student Judicial Affairs. Student Judicial Affairs advisors refer students to needed resources, counsel them, or in a few cases, recommend expulsion.

Officer Kirkendoll, as a campus officer, also works with the city police, especially on campus events such as athletics, music concerts and "block parties." The campus police have the authority to shut down any event that becomes disruptive. If the event gets out of control, the municipal police are available and are often called in.

BACKGROUND   Although there are no law enforcement professionals in her family, Officer Kirkendoll has always been intrigued by the justice system and found herself "policing" her friends, cautioning them away from dangerous or bad behavior. Her freshman year in high school, Officer Kirkendoll told her school's guidance counselor that she wanted to be a police officer. The counselor stated emphatically that Officer Kirkendoll did not want to be a police officer, but instead advised her to consider becoming a lawyer, stating that the law profession was more fitting for a woman. Her mother, like Kirkendoll, was dumbfounded that a counselor responded so negatively. Her parents had always been supportive of her desire to be a police officer. She was brought up to believe that if she worked hard, she could be and accomplish anything.

After high school, Kirkendoll pursued her dream by obtaining a college degree in criminal justice. While working on her college degree, she heard about and applied to the Police Corps program, a federally funded program that pays or reimburses students' college expenses if they attend and successfully complete a rigorous basic law enforcement program and agree to serve with their selected law enforcement agency for four years.

The Police Corps selection process is thorough and follows the procedures required to be hired by most law enforcement agencies. Applicants must pass a written test, a physical agility test, an extensive background investigation, as well as a computer voice stress analysis or polygraph. The training itself is grueling. The students attend class 14 hours daily, six days a week, for a total of 20 weeks of residential training. In Kirkendoll's class, 14 students started and 10 graduated. She was the only female to graduate.

Kirkendoll is one of two females with her agency. After a year with the agency, Kirkendoll believes that she has earned the respect of many of her fellow officers. In the past, her agency has had a hard time retaining female officers. The administration now in charge of the agency is working hard to recruit a diverse group of qualified individuals, including women.

COUNSEL   Know your community that you will be serving. Don't expect "hot calls," such as major crimes, but instead a great deal of report writing for minor offenses such as stolen purses. Because campus politics are a large part of the university culture, officers must be aware and sensitive to them. Universities have a diverse student body; be aware of cultural differences. As an officer, you must be able to understand and respect the different values of other cultures. Not all cultures see the police as helping people and fear them. There are certain taboos of different cultures, and it is important to understand them. In certain cultures, female citizens find it easier to talk to female officers. For example, a Japanese female student worker was being stalked and subjected to indecent exposure at work by a Chinese male graduate student. She was so embarrassed by and afraid of these aggressive acts that she quit her job. Her employer reported the actions by the Chinese male graduate student. The female student believed that she was expected to accept such behavior.

Lenore Barbour, Crime Scene Supervisor, Large Police Agency, Southeastern State

RESPONSIBILITIES   Lenore Barbour supervises between 18 and 20 crime scene technicians, who detect, collect, preserve, and submit physical evidence from major crime scenes. She finds her job fulfilling. Having a great deal of passion for whatever she does, her current job is challenging, physically and mentally. Barbour believes she is speaking for those victims who can no longer speak. Evidence doesn't lie, so the crime scene technicians must be able to detect and read the evidence. If the technicians do their job, the victim and the accused are more likely to receive the justice they deserve.

She is proud of her department's crime scene team specialists, who are very dedicated and tenacious. Crime scene technical work is attractive to females, and her unit has a high percentage of females. Women are intrigued by the need to use their brain. The work has a physical aspect but is still different from regular patrol work. The turnover rate of employees is high because the job is not glamorous but instead is stressful, with long hours. The technicians must deal with everybody's tragedies, and there always seem to be 15 officers on the crime scene making demands of the technicians.

BACKGROUND   Ms. Barbour had a coach in high school who encouraged her to consider a career in law enforcement. Lenore was rather rough in sports and had an attitude. She wasn't even sure about going to college, but her mother talked her into attending the local community college. There, one instructor really caught her attention with mock crime scenes. After exploring criminal justice, Ms. Barbour liked it well enough to transfer as a criminal justice major to a four-year college. There, Ms. Barbour was able to obtain an internship with one of the major crime scene units in the state. Within two months of graduating, she started working as a chemical analyst and fingerprint technician, as well as operating the equipment for drunk drivers and photography development. The technicians with the crime scene unit were sworn agents (deputies), so Ms. Barbour could never become an actual technician without becoming a deputy; however, her current agency had a crime scene unit with nonsworn technicians. When a position came open, she applied and was hired.

One obstacle Ms. Barbour has had to face is within herself. She likes to control the entire job, but she has had to learn to hold back and let others take on responsibilities of the job. Her job can also be frustrating. Although she wants to help the victim or the victim's family, sometimes nothing can be done. For instance, a surface area may not be conducive to prints, or a case is thrown out of court after a great deal of time and effort. Finally, the job comes with a price. Often it is the sacrifice of personal time with family. Ms. Barbour is divorced and knows the job can be consuming if she allows it.

COUNSEL   When new people are hired, few know what is involved in the job. First find out everything you can before you take the job; don't just look at the glamour as it is depicted on television. Crime scene investigation needs to be seen first as a career, so be willing to learn the skills and invest the time needed for your new career. Some courses in college will help you, such as criminal justice and psychology. Testifying is an important component of your crime scene responsibilities. If you have any fears of talking in front of people, you also may want to take a speech class. You need to have a certain level of confidence. Confidence will allow you to remain calm, to be assertive, to ask questions and keep focused. You need to have professional compassion. Hopefully you will never look at a dead body as a thing. Being objective, but respectful of human life is a critical component of the job.

Deputy Annadennise Wollenzier, Deputy and Negotiator, Large Sheriff's Office, Pacific State

RESPONSIBILITIES   Deputy Wollenzier is currently assigned to a correctional facility. She is part of a three-year, federally funded research grant for the purpose of working with incarcerated women with co-occurring disorders (major mental illness with alcohol and/or drug abuse) who are mothers and are homeless or at a high risk of homelessness. Her responsibilities are to work with a multidisciplinary treatment team consisting of members from the Department of Mental Health and fellow sworn staff to provide services to women, who are randomly assigned to one of four treatment groups. Deputy Wollenzier is also a member of the hostage/crisis negotiations unit. As part of approximately a six-member negotiations team, she can be called out anytime with the special weapons and tactical (SWAT) team for such situations as barricaded hostage incidents and/or suicide attempts. The agency has three rotating teams that answer an average of 150 calls annually.

Deputy Wollenzier finds all her responsibilities fulfilling. There is a challenge in making a difference in somebody's life when he or she is in crisis. Also, with the incarcerated women, she is able to see a change from rage to a desire to take responsibility for themselves. The main goal is to keep these women from coming back to jail, getting them to realize they can change and get treatment for their psychological problems.

BACKGROUND   Annadennise began her police career at a later age than many deputies. Her original profession as a licensed psychiatric technician was with a mental health clinic helping people in crisis and the homeless. She then became a member of the mental health evaluation team (MET), which is a joint mental health and law enforcement endeavor supporting deputies when they are interacting with individuals who may have mental health or emotional problems. Annadennise admired the compassion demonstrated by the deputies working on the MET team and was further inspired by the director of the sheriff's office psychological unit. So after six years as a psychiatric technician with the MET team, she decided to enter the profession of law enforcement.

She began a physical fitness program before entering basic training for the sheriff's office. She had never been interested in exercise, and now she was "middle aged." She also worked to overcome her fear of physical contact.

The sheriff's office requires all its deputies to work a certain period of time in detention before being placed on patrol or in other specialized areas. Although Annadennise was working in detention, the sheriff's office was aware of her skills and experience working in the mental health area, so she was quickly asked her to become part of its crisis/hostage negotiations team.

Although Annadennise has heard a few negative remarks from some of the older deputies about women in law enforcement, overall her experience has been positive and satisfying. As a negotiator, being female has helped her. Because they are often afraid of law enforcement officers, the offenders are usually willing to talk to her, finding her less intimidating. She tends to calm them and talk to them openly.

With three young daughters at home, Annadennise has found it difficult to leave her children to work odd hours and holidays. Her husband has been supportive, and she has a nanny staying in her home during the week. Annadennise has told her girls about her job and its related potential dangers, and they are very proud of their mother in uniform.

Annadennise's parents encouraged her to obtain a good education. Her father instilled in her and her siblings pride in their culture and religion, so these two things, along with the support of her entire family, have helped her to get to where she is now. Without any of this, she states, it would have been impossible.

COUNSEL   If you are interested in law enforcement or any nontraditional profession, do it. Don't let anybody talk you out of it. It would have been easy for me to decide I was too old, but I didn't and I really enjoy my work. Education is very important. Complete your college degree and then become as knowledgeable about your job as you can. Don't ever stop believing in yourself and in the good out there. We are constantly surrounded by the negatives so that many times we lose sight of the good in everybody (well, almost everybody) and of the many beautiful, simple things in life that bring about pleasure and happiness. If you want something bad enough—GO FOR IT! You can do it. I did.

Monica Geddry

Monica Geddry, Traffic Officer, Midsize Police Agency, Western State

RESPONSIBILITIES   Officer Geddry currently enforces traffic laws, including speed regulations, traffic lights and signs enforcement, and drunk driving enforcement. She also investigates crashes and educates the public about safe driving. One of the areas that Officer Geddry has found most fulfilling is developing and conducting a drunk-driving prevention program, which is especially designed for teenage drivers. The National Highway Traffic and Safety Agency (NHTSA) plans to use it as a national model program. Officer Geddry enjoys interacting with teenagers and keeping them alive. They don't understand what law enforcement is all about, but are willing to learn if she lets them be themselves.

BACKGROUND   Officer Geddry was born in upstate New York as the middle child of seven, three brothers and three sisters. Her father, who had a business career, and her mother, who stayed at home, were supportive of whatever career any of their children chose. Her parents did make it clear that the children would be expected to work for what they wanted. Her parents separated while Geddry was still fairly young, and her father moved them first to Chicago and then to a small town in California. Officer Geddry still remembers the complete culture shock of living in a small town. By the time the family had moved to her current western town in her early teen years, she was active in riding horses, playing basketball, snow skiing, water skiing, and long-distance running. She started college as an elementary education major, but in her last year, Geddry applied to the police department for a summer job. Although she was not hired, she was high on the list, and she decided that she wanted to find out more about policing. She joined the reserve officers and changed her major to criminal justice.

Officer Geddry was hired by her current police agency and worked hard. At first, she was warned that the older officers didn't want to work with female officers. Officer Geddry was careful never to use "gender," and these older officers supported her efforts and taught her the "streets."

When Officer Geddry was first asked to join the motor patrol, she was not interested; however, when her uncle died, she inherited several Harley-Davidson motorcycles. Monica decided to attend the motorcycle school sponsored by her police agency. She liked riding the motorcycles, so decided to join the traffic unit.

COUNSEL   You should know all you can about the police department in your town. Do a ride-along and talk to the officers. If you think you are interested, take a criminal justice introductory class and see if the material interests you. Be confident in doing whatever you must do to meet your goals. If you decide to become a police officer, communicating with people is essential. You will need to be in good physical shape and work hard to achieve high scores on all the tests. Be prepared to prove yourself. Do not use gender to try and get where or what you want. Be wary of which paths you consider. Plan to be a patrol officer for three to five years and then consider promotions and transfers. A behavior a female officer should avoid is trying to act like a man. While this job has always been viewed a man's job, who cares? We should never lose our identity. Be who you are! Get in, do a good job, and you will be respected. Policing is a great job. There is no need to get burned out because there are so many areas to explore.

Laura Conklin, Police Officer and Sniper, Midsize Police Agency, Western State

RESPONSIBILITIES   Officer Conklin's primary duty is patrolling the north district of her city; however, her collateral duty is membership on her department's SWAT team. SWAT consists of 26 officers who are called out for such incidents as armed barricaded subjects with or without hostages, armed suicidal subjects, and the serving of high-risk warrants. Although trained to carry out any function on the SWAT team, Officer Conklin is also one of the few designated snipers for the team.

Representing the prevention side of law enforcement, Conklin also teaches DARE and has adopted one of her city's "at-risk" elementary schools. Through a federally funded "Weed & Seed" program, Conklin spends some of her off-duty hours in uniform, helping children at the "at-risk" elementary school with their studies and coordinating intramural sports events such as soccer tournaments. The children are able to see her in her police uniform as a helper rather than an enforcer.

Being female has helped Officer Conklin in her police agency. The agency is always looking for strong, effective women to promote, but on the negative side of that search are other officers' perceptions that a female officer receives an appointment "because she is a female." Conklin also believes women officers have negotiation skills that men are less likely to possess. These negotiation skills are derived from both interpersonal communication

Laura Conklin

skills and the ability to consider other alternatives besides aggression. Male offenders are also less apt to fight a female officer because they view the female as their sister or mother.

Officer Conklin prepared extensively for SWAT. She talked to other SWAT members in order to visualize what skills might be demanded during the testing for new SWAT members. She discovered that there would first be agility and shooting tests, and then an oral interview by a board consisting of SWAT members, for those who passed the physical tests. Six months before the test, Conklin began to work out, carrying 50 pounds on her back and shooting more. She also reviewed oral interview questions that had been used in the past. She knew that the members wanted to see if the candidate could think on his or her feet, make ethical decisions, and problem solve. Any complaint and commendation in her personnel file would be reviewed. After all the hard work she invested, she was accepted on the SWAT team. After about a year on the team, she tried out for a sniper position. The test for the sniper position was also difficult. She had to demonstrate her ability to shoot after a 50-yard sprint and 25 push-ups. In addition to ethical and problem-solving interview questions, Conklin also had to answer math questions.

BACKGROUND   The youngest of five children, Conklin grew up in a very close family. With three older brothers, she played hard and participated in sports. Her parents were supportive, encouraging all their children to achieve what they wanted out of life. When Conklin entered college, she was interested in criminal justice and interned with a local fire department's arson investigation unit. Like one of her brothers, she decided she wanted to be a firefighter, but after testing unsuccessfully several times, she decided to train as a probation/parole officer. Unlike other states, her particular state first provides common training for all criminal justice personnel, such as adult and juvenile probation, fire, and police. In addition to testing successfully for probation, Conklin had also tested successfully for the municipal police agency. Although she was three months into her training for probation, with the support of her staff officer, she was allowed to switch over to a career with the police. In the five years that she has been a police officer, she has never regretted that decision.

COUNSEL   You will be better at firearms than you think. If you have never handled firearms, you won't have bad habits to eliminate. Just be confident that you can do it. Analyze your personal assets. For example, you may find that you are a good communicator and presenter so you may want to include DARE teaching as part of your responsibilities. Get a college degree before applying. You will find it helpful in dealing with people and problem solving, and you are usually paid more. Once in the profession, you may want to work towards a graduate degree. Many police departments will help pay for the degree, and many agencies require a graduate degree for higher administrative positions. Policing is fun. I'm a different person than when I worked in the warehousing profession. I now enjoy coming to work. Women often seem to come into the police business later in life, which is probably an advantage.

Detective Sylvia Connor, Youth Investigator, Large Police Agency, Southeastern State

RESPONSIBILITIES   As youth investigator, Detective Connor investigates cases of child abuse and neglect and equivocal infant deaths. Child abuse includes children who have been physically, emotionally, and sexually abused, and neglect comprises such areas as lack of adequate supervision, shelter, and food. She works with personnel from the medical field, social services, mental health, and child advocacy. Connor finds working with children and stopping offenders from further hurting children particularly satisfying.

Sylvia Connor

BACKGROUND   Detective Connor had several jobs before she entered law enforcement, including waitress, factory worker, and secretary. During the time she was a secretary, a friend, whose boyfriend was a police officer and responsible for recruiting, kept trying to convince her to apply to the police department. Detective Connor refused until she was assaulted by her former boyfriend. The trauma convinced her that she needed to be able to protect herself.

Her mother didn't like her decision to enter law enforcement. She was worried about the danger; however, she did support her daughter's choice and, most importantly, was willing to provide childcare for her granddaughter. Detective Connor did learn that her family became anxious if she discussed her experiences at work. So she began to talk to other officers, leaving the daily incidents at work.

She completed basic law enforcement training at a time in which the structure was paramilitary with emphasis on physical training. Although she had to work hard, the fact that all of the students liked each other and that there were six other females helped. They studied together after class and supported each other in all areas.

Detective Connor began her patrol experience in the west/southwest part of town, which had high-crime areas. She continued for 10 years there, working a variety of different crimes and interacting with a diverse group of people. Detective Connor took an assignment as a school resource officer for one year and then was promoted to master police officer. During these 11 years, she was also a field training officer (FTO), becoming the first black female in that capacity for the department. Detective Connor was then promoted to the Family Services Bureau as a youth investigator, where she has worked for the past 13 years.

Beginning policing in the 1970s, Detective Connor faced a number of citizens who would say, "I want a real police officer. You can leave. Tell them to send somebody else." On the other hand, she would receive a number of flirtatious comments with sexual innuendos. For example, men she was wrestling down to cuff would get an erection. Or when she searched (it is important to search the groin area), the offender would squeal and say "Do that again."

When Detective Connor first began patrol, there were fewer than 20 female officers with the department. Several of the female officers told her that if she wanted to stay in police work, she would need to put up with "whatever was dished out." When other officers or superiors would make sexual comments or invitations, Detective Connor refused their advances or ignored their comments, but when that was not enough, she threatened to file a complaint (but never did). She did feel that she was not harassed as badly as other female officers who remained passive.

Detective Connor also experienced sexual and racial discrimination. The most serious example was lack of promotion. She participated in the sergeants' promotional process six times, and each time she was on the eligibility list. Prior to 1995, the chronological list of eligible officers was not publicized, allowing the selection to be more subjective. Detective Connor believes that one of her sergeants deliberately gave her a poor evaluation, a rating that was not justified, so that she would have a low score on the eligibility list. When she complained to her chain of command, she was told that nothing could be done.

In retrospect, Detective Connor believes a mentor would have been helpful to her, but for several years there were no black female supervisors and few experienced white female supervisors who would have been good role models. If experienced male officers or superiors tried to mentor a female officer, then they were often accused of sleeping with her. Even now, women officers are assigned throughout the city in satellite district offices, so it is hard for them to network. In the past when everybody was in one building, it was possible to communicate with women on the same shift, even if they were not in the same district.

To prepare for investigations, Detective Connor had a number of relevant qualifications that helped her meet the requirements for youth investigations. First, she was experienced as a school resource officer. Second, she had shown and taken special interest in cases involving juveniles, such as initiating requests to answer calls involving juveniles, conducting follow-ups on misdemeanor juvenile-related cases, or supporting the investigators on juvenile felony cases. Still she applied four times before she received the position. After the third time, Detective Connor felt certain that discrimination was involved. She knew that less experienced or qualified white officers were receiving promotions. Although not desiring to complain formally, Detective Connor did go to a police chaplain and explained the situation. She wanted to stay in police work, but after 10 years on patrol, she needed a change. She told him that she had applied several times and was discouraged. Detective Connor is not sure how the conversation with the chaplain influenced the promotional decision, but after her conversation, she received the position.

COUNSEL   Respect yourself. Only with self-respect can you have the courage to speak out when necessary to defend yourself. Have the determination to take the extra step; do more than the next officer. This extra work translates into doing a better job, writing a better report. Taking the extra step will give you the confidence to strive for those promotions when the time is right, and you are qualified. As a black female, you must always do better in any profession, not just law enforcement. If you work hard and persevere for three to five years, you will find policing is very rewarding. Expect to be required to "prove yourself" in a dangerous or highly volatile situation. Other officers need to know that you can handle yourself and will also back them up. If you are ever tagged a coward, you may as well resign. Have good interpersonal communication skills. You must be able to reach out and initiate those conversations with other officers and the community. Don't let them alienate you, but instead be willing to help. Try to reach out to other female and minority officers any chance you get. Finding a black female mentor with a positive attitude is valuable. Although discrimination is still present, it is more subtle. Don't go looking for it, but don't be passive when experiencing it. Learn to manage stress by exercising, limiting alcohol consumption and spending time with your family and friends. Grow spiritually.

Detective Linda Holmes, Homicide Detective, Large Police Agency, Southeastern State

RESPONSIBILITIES   Detective Holmes's current responsibilities are investigating deaths, kidnappings, suicides, serious assaults with deadly weapons with intent to kill, and some natural deaths. She works with a partner who, after 13 years in the homicide unit, is a wealth of information. As a squad of five detectives, they are called out to major cases, carrying out the variety of different tasks required.

Having worked more than five years with the sexual assault unit, Detective Holmes is now faced with different challenges in the homicide unit. While still utilizing general investigative techniques, she has learned new technical skills, such as ballistics, and also the internal politics of the unit considered the most elite and where many officers would like to

Linda Holmes

be. The unit is still adjusting to women detectives, and the women have to learn to work as part of a team. The female detectives also work hard to prove themselves, so an undercurrent of tension often seems to exist that hopefully will lessen as female homicide detectives become more commonplace.

Being a female has not been a hindrance to Detective Holmes as she has progressed, but has helped her deal with victims and families of victims better. Families of suicide victims especially seem to have a hard time adjusting to the death of their family member, and she relates particularly well to these families.

BACKGROUND   Detective Holmes's love for the uniform began early. When she was 5, she loved watching "meter maids," believing they were women in policing. As women began to appear on television in such investigative roles as Angie Dickinson in "Police Woman," she decided that she wanted to go into policing. She began as a criminal justice major at Kent State in Ohio, but chose to go to work for a sheriff's office in North Carolina rather than complete her degree. She became the first female road deputy for that agency and continued in that role for four years. Detective Holmes decided to move back to a large metropolitan area and went to work for the airport police. Then after four years working there, she joined the city's police department. After two years on patrol, she made a career decision that she now realizes might not have been a wise choice in facilitating a future career in investigations. She transferred to the expeditor unit, a unit that helps citizens with minor and noncriminal offenses. Detective Holmes did well in the expeditor's unit, and when time allowed would pull rape reports and read the investigative notes, learning what she could about investigating sexual assault cases. Her interest and preparation paid off. After eight years in the expeditor unit, she was promoted to the sexual assault unit as detective. Five years later, a sergeant in the homicide unit suggested that she compete for an opening, which she did.

COUNSEL   If your goal is to become a homicide detective, you must realize that the only route in reaching your goal is to do a good job from the very beginning of your career. You first must be a good patrol officer, one who is known for going the extra mile attempting to obtain information and writing excellent reports. Then you must express your interest. Go and talk to a supervisor in the homicide unit, ask to spend some time with the unit, perhaps even on your own time if your department won't allow temporary assignments. You will need to consider working in other investigative units first in order to learn basic investigative skills. Whenever you apply for a new assignment, get to know the captain or major. Let them know that they have your paperwork, but you would like to talk to them about the position. You need to get as much exposure as possible. Make sure you can emotionally handle a homicide crime scene. When still a patrol officer, take every opportunity possible to provide support to a homicide case that is being worked. You must be prepared to deal with the extra pressure that comes from the public, media, and the administration to find the perpetrator and make the case.

Detective P. J. Allen, Repeat Offender Program, Midsize Police Agency, Western State

RESPONSIBILITIES   Detective Allen's unit monitors the "most serious felons," the violent and habitual offenders in the region. The criteria for most serious felons are two separate prison terms and three non-drug-related felonies. The repeat offender program (ROP) unit originated after a study revealed that 20 percent of offenders commit 80 percent of the

P. J. Allen

crimes in the United States. So the ROP unit monitors inmates while they are in prison and when they are released. This activity requires extensive surveillance. The ROP's unit officers put cases together for court and testify, striving for maximum sentences.

The ROP unit has bimonthly meetings with other law enforcement and criminal justice agencies such as probation and parole, the district attorney's office, and gaming control. They exchange information and pass out fliers on offenders. There is also a review committee, comprised of non-ROP officers, that meets monthly to evaluate those individuals who should be considered ROP offenders and also inmates coming up for parole. These committee members decide about whom the parole board should receive information in an effort to persuade the board that these designated offenders should not receive parole. Allen is responsible for compiling the material and writing a letter to the parole board outlining reasons that specific inmates should not be released.

Detective Allen finds her job fulfilling. After a great deal of time and effort, she is able to see violent habitual offenders receive maximum sentences. She also works with a really great team of investigators. Detective Allen does not believe being female has hindered her progress. Ten years ago, females were just coming on the force, and male officers weren't sure how to treat them, but now there are enough women in her agency that it is no longer a problem. Sometimes it helps to be a female. Some female suspects believe female investigators are more understanding, making it easier to build rapport with offenders.

BACKGROUND   Detective Allen's parents told her that she would either be a crook or a cop. She was a "hell-raiser" in high school and had some pretty interesting friends; some she arrested later. Living on a ranch, Detective Allen was used to working hard and spending a great deal of time outdoors. She was raised around horses and livestock, and fished and camped with four step-brothers.

For three years Detective Allen was an animal control officer. One day when she was attempting to take a dog away from an owner and put it in quarantine, the owner threatened to kill her. Detective Allen had to call for police backup, so she decided it would be better and safer to be trained as a police officer. As a police officer, she began on the graveyard patrol shift and remained there for several years. During that time, she heard over the radio that a specific individual was suicidal. She had helped the individual earlier to solve a problem, so she told the dispatcher about her experience with the subject. After talking directly to the subject and facilitating his subsequent decision to surrender, Detective Allen was asked to join the critical incident negotiation team as a negotiator.

After leaving patrol, she became a homeless evaluator, interacting with homeless citizens and attempting to reunite them with their families and/or get them resources. Detective Allen became known as the "Troll Queen," because she spent so much time under bridges. From the position of homeless evaluator, Detective Allen transferred to the horse patrol for four years and then returned to patrol. Soon after her return to patrol, she was able to make detective with the ROP.

Detective Allen had a couple of obstacles that she worked hard to overcome. She had a difficult time with public speaking, an important skill for conducting meetings and testifying in court. A great deal of training and teaching students DARE helped her work on her presentation skills and reduced her public-speaking anxieties. Also, Detective Allen is not a large woman, so she has had to learn to depend on communication skills as well as to think and move decisively. On the other hand, she has learned her limits and to work within those limits.

COUNSEL   Take a long hard look at yourself and identify who you have at home who means the most to you. Talk to them about your desire to become a police officer. Then research the field, talk to professionals, and listen to their stories. Look at policing as a career, a way of life. Your lifestyle will be different; people will look at you differently and you will look at life differently. This is not a job to meet men! Do not enter the profession for that reason. Take all the training seriously. What you do in the profession will make a difference, possibly with your life or others lives. Don't take anything for granted. For the right person, the job is like a party—fun and entertaining with new opportunities and new people.

Sergeant Katherine Kasell, Internal Affairs, Large Police Agency, Southeastern State

RESPONSIBILITIES   Sergeant Kasell investigates complaints against police officers. These cases include criminal wrongdoing, but also administrative problems and incidents that can lead to civil liability. She investigates and compiles the cases that will be reviewed by the department's administration.

     Sergeant Kasell believes that internal affairs is the hardest assignment she has had, because unlike past, specialized investigative assignments, internal affairs cases can fall into any area. She must understand all laws, including civil laws, and she must keep a delicate balance between protecting citizens against the wrongdoing of an officer and also protecting officers. Sergeant Kasell finds her job particularly fulfilling when she investigates a complaint about an officer and finds it is unfounded. She is able to phone the officer and confirm that he or she didn't violate procedures, so "keep up the good work."

Katherine Kasell

BACKGROUND   Sergeant Kasell was taught discipline early. By 12 years of age, she was practicing the piano three hours daily. She had her own business teaching piano in high school, incorporating her students into her own piano recital each year.

Sergeant Kasell went to college to study classical piano, but "burned out" practicing and studying piano five to six hours daily. She got out the college catalogue and looked at courses that might interest her. She found criminal justice, and became particularly interested in the legal area. Sergeant Kasell considered law school and also contacted federal law enforcement agencies. The different federal agencies told her that she needed to have two years of law enforcement experience before she would be considered, so she talked to recruiters for the state highway patrol. Their statements that she would be required to cut her hair and other discouraging remarks made her believe that the state highway patrol did not want women. Discovering that her current police agency ranked highly nationally, she applied.

Sergeant Kasell first worked patrol on the west side of the city. At that time it was very crime-ridden with drug-related problems, so she became interested in drug work. When community-oriented policing began, she was assigned to a group of housing projects with high crime rates. After three years on patrol, she decided to go to the vice unit so that she could work more directly on the drug problem. She worked undercover in both drugs and prostitution. Sergeant Kasell was also part of a federal investigative task force on organized crime and conducted drug interdictions at the airport for eight years. After a one-year assignment regulating sex-oriented businesses in the city, she was promoted to sergeant.

Sergeant Kasell went back to patrol on the lower-west side of town on the midnight shift. Adjusting to patrol, she let her officers know that she would need their help. She wanted to "lead from the front" and not expect them to do anything that she wouldn't do. Sergeant Kasell made sure that she sought guidance from the older officers, who might be more reluctant to have a female supervisor.

With every assignment, Sergeant Kasell has had to prove herself. She helps new female sergeants assigned to her area by mentoring and encouraging officers to support them. Being female does help in some areas, and female officers before her have built the foundation. Females have a certain demeanor and outlook on life that provide them special interviewing capabilities and the willingness to serve the public. It is still a male-oriented field, so females who are successful are given respect.

When people first see her in internal affairs, they think she is the secretary; however, when she explains that she is a sergeant and can help them, there is no problem. She just has to get them beyond the stereotype.

One of Sergeant Kasell's main obstacles came early in her career. When she first started with the department, she had a number of ideas that were ignored because there was not much empowerment at that time. For example, she had to convince her superiors that it would be a good idea for her to be assigned to the housing project and dedicate her time to answering calls in that specific area. Now the administration is more open to new ideas. Sergeant Kasell also faced a hostile work environment when she was to be promoted to sergeant. She had a superior who did not like her enforcing the regulations on a particular sex-related business. The superior harassed her about bothering that business. She didn't want to have any problems right before promotion so she kept trying to stay out of the superior's way. The harassment was finally reported by another officer.

COUNSEL   There is nothing you can't do if you make up your mind to do it. Don't worry what others think. Figure out your weaknesses and concentrate on them. When I was first assigned to patrol, I was intimidated about stopping and talking to people, so I really forced myself to get out and talk to people. Now I can talk to anybody. More recently I wanted to improve my paperwork skills. Well, in Internal Affairs, there is a great deal of paperwork!

A women's mentoring group is important and instrumental in retaining new female officers, so select an agency that has an active women's group.

Lieutenant Leigha Struffert, Patrol Supervisor, Midsize Police Agency, Western State

RESPONSIBILITIES   Until recently, Lieutenant Struffert was the direct line supervisor for the training division of her agency. She supervised the training of new hires, academy recruits, probationary employees, and sworn officers. She was also in charge of tracking the training received by each officer, scheduling the training, approving what training would be offered, and counseling officers about their formal education. Training is a controversial assignment due to the litigation every police agency now faces. Now more than ever, it is important for police departments to keep a detailed, accurate record of each employee's training information.

Although just recently promoted and transferred back to patrol, Lieutenant Struffert found particularly fulfilling the opportunity to work closely with outside agencies to regionalize training. She credits the training staff of her agency with launching its division into the 21st century with the most current tracking technology available. It also gave her insight into what is considered important training for the line officers, which often focuses

Leigha Struffert

on critical areas such as defensive tactics, firearms, small-team tactics, and communication skills. The most rewarding aspect of her position was recruiting instructors from within the agency and observing how they seem to become rejuvenated by training their peers.

Being a female is a challenge in law enforcement no matter what area one is assigned. Lieutenant Struffert received a great deal of feedback from her male peers, some negative, some positive, after her promotion to training. On the other hand, the public seemed to be supportive of females in law enforcement and pleased when they found out that the training sergeant was a woman. The new hires were surprised when they met her for the first time.

BACKGROUND   Lieutenant Struffert's upbringing has been a big factor in her decision to choose law enforcement. Her mother was a single parent and emphasized how important it was to be independent, both physically and financially. She also encouraged all six of her children to get an education. Lieutenant Struffert continued with her education until she earned a bachelor's degree in criminal justice and a master's degree in education.

Lieutenant Struffert applied to her current police agency when she was 21 years old, single, and a sophomore in college. Her older sister and she decided that they needed to focus on their careers. The sister dared her to test with the police agency while she applied to medical school. Fifteen years later, Struffert is a lieutenant and her sister practices medicine in Illinois. As an officer, Lieutenant Struffert was assigned to patrol, investigations (auto theft and fraud), housing authority developments, the training academy, and background investigations. Each assignment gave her the tools needed in her next assignment. In 1999, she was promoted to sergeant and returned to patrol. Soon after her promotion she was assigned to the training division. She was the first female officer in her agency to be promoted to sergeant in 11 years.

When she was promoted to sergeant, she had an infant at home. Upon meeting with her deputy chief of police, Struffert informed him that she was looking forward to her new assignments, but that she would need to go home around 11:00 each night to nurse her infant son. The deputy chief didn't know what to say; he just stood there and looked at her. Then he muttered something about his wife having breastfed his daughter and to make arrangements with her training sergeant.

Lieutenant Struffert feels that she faces the same obstacles that other women face in policing, such as returning to work full time after having a child without flexibility in work hours. It is a challenge to maintain a balance between her professional and personal life.

COUNSEL   Law enforcement is a rewarding job that will teach you about yourself. Women have different challenges than their male counterparts so it is important to know your limitations. Focus on the job of policing. After having two children, I became more fearful of being on the street and decided that if I was going to stay in law enforcement, I would need to refocus and make the commitment. I made the effort to stay in good physical shape, become more informed, and be more alert when in my patrol car. Some women officers become emotionally hard from their police experiences. Some of them become masculine, whether it is to fit in better or to compensate for what they are seeing and/or feeling. Policing is not good for some people. If you ever get to the point where you don't want to come into work, take six months to evaluate the reason, and if you still feel the same way—get out! Policing can be very hard on a person mentally and emotionally. Don't get stuck working in policing by the "three B's—booze, babes and bills." Do it because you love it! Policing is a progressive career that will continue to evolve. Women need to be part of that evolution. Just as we have proven to be a valuable part of the workforce, so must we continue to be a valuable part of policing's future.

Lieutenant Julia Grimes, Supervisor of the Major Crime Unit and Staff to the Colonel of the Alaska State Troopers

RESPONSIBILITIES   Lieutenant Grimes is currently assigned as supervisor of the major crime unit for the Alaska State Troopers. Her permanent assignment is staff to the director of the Alaska State Troopers. In this capacity, she interacts as a liaison with the different legislative bodies, introducing legislation that may have an impact on the Department of Public Safety's oversight of the State Troopers. She testifies before legislative committees, prepares analyses for the governor's office of bills that pass legislation, and writes fiscal assessments describing the fiscal impact of any proposed legislation on the Department of Public Safety. She also supervises the civilian staff who operate the concealed handgun permit program and licenses security guards for the state.

Lieutenant Grimes finds it especially fulfilling to be part of the homicide response team. Teamwork is required, not only within the unit and department but also across agencies. Criminal investigations frequently cross jurisdictions, and the ultimate goal of solving the crime overshadows any turf or recognition issues. It is also necessary to work with the district attorney's office to coordinate evidence gathering that will ensure successful prosecution of defendants. There is a feeling of justice served, especially in homicide cases. Although she can't bring back a life, she at least is part of taking the victim's killer off the

Julia Grimes

streets and allowing the victim's family some sense of closure. When she is able to see the jury hand down a sentence, Lieutenant Grimes considers it an example of the criminal justice system working.

While working as staff to the director is not the type of police work to which she is accustomed, there is satisfaction in learning how the agency operates. As a trooper, Lieutenant Grimes used different types of equipment, never thinking about their origins or how they were purchased. It was her job to use it to meet the goals of the State Troopers. Now she writes and administers grants and works with governmental bodies to ensure resources are available for the troopers to do their job.

BACKGROUND   When she was 14, Lieutenant Grimes's father allowed her to take flying lessons. She soloed at 16, and when it was time for college, she attended an aviation college. After a short stint as a flight instructor, she was hired by United Airlines as a pilot and flight engineer. For the next three years, she flew 727s as the flight engineer. Unfortunately, this was the early 1980s, and the oil embargo placed United Airlines in a position in which they had to furlough 1,000 pilots, Grimes being among them. She was hired for seasonal work flying pontoon planes, first around New York City and Long Island and then Ketchikan, Alaska. Near the end of one season, she was flying some Alaska state troopers, and they suggested to her that she might want to apply to their department. So Grimes soon entered the 14-week Public Safety Academy in Sitka, Alaska.

Before Lieutenant Grimes completed her one-year probationary period, the colonel asked her if she would consider participating in a secretive undercover assignment in the state's capital, Juneau. In response to a complaint by one legislator about the rampant use of drugs among members of the political and legislative bodies, the Alaska State Trooper's drug enforcement unit had been requested to conduct a long-term undercover operation. On paper, Lieutenant Grimes was shown to have quit the State Troopers and become a cocktail waitress. After a successful drug operation, she was asked to continue with the drug unit, and there she remained for ten years. During those years, Lieutenant Grimes continued to work undercover, became a scent-detection canine handler, and managed many major drug cases all over the state of Alaska. She continued to use her pilot skills when the drug unit had surveillance operations and for aerial photography operations.

Lieutenant Grimes then decided to take a position as trooper pilot in a rural enforcement detachment. Although the trooper post was in the small town of King Salmon, she was actually responsible for a series of isolated villages north of King Salmon in which the only possible mode of transportation was bush plane or boat. She was responsible for handling any complaints of criminal activity and calls for search and rescue from the villages. The State Troopers have historically performed this basic police work, in which one trooper responds alone to calls. Lieutenant Grimes had to learn to depend on her own skills in deescalating situations involving hostile or intoxicated subjects and rely on villagers' support and assistance in making apprehensions. Some villages employed village public safety officers. These officers are armed only with a baton and an aerosol that stuns an assailant but have received first responder training, as well additional training to secure crime scenes and assist troopers. She would go to council meetings, teach DARE in schools, and do many of the activities considered community policing today. Although the work could be discouraging at times, with a great deal of domestic violence, sexual assaults on minors, and alcohol-related crimes, she found the job challenging. The Alaskan native population has its own unique culture that must be respected, but at the same time, the state troopers have a job to do and laws to uphold. Thus she always had to keep the dual cultures in mind and remember that underlying tension may be reduced or increased by how the troopers treat the public they are protecting.

After five years as a trooper pilot, Lieutenant Grimes returned to Anchorage to serve as an investigator in the major crime unit. At that point in her career, she had 17 years of service, so she decided to compete for sergeant. She could have applied for a promotion much earlier, but she was not mentally prepared. Grimes was promoted to sergeant and assigned to the judicial services unit in charge of the warrant/fugitive task force. After serving there for about a year, she was assigned to the airport interdiction team, which was primarily concerned with interdicting the large quantities of drugs being smuggled into the state. Sergeant Grimes then became a lieutenant, assigned to the director.

Being a female never seemed to hinder her. She became Alaska's first female trooper pilot as well as its first female canine handler. She never doubted her ability to do the jobs, nor felt that the agency would hinder her in any way. In fact, the troopers encouraged her to participate in these specialty units. Possibly, being a female helped her, particularly in rural enforcement. Lieutenant Grimes was especially able to develop a good rapport with the elders and children. Often the people she arrested would later thank her for treating them with respect.

If she had any obstacles to overcome, they came from within herself. She knew she could aviate, and when she came out of basic training, she knew she could be a trooper. Supervising other officers was a different responsibility, and she was not prepared for that role until she had a number of years experience and was ready for a new challenge.

COUNSEL   If you have a chip on your shoulder or the attitude that you are owed something, get rid of it. Don't go in with the expectation of being treated poorly or special because you are a woman. You need to enter law enforcement with the attitude that you are as good as anybody else so you don't need special treatment. Just get in there and do the job. It is important to have good work ethics. You want to be respected for your competence. Unfortunately because there are so few women in law enforcement, an obnoxious, incompetent female is more noticeable than an obnoxious, incompetent male, and she reflects on all female officers. If you want to be promoted, find out what your law enforcement agency expects of people they promote and then try and do those things. Don't be afraid to move up, but don't whine if you first fail; just try again. With the Alaskan State Troopers, they expect their supervisors to be well rounded and to have worked in a number of different assignments within the division. If you accept responsibility and are accountable for your actions, respect and success will come.

FEDERAL AGENTS

Lisa Holman, Federal Postal Inspector, Mid-Atlantic Division

RESPONSIBILITIES   Inspector Holman is currently assigned to the child exploitation unit, consisting of five members who cover five states. She investigates illegal use of mail or the Internet to send or receive child pornography or to coerce a child to engage in sexual activity for the purpose of child pornography. Inspector Holman is also the public relations officer for the postal inspection services for two southern states. In addition to all of these duties, she still works with evidence for the forensic unit.

United States postal inspectors have been in service for 200 years; it was the first federal agency to investigate child exploitation. Inspector Holman finds her job especially fulfilling, knowing that she is protecting and helping children. When the offenders are in prison, they can't exploit children. Also, children coerced into pornography normally never tell anybody and are left to deal with the aftermath, but because children can be identified in pornography, it is possible to get them help. Teamwork is very important, and Inspector Holman works well with local and state agencies, knowing she can't do it alone with only four other agents. She never dominates a case, but rather gives credit to whom it is due.

BACKGROUND Her family background includes a father and a brother who are Marines, so from early childhood she was taught discipline, loyalty, and dedication. Inspector Holman began college as a chemistry major but also enjoyed journalism and drama. She knew she did not want to end up in a lab. Having been given the opportunity to complete an extended (six months) internship with the Drug Enforcement Administration (DEA), she then returned to school for one semester, graduated, and then returned to DEA.

Inspector Holman remained in forensics for 16 years, first in evidence from clandestine drug labs for the DEA and then forensic drug analysis for the postal inspection services. She then knew that she wanted to do something different, so she took an assignment with the Congressional and Public Affairs Division, working on publications and writing the postal inspector's presentations. The time in Congressional and Public Affairs helped her appreciate the diversity of the postal inspection service and solidified her desire to stay in the department, but as a postal inspector.

To become an inspector, she had to attend the 14-week federal academy. She had taught at the academy for 10 years in the forensic area, so the instructors knew her as a friend and colleague, but she had to become a student and learn the new world of law enforcement. Her class was very cohesive; 24 students started and 24 graduated. They worked as a team and never left anybody behind.

In general, her field is dominated by males, but being a female helps, especially in child exploitation cases. She is very much a "people" person—Inspector Holman can talk to offenders and get them to confess. She also believes it is less intimidating to talk to a woman. Children gravitate to her, and even teens don't see her as a "typical federal officer." Her forensic background helped her in her different assignments. She was experienced in handling evidence and trained many of the inspectors in drug investigations. When she wanted a change, the Congressional and Public Affairs Division was a good transition to find out more about the department. She talked to other inspectors and knew they wanted her to join them

Inspector Holman believes that the agency did nothing to hinder her, and her supervisors were supportive of what she wanted to do. For example, while she was in forensics, she wanted to go beyond the obvious when working cases, explore new ways to work a case, and was encouraged to be creative. Inspector Holman has stood in front of 200 men to give drug lectures and has always been given respect and not pressured to know everything. She is willing to say she doesn't know all the answers, and they are willing accept it.

Her main shortcoming is her own inability to say no. She always wants to help, so it sometimes gets overwhelming and hard to set priorities.

COUNSEL   Education is the most important quality you can possess. Then work in the real world. Be realistic; it takes many more hours to close a case than television depicts. If you are going to consider forensics, diversify your field. Don't become too specialized in one area, for example, DNA analysis only. You need to be willing to make an enormous commitment. This commitment includes dedication and long hours, but you also need to learn to balance your profession with your personal life. Child exploitation cases can really consume your life. You have to be independent and willing to move, especially if unmarried. I moved to my current job site after 20 years in Washington D.C., but it was easy to adapt and make new friends. When accepting a job, accept it as it is. You can't put parameters around it, or criteria. It is a great life, exhausting and trying, but a lot of fun with so many opportunities. I have traveled all over the United States, and my career opened an entire new world for me.

Agent Jacqueline Madison, Special Agent, Alcohol, Tobacco and Firearms (ATF), Southeastern District

RESPONSIBILITIES   Agent Madison is part of a team responsible for investigating firearms, explosives, and arson. She works with local police departments, who usually call her if weapons or federal offenses are involved. She is also part of a task force consisting of the state bureaus of investigations, the DEA, and local police departments. It is particularly important for ATF to work with agencies in small counties who are not large enough to have arson or explosive experts. Agent Madison feels that she is making a difference. She is part of a team whose job involves putting away violent, repeat offenders. Agent Madison also enjoys working in the field and interacting with other law enforcement officers. She indicates that it is less satisfying to complete all of the paperwork involved in the investigations; however, Agent Madison realizes this is an integral part of her job.

Agent Madison has been told on several occasions that she doesn't resemble a typical agent. When she hears these comments, she takes them as a compliment. Although she thought it would be a problem being a black female in a rural county, it hasn't been. In the short time that Agent Madison has been an ATF agent, she has been accepted as a professional investigator in her assigned counties. Sometimes she is questioned about her presence at a crime scene and has to identify herself as an ATF agent. The questioning is not done in hostility, but rather more in terms of people getting used to black female agents. Agent Madison realizes that she is not "one of the guys" and somewhat limited physically. The male agents are sometimes protective, so she has to let them know she can "handle her own."

BACKGROUND   When Agent Madison was growing up, the values she was taught by her parents included, "be self-sufficient and get an education." Her father was old-fashioned in his expectations of his children. For example, every Saturday morning they all had to do housework, and her father expected the children to be busy. In high school, Agent Madison knew that she wanted to go to college, although she and her siblings would be the first generation in her family to attend. When she entered college, she decided that marketing would be a good area. In her last year in school, she worked for the Army Corps of Engineers; her family did not want her to continue beyond school, but instead return home to Washington, D.C. A relative who had contacts with ATF suggested that she consider employment with ATF.

Agent Madison began working for ATF, first in the seized property/asset forfeiture section and then in the office of training and professional development as a management analyst. Physical fitness has always been important to her, and she regularly worked out in the gym. The agents who also exercised in the gym told her that she should apply to be an agent, so she began to gather more information. The first time she applied she wasn't selected. Trying again, she was accepted. At the same time she was told that she had the job, Agent Madison was notified that she would have to move to her current city. All her family lived in Washington, D.C., and it was very hard to leave. Her family was worried about her safety but continued to be supportive of her career.

Agent Madison's training consisted of 11 weeks of criminal investigator school and 13 weeks of new professional training at the Federal Law Enforcement Training Center in Glynco, Georgia. Her on-the-job-training included an assignment to a veteran ATF agent. She first observed and then began to help with such areas as surveillances, interviews, and report writing.

Although Agent Madison joined ATF because her family wanted her to return home to Washington, D.C., she knew she wanted a job that made a difference. She also knew that she wanted to gain her independence, thus she accepted the position as an ATF agent. Agent Madison was first nervous about moving to a new area, but she was quickly involved in work. She has been introduced to many different people through both local law enforcement officers and her team at ATF, and her office partners have made her feel comfortable.

COUNSEL   Believe you can do it. You may not get what you are striving for the first time, but keep trying if it is important to you. Go beyond the negative feedback of peers. Never give up! Find out all you can about the job in which you are interested, so that you understand the requirements and expectations of the job. Make sure you are the right person for that job. Talk to somebody who has recently successfully completed it so you understand what you will be facing. Practice certain areas in which you know you may be weak or difficult. One of my obstacles is shooting a firearm, so I practice a great deal on my own. Be prepared to be uprooted if you are interested in becoming a federal agent. Federal agents are required to sign a mobility clause agreeing to move upon request. Don't expect traditional relationships. You must be available 24 hours/day. I am now engaged and have talked in-depth with my fiancé about the requirements of my job. He is willing to move if necessary and understands the long hours I must work.

Agent Michelle Larouche, Special Agent, Immigration and Naturalization Services, Southern District

RESPONSIBILITIES   Agent Larouche targets and arrests criminal aliens. She works with probation officers, interviews in the jail, and checks gun permits. Often, local police agencies will phone concerning individuals they have arrested. If Larouche believes they are illegal and have committed criminal offenses, she will follow up and detain those who are found guilty. If she identifies previously deported illegal aliens, they will be prosecuted, convicted, and sentenced. Once they have completed their prison sentences, they are then deported. If an alien has been convicted and deported on an aggravated felony, he or she cannot return to the United States. Even if in possession of a green card, the alien can be deported if convicted of an aggravated offense. Larouche and the other agents in her office have a large area to cover and an overwhelming number of cases. Because many criminal aliens are prosecuted for drug or sexual abuse of minors and because of the current concern for homeland security, she finds her job very fulfilling.

BACKGROUND   Agent Larouche was a tomboy. When she was young, she played baseball with her brothers and other boys. Being very competitive, she worked until she could kick a ball farther than any of her brothers. She also developed quite a "gutter" mouth. She believed that her mother liked boys better than girls, so she strived to be like a boy. As the oldest of eight children, she was responsible for taking care of her younger siblings. Agent Larouche believes her temperament is similar to that of her father; it takes a great deal to get her angry, but when she becomes angry, she is furious.

Agent Larouche majored in Spanish in college with the thought of working in airline customer services. While at college, she took the written test for both border patrol and customs. Customs interviewed her first, but they didn't seem to really want women. Border patrol recruiters were much nicer and hired her on the spot. At that time she didn't really know what border patrol did.

She went through 19 weeks of training that emphasized the physical aspect of law enforcement. She lifted weights during any off time to help make it through all the upper-body tests of strength. With few other women in the border patrol or in her training, she was made to feel that women really had no place in the border patrol. Agent Larouche spent more than seven years with the border patrol and enjoyed it. The male officers were hostile at first, letting her know that they felt she had taken a job from a man, but she did her job well and stayed busy. She would ride out by herself and apprehend large groups of illegal Mexican aliens coming over the border. (Now, the job might be much more dangerous; the aliens are more frustrated and violent, and there are more assaults against officers.)

She then transferred into the adjudications unit, where she was directly involved with approvals for immigration. She was promoted first to supervisor and then branch chief. Then moving to New Mexico, she taught immigration law for advanced training classes. Agent Larouche wanted to move back into the law enforcement area of Immigrations, so she applied for and accepted her current position as special agent. In Immigrations, internal announcements are made concerning all openings. Employees who meet the requirements can apply and are tested, with years of experience and other factors also weighing in.

Being a female in Immigrations was difficult. Male officers didn't want her to be there. They were harder on her than the other new agents in field training, giving her all the menial jobs (if there was a tire to be changed, she was told to change it). Agent Larouche made sure she was good at her job. As she became more experienced and trainees were assigned to her, the male trainees would often question why they had to ride with her. Later, they would tell her how much they appreciated working with her, but she always felt that she had to be twice as good. For the first four or five years of her career, she was always proving herself. It was difficult to come to work every day knowing she would be judged. Many things that occurred would have been enough for a discrimination or harassment complaint, but she never filed one. Agent Larouche would not internalize the negative messages male agents gave her. She was determined that she would not quit. She knew that she was as good as they were. Agent Larouche does believe it is better now that more women have been hired.

In her current office, her relationship with the male agents is good. She has a great deal of experience and knowledge to share; they realize she really knows the law. There is also another female agent who is very good. All the male agents are relatively young and so more accepting of women. Currently, Immigrations is a good place for women; there are many opportunities within the agency and in other federal positions.

COUNSEL   You really need to understand the job. Border patrol is a very good job with a great deal of autonomy. It is the kind of job that you can make what you want. You can sit and do nothing or stay busy all the time. If you are interested in legal issues, then the adjudication section is ideal. It will really allow you to learn local and immigration laws. You must be able to remain professional and not internalize any negative comments made about women in the profession. It is still a pioneering field for women.

Agent Amelia Martinez, Special Agent, Applicant Coordinator, and Principal Firearms Instructor, FBI, North Carolina Office

RESPONSIBILITIES   As applicant coordinator, Agent Martinez tries to find the right people, especially women and minorities, who have what it takes to be FBI agents. Once they are identified, she begins the process of selection, selecting those who meet the initial criteria and allowing them to take the written exam. Martinez then goes over the applications of those who pass the written test thoroughly, because only a specified percentage can be selected for interviews by trained assessors. She then works with selected applicants, preparing them for the interview so that they each have the best opportunity possible.

Furthermore, as principal firearms instructor for the FBI, Martinez provides firearms training for the FBI agents in her region. The agents qualify six times a year, so she must arrange for the use of the different firearms ranges of local law enforcement agencies. In addition, she gives most of the speeches requested by community groups. She has always felt that she was doing something positive—fighting crime, training others to fight crime, empowering victims, and helping put offenders in prison.

BACKGROUND   Agent Martinez remembers watching the original *Untouchables* on television when she was 5 years old, so she grew up wanting to be a FBI agent. She usually played with her older brother and his friends. Her father, a member of the Coast Guard, instilled in his entire family a sense of patriotism. Although neither of her parents

Amelia Martinez

had completed high school, they reinforced the message that education was important if she wanted to live a life different from theirs. Being a member of a military family, Agent Martinez attended 11 different schools while she was growing up, making her very adaptable and familiar with different types of people.

Until 1972, Agent Martinez was always told she could never be an FBI agent (former director J. Edgar Hoover would never let women in), so upon graduating from college, she took a job with the U.S. Department of Agriculture (USDA) as a special agent, with the ultimate goal of joining the FBI. Her college degree was in public/urban affairs with a criminology emphasis. As a special agent with USDA, she conducted long-term undercover work investigating food stamp fraud. Criminals buy drugs and guns using food stamps, produce counterfeit food stamps, or break into stores and steal food stamps. When Agent Martinez left her undercover assignment, she worked white-collar crime in the collateral loans area. The move to the FBI was fairly smooth at that point, as she was already a federal agent and had already been to the Federal Law Enforcement Training Center in Glynco, Georgia.

As a special agent with the FBI, Agent Martinez's first assignment was in Albany, New York with the fugitive and theft unit. She was part of the FBI's SWAT team, as well as involved in various undercover assignments. Agent Martinez was then transferred to New York City to work with the auto theft task force. With the New York Police Department, she worked on truck hijacking and organized crime. Agent Martinez then joined the staff at the FBI Academy at Quantico as supervising special agent. There she taught firearms and arrest procedures to new FBI recruits and others at the academy. Agent Martinez also provided in-service training for other field and task force agents.

In her current location, Agent Martinez first worked white-collar crime, including Internet fraud and bank embezzlement, before becoming the applicant coordinator. Her duties as firearms instructor has extended over the past 15 years with the FBI.

Agent Martinez believes being female has benefited her in a number of ways. First, while conducting undercover assignments, the criminals never suspected who she was. In the 1980's, men, especially those in management, would answer her questions, thinking she was too stupid to understand. The truck hijackers would often talk to her because of their need to brag. Victims were often more at ease talking to her, and now potential female recruits are comfortable talking to her. The FBI never hindered her; the agency was ready to accept women when she was hired.

COUNSEL   Be unique. The FBI gets 30,000 applicants with a criminal justice degree and three years of law enforcement experience. Advanced computer skills, physical science degrees, and language fluency are particularly important. You can stay current with the critical needs of the FBI by going to the Internet address: www.fbi.gov. Be a leader. Show you can work independently. Community service is important. It shows that you have given a little extra back to your community. Stay in shape and out of trouble. Be well rounded and interact with a variety of people. Good interpersonal communication skills are critical.

SUMMARY

The examples provided by the women in this chapter demonstrate that this is a very exciting time to enter law enforcement. The field has become recognized as a profession requiring educated and thinking individuals—people who must deal with the public's survival in an era when danger seems to be everywhere. Although it is important for officers to be physically fit, their intellect plays a major role in getting the job done and striving to meet new challenges.

The women whose personal and professional stories were included in this chapter are certainly not representative of all women in policing, but they have had several traits in common:

- They tended to grow up in a very supportive family, one where young women were taught to be independent, and to "be all that you can be."
- They typically have had a gratifying overall experience in law enforcement—some more than others having to initially negotiate a few "bumps in the road"—in terms of being accepted.
- They have worked in a wide variety of specialized assignments at the federal, state, and local levels.
- They believe that being a woman is not a hindrance to their work. In fact, their gender is often an asset, especially when dealing with certain types of offenses.
- They believe that females should not attempt to exploit their gender; one is a police officer first and a woman second.
- They believe that new female officers should take seriously—and soak up like a sponge—all available training and educational opportunities, to learn and better perform their assigned duties.

READER LEARNING OUTCOMES

Having examined this chapter, the reader should understand:

- females should find out all they can about the career in which they have an interest
- female officers are active in responsibilities ranging from patrol to piloting, school resource officer to homicide investigations
- education and training need to be taken very seriously for remaining safe, performing specific tasks, and striving for promotions
- policing is a career, not a job, and dedication to the profession is critical

Chapter 9
Challenges: Looking Forward

❖

Key Chapter Terms

Androgynous models
Diversity
Flextime

Interpersonal communication
Leadership roles
Physical abilities

Sex-role norms
Spouse academies
"Tip-over"

Have you seen Robocop? Robocop *was in the next century, and it was really high tech. It showed men and women showering and changing clothes—they were all police officers—it showed them all in one locker room, and not to say that we want to do that, but they had reached that point where they worked as one and they all worked together and there was no more line between. . . .*

—Veteran female officer[1]

Some men see things as they are, and ask why? I dream things that never were, and ask why not?

—Robert F. Kennedy

At every crossing on the road, each progressive spirit is opposed by a thousand appointed to guard the gates of the past.

—Maurice Maeterlinck

Introduction

In 1980, Susan Martin wrote in her groundbreaking book *Breaking and Entering: Police-women on Patrol*:

> Social structures adapt as cultural mandates change. The more frequent the occurrence of patterned conflict, the more likely it is that new norms will evolve to govern these situations by assigning or revising priorities of obligation. Growing numbers of women in policing as well as in other nontraditional occupations make it likely that the trend of change in **sex-role norms** which has occurred in the past decade will continue and accelerate. Some of the conflicts currently faced by policewomen and others in nontraditional occupations will be eased. These changes plus strong efforts in the past decade to eliminate sexism and sex-role stereotyping in education are likely to result in a generation of women who have a more positive view of themselves and their occupational options, and are more willing to assert themselves to assure that opportunities materialize. Increased athletic opportunities for girls and encouragement to develop their physical skills are likely to diminish the physical differences between men and women.[2]

As we enter the 21st century, what are some of the issues facing both women entering law enforcement and police administrators? Some researchers argue that it is women who are changing, not the police organizations;[3] however, women are experiencing greater economic and political power than ever before so some general issues such as **leadership roles**, selection criteria, family needs and ethnic **diversity** can't be ignored. It has been said that the only thing that is permanent is change. Given that, the question at the forefront of our minds is, what will the future bring? What changes will be brought to policing, both by its own hand and by outside forces? And what role will women play in those changes?

Predicting the future is not a simple undertaking. Many variables—such as war, technology, and economic upheaval—can greatly affect otherwise sound predictions and trends. All predictions are grounded in past trends and on future likelihood, but unforeseen variables and major events can and do change the course of the future in ways that no one could have anticipated. In other words, the best we can possibly do is render an educated guess.

With that in mind, this chapter begins by examining how America is changing, primarily with respect to its people and its crime. Then the focus shifts to what all of these anticipated changes portend for the police, especially in the areas of homeland defense, the need to become more diversified, and the community-oriented policing and problem-solving (COPPS) strategy, which was discussed in Chapter 1. The chapter concludes with a discussion of the future role of the rank-and-file officer.

CHANGES COMING TO AMERICA

A Demographic Shift

Future police recruiting and leadership efforts will be greatly affected by the demographic shift in the nation's makeup. A trend toward older workers, fewer entry-level workers, and more women, minorities, and immigrants in the population will force criminal justice organizations and private industry to become more flexible in order to compete for qualified applicants. Agencies must devise new strategies to offer better wage and benefits packages in order to compete with private businesses, and these packages will need to include day care, flexible hours, and paid maternity leave.[4]

We are rapidly becoming a more diverse and older society. By 2010 one in every four Americans will be 55 or older. The elderly are more likely to suffer the more harmful consequences of victimization, such as sustaining injury or requiring medical care.[5] The minority population is also increasing rapidly; in less than 100 years we can expect the white majority in the United States to end, as the growing number of blacks, Hispanics, and Asians together become the new majority. And when these various minority groups are forced to compete for increasingly scarce, low-paying service jobs, intergroup relations can be damaged and even become combative, as has already occurred in several large American cities. The gap between the "haves" and "have-nots" is widening. An underclass of people, those who are chronically poor and live outside of society's rules, is growing.[6]

Crime and Violence

There are about 29 million violent and property crimes per year in this country.[7] A number of factors contribute to this criminality: immediate access to firearms, alcohol and substance abuse, drug trafficking, poverty, racial discrimination, and cultural acceptance of violent behavior.[8] Serious challenges exist with respect to our crime problem. New criminal types will dot the national landscape in the future: better educated, upscale, older, and increasingly female. The people who make up this culture—gangs, pseudogangs, well-armed young people, and others—engage in the wanton use of violence, that is, aggression for the sake of aggression. In the future, the police will have to be trained and educated to understand violent behavior far beyond what they are today.[9]

Homeland Defense

Unquestionably, future historians will maintain that terrorist acts and the Iraqi war of the early 21st century changed forever the nature of policing and of security efforts in the United States. Local police departments are our first line of defense. Within the 50 states, there are 3,000 counties and 18,000 cities that must be protected. The job of getting law enforcement, emergency services, public health agencies, and private enterprise coordinated and working together at local, state, and federal levels is a daunting task.[10]

There are four major aspects of dealing with terrorist organizations:

1. gathering raw intelligence on the organization's structure, its members, and its plans (or potential for the use of violence)
2. determining what measures can be taken to counter, or thwart, terrorist activities
3. assessing how the damage caused by terrorists can be minimized through rapid response and containment of the damage
4. apprehending and convicting individual terrorists and dismantling their organizations[11]

The World Trade Center attacks have changed law enforcement forever.

MAJOR ISSUES FOR WOMEN IN LAW ENFORCEMENT

Changes in Selection, Training, and Performance Criteria

Selection Women are helping agencies continue to modify selection and performance criteria. For example, women entering law enforcement soon questioned the job validity of height requirements, which also allowed short men to enter a field previously closed to them. Police agencies need to continue assessing the job relatedness of their selection and training process. **Physical abilities** will continue to be important in law enforcement, but as technology and training place less emphasis on strength, height, and weight and more on agility and intelligence, requirements will evolve. Unfocused, random recruiting is unlikely to attract women and minorities; agencies should go to several locations (local colleges, women's groups, female community leaders, gyms, martial arts schools) and use all types of media to attract qualified applicants. (Appendix II shows what some law enforcement agencies have done to successfully recruit women.)

Academy Training In the past, particularly under the professional model of policing, during the academy phase of their training recruits adopted a new identity and a system of discipline; they learned to take orders and not to question authority. Indeed, much of the emphasis was on submission to authority. Recruits learned that loyalty to fellow officers, a professional demeanor and bearing, and respect for authority were highly valued qualities. That theme—and the police executive's expectations for recruits—must change. Officers of the future must be hired for their ability to think critically, plan, and evaluate. Female instructors are especially important during academy training, both as positive role models and to help female rookies develop skills and confidence. One study of an all-female police class[12] concluded with the following recommendations for female recruits:

1. emphasize karate and judo that uses lower body strength
2. lift progressively heavier weights
3. utilize special exercises to strengthen their grip necessary for shooting
4. box to overcome women's resistance to using force
5. simulate stressful situations to teach how to handle stress
6. develop strong, positive mental attitudes toward their ability and a keen awareness of who they are, where they are, what they are doing, and with whom they are dealing
7. teach through awareness and quick reaction time how to avoid an attack or delay an attack
8. teach techniques of dealing with close-quarter confrontations

Performance Criteria A great deal of effort is invested in designing objective performance evaluations that reflect the values of the police agency. Decisions on merit pay, specialty assignments, and promotions depend heavily on officers' evaluations. Traditional gender-role expectations of female officers may play a part in how these officers are evaluated if the evaluation instrument and the supervisor conducting the evaluation are biased.[13] Female officers in police agencies that have implemented community policing AND have updated their performance evaluation systems are more likely to receive a fair and unbiased evaluation that reflects their policing abilities. As policing focuses on partnerships and facilitating problem solving, which are components of community policing, controlling by force will receive less positive organizational reinforcement and positive alternatives to the use of force and arrests will garner more recognition.

The Role of Community Policing

As noted in Chapter 1, skills of **interpersonal communication**, prevention, and informal conflict negotiation that were denigrated in the past as feminine are now recognized as essential for success in community policing. What we conceptualize as masculine and feminine is socially learned and reinforced, not biologically determined. Behavior we consider appropriately feminine or masculine is socially constructed. In the past, this gender-role dichotomy was particularly clear in the world of the police officer. A new goal will be to convince all police officers to follow **androgynous models**, in which they, as professionals, recognize that the ideal repertoire of skills includes a range of behaviors considered both masculine and feminine. Relying on a wide range of behaviors and emotions neither feminizes the police occupation nor prevents the responsibilities of officers from being fulfilled.[14]

Author Rhonda DeLong views women's desire and gift for peacemaking as important for community policing.[15] Focusing on nonviolent solutions to crime, peacemaking includes four concepts: (1) awareness of human suffering, (2) identification of the basis for human suffering, (3) "compassion and service"—awareness of the needs of others and service in the capacity of peace officer that move beyond traditional law enforcement, and (4) "the way of peace and social justice"—human actions rooted in compassion. Peacemaking, an acceptable trait in women, is now becoming core to community policing. Partnering with community members, law enforcement officers identify and help solve problems within neighborhoods that cause suffering and lead to crime. Another characteristic of peacemaking, tied to the community-policing philosophy, is a victim-centered rather than an offender-centered approach. Typically, the victim is the forgotten component of crime while officers aggressively seek the offender, asking the victim only for a physical description and neglecting his or her needs and concerns.[16] Including victims in the investigative and judicial process keeps them involved and demonstrates law enforcement's concern for them.

Community policing is an important means by which women can be accepted in modern policing as it moves from "police force" to "police service." Women are less likely to oppose change; they won't be thinking nostalgically about the "good old days" when crime was controlled by force.[17] Another area of anticipated change due to COPPS involves greater participative management. Because law enforcement officers of the future will not normally possess military experience and its inherent training in obedience to authority, but will have higher levels of education, they will tend to be more independent and less responsive to traditional, authoritative approaches to their work. They will have been exposed to more participative, supportive, and humanistic approaches. These officers will want more opportunities to provide input in their work and to address the challenges posed by neighborhood problem solving. In short, they will not want to function like automatons during their tour of duty, blindly following general orders, policies and procedures, and rules and regulations. These officers will be, according to author J. R. Metts,[18] "bright, resourceful, and versatile, cross-trained in law enforcement, firefighting, and paramedical services. Administrators will care less about marksmanship and physical size and more about mental capacity and diplomas."

Women in Leadership Roles

One measure of progress for women in law enforcement will be the percentage of women in leadership roles. As stated in Chapter 4, fewer than 5 percent of the supervisory positions and fewer than 4 percent of the top administration positions are held by women in small departments, compared with 10 percent of supervisory and 7 percent of top administration positions held by women officers in large departments. Likewise, as noted in Chapter 7, the visibility of top women administrators facilitates the recruitment of women. There are a number of reasons that women choose not to strive toward higher ranks. The primary reasons center around having time for their families and male officers' perception that women gain rank only because of their gender. Encouraging women to advance and having enough qualified women becomes something of a challenge. The more women advance, the more they will be accepted as administrators, but there must also be qualified women proceeding through the promotional process. Author Jennifer Brown has coined the term, "**tipover**,"[19] meaning that women will be considered tokens and on the fringe until there are 25 percent of them in any given agency. When women officers and then women supervisors reach 25 percent, play a fuller role in all aspects of policing, and achieve higher rank in greater numbers, they will have a greater impact on the character and style of policing.

Leadership training is one strategy to be considered. Women should be encouraged to participate in the training that would provide them (and male officers) the skills necessary to step right into managerial roles. The training would also increase their confidence and comfort in leading other officers. Mentoring is another strategy that must be encouraged, first to retain new female officers but then to continue into the promotion stage with ranking female officers providing information and support.

Need for Diversity

As noted earlier in this chapter, the minority population is rapidly increasing, but few citizens from these minority populations are becoming police officers. Women of color only hold 4.9 percent of sworn positions and one-third of the nonsworn positions.[20] An overall increase in ethnic diversity is critical. Strategies are needed to attract women who are African American, Hispanic, Asian, and American Indian to law enforcement. Cultural barriers need to be overcome and police service presented in a way that will interest minority females.

Family Care

Police families must be supported and preserved. Strategies to reduce the conflict between the demands of the workplace and the demands of the family are needed to attract and retain officers with families.

To encourage spousal understanding and support for officers, **spouse academies** are needed (with child care provided). Usually, several weekly sessions are held for spouses of new officers to educate them about officers' responsibilities and potential areas of stress. Many agencies allow spouses to participate in a ride-along with other officers so that they might better understand what is involved in policing.

At present, although the government mandates a minimum of 12 weeks unpaid parental leave,[21] many officers cannot afford to take such a length of time without a salary. Once a child is born, finding quality child care, especially care available 24 hours daily, is difficult. Plans to provide on-site day care need to be explored.

Other means of balancing time and priorities, such as programs like **flextime**, reduced work hours, job sharing, a variety of personal leaves, or combinations of these strategies also should be considered. Of course, there is the accompanying danger that these benefits would be used by some, but not all, women, and rarely by men. Women who choose to take advantage of the benefits might therefore become marginal workers.[22]

SUMMARY

This is a very exciting time in the history of law enforcement. One thing is certain: no matter what crime and homeland security issues lie ahead, the public will always expect a high degree of service from its police. It is hoped that at some point in the future Americans will reflect back on the challenges facing women and law enforcement today and say with certainty that "the police are in the lead. They're showing the world how things might better be done."[23] The best hope for this to occur may lie with women themselves. They should and must work hard, unite, and try to expand their role in what is certainly one of the most challenging and rewarding occupations in the United States.

READER LEARNING OUTCOMES

Having examined this chapter, the reader should understand:

- the future challenges that women will face in the field of policing
- the major issues concerning changes in selection criteria and performance ratings that may affect women in law enforcement
- the importance of increasing the numbers of women in leadership roles
- why many women do not pursue advancement in policing

NOTES

1. Frances Heidensohn, *Women in Control? The Role of Women in Law Enforcement* (Oxford: Clarendon Press, 1992), p. 198.

2. Susan Martin, *Breaking and Entering: Policewomen on Patrol* (Berkeley, CA: University of California Press, 1980), p. 221.

3. Peter Horne, *Women In Law Enforcement* (Springfield, IL: Charles C. Thomas, 1980), p. 195.

4. Rob McCord and Elaine Wicker, "Tomorrow's America: Law Enforcement's Coming Challenge," *FBI Law Enforcement Bulletin* 59 (January):31–33.

5. Kenneth J. Peak, *Policing America: Methods, issues, challenges*, 4th ed. (Upper Saddle River, NJ: Prentice Hall, 2003).

6. Ibid.

7. U.S. Department of Justice, Bureau of Justice Statistics Press Release, "National Violent Crime Rate Falls More Than 10 Percent—Violent Victimizations Down One-Third Since 1993," August 27, 2000.

8. Lee P. Brown, "Violent Crime and Community Involvement," *FBI Law Enforcement Bulletin* (May 1992):2–5.

9. Sheldon Greenberg, "Future Issues in Policing: Challenges for Leaders," in *Policing Communities: Understanding Crime and Solving Problems*, in Ronald W. Glensor, Mark E. Correia, and Kenneth J. Peak (eds.) (Los Angeles: Roxbury, 2000), pp. 315–321.

10. J. Meisler, "The new frontier of homeland security," *Government Technology's Tech Trends 2002: Combined Effort* (August 2002):26–30.

11. E. J. Tully and E. L. Willoughby, "Terrorism: The role of local and state police agencies" http://www.neiassociates.org/state-local.htm (accessed 31 July 2002).

12. G. Patterson, *New Jersey's State Police All-Female Police Class* (Trenton, NJ: New Jersey State Police, 2002), p. 163.

13. Susan Miller, *Gender and Community Policing: Walking the Talk* (Boston: Northeastern University Press).

14. Ann Harriman, *Women/Men/Management*, 2nd ed. (Westport, CT: Praeger, 1996), p. 227.

15. Rhonda K. DeLong, *An Analysis of Police Perceptions of Community Policing and Female Officers* (Kalamazoo, MI: Western Michigan University, 1997), p. 18.

16. Ibid., p. 20.

17. Patricia Luneborg, *Women Police Officers: Current Career Profile* (Springfield, IL: Charles C. Thomas, 1989), p. 180.

18. J. R. Metts, "Super Cops: The Police Force of Tomorrow," *The Futurist* (October, 1985):31–36.

19. Jennifer Brown, "Women in Policing: A Comparative Research Perspective," *International Journal of the Sociology of Law* 25 (1997):18.

20. National Center for Women & Policing, *Equality Denied: The Status of Women in Policing* (Los Angeles: Author, 2000), pp. 11–12.

21. Family and Medical Leave Act of 1993, 29 USCS § 2601 (2001).

22. Harriman, *Women/Men/Management*, p. 213.

23. James Q. Wilson, "Six Things Police Leaders Can Do About Juvenile Crime," in *Subject to Debate* (newsletter of the Police Executive Research Forum) (September/October 1997):1.

Appendix I
An Example of Community Policing and Problem Solving

❖

In Chapter 1, we briefly discussed community-oriented policing and problem solving (COPPS) and reviewed the basic elements of the four-step SARA problem-solving process. To allow the reader to better understand this strategy, the following is an example of how this process operates.

First we look at how a neighborhood problem might be treated under the traditional, reactive style of policing versus the community problem-solving approach:

> Police experience a series of disturbances in a relatively quiet and previously stable residential neighborhood. Although the neighborhood's zoning had for years provided for late-night cabaret-style businesses, none had existed until the Nite Life, a live-music dance club, opened. Within a few weeks the police dispatcher received an increased number of complaints about loud music and voices, fighting, and screeching tires late into the night. Within a month's time, at least 50 calls for service (CFS) had been dispatched to the club to restore order. Evening shift officers responded to calls and restored order prior to midnight, but graveyard shift officers would have to again restore order when being called back to the scene by complaining neighbors after midnight.

Under the COPPS approach, this same matter might be handled in the following way (note the variety and innovative nature of the methods used to address the problem, especially when compared with the traditional, "get in, take a report, and get out" approach):

> The evening-shift area patrol sergeant identified the disturbances as a problem. The initial information-gathering phase revealed the following: large increases in CFS in the area on both the evening and graveyard shifts; several realtors complaining to council members about declining market interest in the area and saying that they were considering suing both

the owner of the new business and the city for the degradation of the neighborhood; a local newspaper about to run a story on the increase in vehicle burglaries, and damage done to parked vehicles in and around the cabaret's parking lot. The team also determined that the consolidated narcotics unit was investigating both employees and some of the late-night clientele of the business as a result of several tips that narcotics were being used and sold in the parking lot and inside the business.

The officers and their sergeant gathered information from crime reports, a news reporter about to publish the story, neighboring business owners, and the department's crime analysis unit. Information was also gathered concerning possible zoning and health department violations. Officers then met with the business owner to work out an agreement for reestablishing the quality of life in the neighborhood to its previous levels and decreasing the department's CFS. First, the business licensing division and the owner were brought together to both reestablish the ground rules and provide for a proper licensing of all the players. This resulted in the instant removal of an unsavory partner and in turn his "following" of drug users and other characters at the business. The landlord agreed to hasten landscaping and lighting of the parking lots and to provide a "sound wall" around the business to buffer the area residents. Agreements were reached to limit the hours of operation of the live music of the business. The cabaret's owner and its employees were trained by the area patrol teams in relevant aspects of the city code (such as disturbing the peace, minors in liquor establishments, and trespassing laws). The police experienced a reduction in CFS in the area. Area residents, although not entirely happy with the continuing existence of the business, acknowledged satisfaction with their complaints; no further newspaper stories appeared regarding the noise and disorder in the neighborhood.

In this example, the police not only responded to the concerns of the neighborhood residents, but also developed a better understanding of both the area's businesses and residents and established a working relationship with all involved. By co-opting the services of the other municipal entities, police also learned of new and valuable resources with whom to share some of the burden of future demands for government service.

Appendix II

Successful Strategies for Recruitment of Women: Tales of Six Cities

--- ❖ ---

Philadelphia, Pennsylvania

www.ppdonline.org/ppd_jobs.htm

The Philadelphia Police Department has 7,000 sworn officers, or about 463 officers per 100,000 citizens. From 1990 to 2000, the percentage of those sworn officers who were women rose from 14.7 percent to 24.2 percent.[1]

The Philadelphia Police Department has a very informative and easily navigated website. Each of the nine steps of the selection process is explained.

> Candidates must successfully complete a written examination, an oral interview, a drug screening test, a polygraph examination, a psychological evaluation, a medical examination, background investigation, a 32-week training program, and one-year probationary period.[2]

There is a one-year residency requirement, which would restrict women living out of town from applying.

The Philadelphia Police Department recruiting staff believes the women officers themselves are the best recruiting tool for women applicants. In addition, since the department's deputy commissioner is female, higher visibility has been given to female officers' ability to rise in the ranks.[3] Furthermore, when recruiting at colleges and universities, recruiters encourage students who have declared any major to consider a career in law enforcement. For example, theater majors would have important skills for undercover work, while computer science majors are needed to help support the computer network for the 7,000 officers and investigate white-collar and computer crimes.

Recruiters wear uniforms and civilian attire so that prospective recruits can appreciate the varying nature of police work. They also describe the approximately 170 different units that compose the department. Visiting all the minority communities and such organizations as the Latino Organization, the recruiters encourage women to get their general education diplomas (GED) and apply to the police department. They also offer tours of the police academy to view the training.

The minimum requirement of a high school degree or GED has been found to be attractive to single mothers. They are, of course, encouraged to continue their education, and local colleges offer evening classes at the police department at a reduced tuition rate. As part of their community-policing and recruiting efforts, the police speak in the public schools, helping to increase the positive image of the police officer.

One of the officers who is assigned as a recruiter takes her job more seriously and personally than most. She was in an abusive relationship and realized that she needed to get out. Going from the cosmetology profession to police officer gave her personal and professional confidence. When appropriate, she shares her own life experiences with women applicants.

Recruiters also ensure that prospective applicants are aware of the paid 10-month training period, in which they will learn how to minimize the risk of injury. Knowing that they will receive extensive training in this area affords a greater degree of confidence to those individuals who have had little experience in physical or verbal confrontations.

Omaha, Nebraska

www.opd.ci.omaha.ne.us/media/Police

The Omaha Police Department (OPD) has 750 sworn officers, or about 192 officers per 100,000 citizens. From 1990 to 2000, the number of sworn female officers rose from 8.2 percent to 19.7 percent of the agency.[4] By late 2002, the percentage of female officers had risen to 26.6 percent. Contributing to these increases was a court order placed on the agency to boost the number of women hired and promoted.[5]

The OPD's website is extensive and begins with this message from the chief:

> We are looking for outstanding police applicants who will be able to use new technology, as well as traditional police methods in the fight against crime. Today's police officer must be able to adapt to our ever-changing environment and develop innovative solutions in helping to solve community problems.

The website takes the reader through the selection process, the command structure, salary and benefits, and the Law Enforcement Code of Ethics.

The OPD uses a variety of means to recruit a diverse pool of applicants. Its recruiters work closely with local television, radio, and newspapers to provide publicity spots highlighting various aspects of police work and the department's recruiting efforts. From these publicity spots, OPD and one television channel designed a short video to present at recruiting functions that explains the history of the department, special assignments, duties assigned to patrol officers, and special programs.[6] All written materials, which are also translated into Spanish, are upbeat and illustrate the diversity of the officers' backgrounds. Even background investigators carry business cards designed to be recruiting tools; the cards include not only all the investigators' information, but also all the benefits of the Police Department and a brief description of the entry requirements.

The recruiters work closely with print and electronic media to develop ads that spotlight various aspects of police work and the department's recruiting efforts. They also send a variety of posters, brochures, and entrance examination information to selected sites across the nation, as well as provide application information to colleges, universities, community agencies, churches, health clubs, libraries, female/minority-owned businesses, special interest groups, and community leaders.[7] Effective use of the Internet is accomplished by placing job announcements on local, state, and national employment-related job sites. Recruiters also attend numerous career fairs to disseminate information, answer questions, and set up mock interviews in which interested candidates can participate.

Once recruited, the next important step is preparing candidates for the selection process. When a candidate applies, he or she is given a packet containing information about the written exam, along with a study guide; furthermore, they are given a description of the physical-agility test, including a diagram of the obstacle-course layout. The applicant receives information concerning the minimum qualifications of the position, benefits, duties/responsibilities, promotional levels, and possible special assignments. Each applicant also meets with police personnel, who explain the testing procedure and tips on using the study guide and answering the different types of test questions. They also discuss the selection process and answer questions about the job.[8]

The OPD annually assesses its ability to reach and hire a diverse workforce. A list of recommendations is compiled and implemented the following year.

Chicago, Illinois

www.ci.chi.il.us/CommunityPolicing/Challenge/Challenge.html

The Chicago Police Department (CPD) has 13,466 sworn officers, or about 465 officers per 100,000 citizens. From 1990 to 2000, the percentage of those sworn officers who were women rose from 13.0 percent to 21.3 percent.[9]

The CPD website begins with a strong promotional message:

> The Chicago Police Department is preparing for the 21st century with a diverse workforce and excellent opportunities for career promotions and advancement. The Chicago Police Department offers men and women the opportunity to utilize the latest law enforcement methodologies and technological tools.[10]

The website then describes some of the different career and promotional opportunities, benefits, minimum qualifications, and the hiring process, including specifics about the physical fitness requirements. Applications can also be downloaded from the website.

The CPD's large recruiting division reflects the diversity that the agency is attempting to recruit. These male and female, white, African American, and Hispanic American officers visit community and college job fairs, military installations, community meetings, religious organizations, and neighborhood organizations in their dress uniforms. They believe that first impressions are the most important, so recruiters reflect the professionalism of their job and the importance that is placed on recruitment. The recruiters also travel to other states.

CPD's recruiting efforts, combined into what is termed the Ambassador Program, are promoted in military transition offices and publications, local television ads, public service announcements, newspapers, movie theaters, on marquees at baseball fields, and in public areas of the mass transit system. All major ethnic media outlets—African American, Asian, Polish, and Hispanic—are targeted. Recruitment posters, widely circulated, reflect the diversity seen on the website and include females and minority officers who are on the command staff.

A recent innovation is "Recruitment Day," which in addition to the general public, includes special invitations to the approximately 7,000 individuals who request applications. Many of the different units from within the CPD provide demonstrations for the public so that they can ask questions directly of the officers in the specialized units. More than 2,000 people attend this function.

CPD involves the entire department in its recruiting efforts, underscoring to every officer that he or she is its best recruiting tool. To reflect this philosophy, each year different officers are given an opportunity to have their picture included on recruiting posters.[11]

Buffalo, New York

www.city-buffalo.com

The Buffalo Police Department (BPD) has 928 sworn officers, or about 317 officers per 100,000 citizens. From 1990 to 2000, the percentage of those sworn officers who were women rose from 12.9 percent to 20.9 percent.[12]

About 20 years ago, the BPD, like the OPD, was under a court order to hire more minorities and women. At that time, the pay was not equitable with other job opportunities, but over time the salaries have increased and are now comparable to other jobs, with excellent retirement benefits. Indeed, although its minimum education requirement is two years of college, the salary is more than many four-year graduates are earning. An overall depressed economic situation has provided a large pool of qualified applicants.

The BPD's website is not comprehensive, providing only the bare essentials concerning the department's selection criteria. It is obvious that the Internet is not considered a major tool for attracting interested applicants.

With women in supervisory roles such as the chief of detectives, the BPD reflects the fact that women can advance. Having women in such positions can greatly influence the amount of interest in the law enforcement profession by prospective women recruits.

Nashville, Tennessee

www.police.nashville.org

The Nashville Police Department (NPD) has 1,249 sworn officers, or about 219 officers per 100,000 citizens. From 1990 to 2000, the percentage of those sworn officers who were women rose from 7.8 percent to 21.9 percent.[13]

The NPD's website is efficiently designed so that individuals accessing it can explore a variety of police-related areas, including the department's annual report and information on selection, training, salaries, and benefits. The application for employment can be downloaded from the site.

The recruiting unit of the Nashville Police Department credits the growth of the application pool to substantial pay increases received during the past ten years. In addition, the recruiters attribute the increases in female recruits to female officers, who have demonstrated that women can perform policing responsibilities.[14]

Toledo, Ohio

http://www.toledolink.com/~tpd/empopp.html

The Toledo Police Department (TPD) has 690 sworn officers, which is about 220 officers per 100,000 citizens. From 1990 to 2000, the percentage of those sworn officers who were women rose from 13.9 percent to 21.0 percent.[15]

Toledo is a midsize, industrial city, with a low crime rate. The TPD has one of the best unions in the state, resulting in excellent entry-level salaries and benefits. In addition, the agency offers opportunities for advancement to all officers, including female officers of all races.[16] Its sergeants include two white females, one African American female, one Hispanic female, a retired African American lieutenant, and a Hispanic captain.

Its website is comprehensive and includes a description of the specific job benefits offered, including maternity pay, a prescription drug purchase program, a career enhancement program, promotional opportunities, job descriptions of the different ranks, and each rank's pay.

Although the TPD does not have a permanent recruiting section (every two years, for 90 days duration), the state of Ohio and the surrounding states are saturated with ads when it does recruit. Personnel who are temporarily assigned to engage in recruiting attempt to locate every female and minority organization. They disseminate information and give presentations at women-only events and fitness gyms in their effort to reach all females.

ALBUQUERQUE ADDRESSES SEXUAL HARASSMENT TO INCREASE RECRUITMENT OF WOMEN

After implementing a number of different strategies, the Albuquerque, New Mexico, Police Department (APD) increased its number of female recruits from ten to 25 percent within two years. One of the areas of concern was its sexual harassment policy and preventive actions. First, the administration instituted a zero-tolerance policy that was supported with specific training on preventing sexual harassment. This training incorporated the analysis of legal cases and discussions of different types of situations. Officers were informed that there would be surprise inspections of lockers to check for pin-ups and cartoons. The promotional exam included questions from the department's sexual harassment policy and procedures, and the investigation of sexual harassment complaints was assigned to an external city agency. Employees were permitted to circumvent their chain of command when making a complaint. When queried, APD women stated that the work environment had dramatically improved in the past three years. Not only has the recruiting of women increased, but also the women's retention rate now equals that of male officers.

Source: "Recruiting Women to Policing: Strategies that Work."
http://www.iwitts.com/html/recruitment.htm (accessed February 18, 2004).

NOTES

1.   http://www.ppdonline.org/ppd_report.htm (accessed September 18, 2003).

2.   www.ppdonline.org/ppd5processtxt.htm (accessed January 08, 2003).

3. Personal communication with Officer Olga Walsh and Lieutenant Shawn Cary, Philadelphia Police Department, January 8, 2003.

4. Brian Reaves and Timothy Hart, *Police Departments in Large Cities, 1990–2000.* (Washington, DC: Bureau of Justice Statistics, 2002), pp. 10–11.

5. Personal communication with Fredricka Minton, Personnel Department, Omaha Police Department, November 8, 2003.

6. City of Omaha, Nebraska, *2001 Police Officer Recruitment Report* (Author, 2002), p. 2.

7. Ibid., 6.

8. Ibid., 13.

9. Reaves and Hart, pp. 10–11.

10. www.ci.chi.il.us/CommunityPolicing/Challenge/Challenge.html (accessed January 10, 2003).

11. Personal communication with Sergeant Janice Barney, Chicago Police Department, January 14, 2003.

12. Reaves and Hart, pp. 10–11.

13. Ibid.

14. Personal communication with Investigator Marsha Brown, Nashville, Tennessee, Police Department, November 8, 2002.

15. Ibid.

16. Personal communication with Sergeant Gloria Burks, Toledo, Ohio, Police Department, January 28, 2003.

Appendix III

Sample Résumé

---------------------- ❖ ----------------------

Jane Justice

911 Legal Way   Phone: (555)555–5555
Alltown , USA 89500   E-mail: Jjustice@****

Career Objective	To obtain employment in a progressive local law enforcement agency

Education: 1999 to 2002	University of Alltown, Alltown, USA Bachelor's Degree in Criminal Justice, GPA 3.5

Professional Experience

Summer 2002 Intern, Attorney General's Office
Assisted with a variety of investigations, including gathering of background information, compilation of relevant facts and legal opinions, and documentation of activities.

January–May 2001, Independent Study Project, Alltown Police Department
Participated in a community-oriented policing project with a local police department directed at improving community participation in neighborhood watch program. Duties consisted of assisting the law enforcement representatives with coordinating volunteer training, interpreting crime mapping and statistical data, developing presentation material, and obtaining grant funding.

Fall 2001 Class Project
Researched the impact of a law that would require homeless individuals to register with a state-funded substance abuse agency within a two-week period of a third arrest and conviction for a vagrancy or alcohol violation.

Other Employment

June 1999–July 2002, Macy's Loss Prevention
Trained in and performed general surveillance duties, apprehending shoplifters, investigating internal theft, and participating in prosecution of same.

May 2000–June 2002, Alltown School District Lifeguard

Organizations and Awards

University Criminal Justice Students Association, President, 2001 to Present
Sierra Club, Secretary, 2000–2001
Dean's List, 2001–2002

References: See attached

Appendix IV
Selected Police-Related Websites

❖

International Association of Women Police (IAWP)	*http://www.iawp.org/*
Women Peace Officers Association job listings	*http://www.wpoaca.com/job.html*
Bureau of Alcohol, Tobacco and Firearms (ATF)	*http://www.atf.treas.gov/*
Drug Enforcement Administration (DEA)	*http://www.usdoj.gov/dea/*
Federal Bureau of Investigation (FBI)	*http://www.fbi.gov*
United States Marshals Service	*http://www.usdoj.gov/marshals*
United States Customs Service	*http://www.customs.gov/*
The International Association of Chiefs of Police (IACP)	*http://www.theiacp.org/*
U.S. Government jobs	*http://www.usjobs.opm.gov/a.htm*, or *http://www.usdoj.gov/06employment/index.html*
University-based criminal justice careers and job sites	*http://www.unl.edu/crimjust/crimtreemenu/EMPLOYMENT.html*, or *http://www.fsu.edu/~crimdo/feds.html*

Glossary

❖

Academy training—formal classroom training provided to new police officers to teach them the legal and procedural knowledge and skills to carry out their duties

Administrative code—rules that govern the operation of an organization or governmental entity

Administrative positions—professional areas that are considered managerial

Affirmative action—encouragement of increased representation of females and minority-group members in employment or education

Androgynous models—models that consist of male and female traits

Androgyny—having male and female characteristics

Background investigation—a step in the police selection process in which an applicant's personal, educational, and professional references are interviewed concerning the applicant

Blanket waiver—an intentional relinquishment of all rights pertaining to a specific individual right

Bona fide occupational qualification (BFOQ)—characteristics that are critical for successful performance of a specific job or profession

Cadet programs—police programs for students to promote their interest in policing, provide them with safe policing experiences, and assess their aptitude as a future police officer

Car 47—the patrol car assigned to the first female patrol officers of the Indianapolis, Indiana, Police Department

Community-oriented policing and problem solving (COPPS)—a philosophy of policing that entails partnering with the community in order to solve local problems that are related to criminal behavior and neighborhood disorder

Comparable worth—establishing equal pay for equal jobs

Competitive examination—tests that are usually promotional in nature and given to those individuals who desire an increase in responsibilities and corresponding salary; individuals often are ranked according to their scores

Conditional job offer—offering qualified candidates a position on the condition that they can successfully complete the rest of the selection process (such as the medical exam)

Crime Commission—the President's Commission on Law Enforcement and Administration of Justice, appointed in 1967 to study the state of law enforcement

Crime prevention—those activities carried out by police officers or citizens (usually with the advice or guidance of police officers) that will decrease their probability of becoming victims of crime

Cultural diversity—differences among cultures, races, and ethnicities

Decentralization of power—the distribution of power over a less concentrated area, giving more authority to those lower in the organization

Desk sergeant—the officer who receives complaints from or provides information for citizens who walk into the police agency; before telecommunicators, they also responded to telephone queries or complaints

Diffusion—dissemination, spreading

Discretion—the power to decide or act according to one's own judgment

Discrimination—action in favor of or against a person on the basis of prejudice

Diversity—the state or fact of being different

"Double marginality"—a position in which members of a minority are often placed as they attempt to assimilate into the majority culture, but still remain a part of their specific minority culture

Drug testing—primarily used during the selection process to test an applicant's use of opiates, cocaine, marijuana, amphetamines, and other illegal substances

Ego defense—actions that protect an individual's sense of self-worth

Equality—the state of being the same with another person or thing

Esprit de corps—a sense of unity developed among a group of associated people

Feminist consciousness—an emphasis on the empowerment of women

Field training officer—a veteran police officer who assists and evaluates new officers in their transition into their responsibilities

Flextime—work hours that are arranged to help employees meet both work and personal family needs

Gender-based units—police units that are segregated into men and women officers

GIS-mapping—a geographic information system that identifies patterns of crime and "hot spots"

Hostile work environment—related to sexual harassment, the work environment consisting of persistent, unwelcomed sexual conduct that makes the job performance difficult for the employee

"Hurdle process"—a term used to describe the various kinds of tests (including interviews) that can occur when one is seeking law enforcement employment

Internships—experiential learning for students in professions in which they might have an interest and for which they usually receive academic credit

Interpersonal communication—verbal and written interactions between two or more people that convey a message that is understood by all parties involved

Investigative functions—the activities of collecting physical evidence, interviewing witnesses, and compiling other information to gain the probable cause necessary to arrest an identified suspect

Job assignments—specific activities that an individual is given to do and that usually have a title

Law Enforcement Assistance Administration—federal agency created in 1968 to increase the professionalism of law enforcement through funding for officers, equipment, research, and programs; abolished in 1982

Leadership roles—activities that are assigned to those in leadership positions, for example, policymaking

Leadership style—categories of behaviors that distinguish different types of managers

Manager—one who is in charge, makes decisions, and controls the direction of an agency; normally a lieutenant or captain

Medical exam—a step in the selection process of police applicants that is completed after the conditional job offer; an exam to assess an applicant's ability to carry out police activities

Mentoring group—several experienced people who form a group in order to provide guidance and support to inexperienced individuals in their profession

Midlevel personnel—police leaders who manage supervisors and have some policymaking responsibilities (see "Manager" above)

Moonlighting—holding a second job in addition to a full-time occupation

Occupational self-concept—an individual's descriptions of his or her aptitude to function within a profession or job

Operative—the title or rank of early female police officers; the work pertained to policing, but wasn't considered actual policing

Oral interview—one of the steps during police selection in which the applicant is asked a series of questions by one or more veteran officers and/or police administrators

Organizational structure—the organizational bureaucracy from top administrators down to uniformed officers, including the configuration of specialized units in relation to management.

OSHA—the Occupational Safety and Health Administration, responsible for work conditions related to safety and health

Personal history statement—applications that extensively cover police applicants' lives, including their educational, professional, financial, and criminal history

Physical abilities—the ability to perform the physical aspects of a job, for example, arresting a suspect

Physical abilities test—entrance examination that assesses the applicant's potential ability to perform the physical activities required by the job

Police groupies—individuals, usually females, who are attracted to police officers because of their uniform and the authority and prestige it represents

Police role—police functions that include enforcing the laws, apprehending offenders, preventing crime, protecting citizens from harm and crime, protecting citizens' legal rights, resolving conflict, and facilitating the movement of vehicles and pedestrians

Policewoman—female police officer

PoliceWOMEN—one end of the continuum invented by Susan Martin to distinguish female police officers who emphasize their femininity rather than professionalism

POLICEwomen—the other end of the continuum developed by Susan Martin to emphasize female officers who attempt to model after male officers to be accepted

Polygraph examination—"lie detector" used to substantiate the information collected during the selection process

Positive discrimination—also labeled "reverse discrimination," in which women and minority members are given preferential treatment over majority males

Predelinquents—at-risk juveniles, children who display behaviors that are likely to lead to criminal behavior

Prison matron—females employed in prisons, usually to supervise female inmates

Protected group—groups based on race, color, sex, ethnicity, or national origin who are protected from discrimination

Psychological evaluations—a battery of psychological tests that are used to screen out individuals who have emotional or mental problems, have problems coping with anger or stress, or cannot interact well with different types of people

Punitive damages—payment provided for evidence of intentional discrimination or injury

Quid pro quo—"one thing leads to another," a concept used in terms of sexual harassment in which one individual expects sexual favors in return for a business or professional favor or benefit

Quota—a share or proportional part of a total required or assigned

Recruit—a new member of any organization, a new police officer

Residency requirements—mandates established by a police agency detailing the geographical range in which its police officers must live

Resume—a summary of one's education, employment, and experience submitted in application for a job

Retrospective reasoning—rationalization that occurs when one discusses events that have occurred in the past

Reverse discrimination—also labeled "positive discrimination," in which women and minority members are given preferential treatment over majority males

Ride-along—opportunity for students or other interested citizens to "shadow" a police officer while he or she performs their job duties

Selective omission—an individual's propensity to omit certain events that occurred in the past because they are painful or do not support the image that he/she wishes to portray

Self-efficacy—internal sense of ability; confidence that one can accomplish a task or do well at a job

Seniority—rights and privileges resulting from length of service within an organization

Sex-role norms—characteristics that a culture specifically attributes to men or women

Sex typing—similar to sex-role norms; the action of placing jobs and other activities into categories according to gender

Sexual harassment—unwelcomed sexual advances in the workplace, often with the implication that acceptance is necessary for hiring, job security, promotions, etc.

Sexual misconduct—sexual behavior that is considered inappropriate and at times deviant, based on the norms and rules established by the police organization and/or police culture

Sexualizing the workplace—activities of individuals, often males, who focus their attention and remarks on the gender of fellow employees rather than on the professional job that they are performing

Shift assignment—assignment of officers so that all hours of every day are covered, ranging from 8 to 12 hours in duration

Shoot/don't shoot decisions—decisions referring to the use of deadly force

Social work—a profession that focuses on improving conditions of individuals and communities, especially in poverty areas

Spouse academy—information sessions for the significant others of new officers

Stop-and-frisk—a search ("pat-down") of an individual by a police officer for a weapon for the purpose of officer safety

Supervisors—those persons who work directly with, and oversee activities of rank-and-file officers

Support functions—administrative and technical services that are needed to support the main enforcement and service functions of law enforcement

Sworn personnel—individuals who swear to uphold the laws of the municipality, state, and nation and protect citizens and their rights and who in turn are allowed to carry a weapon and other tools to carry out their responsibilities

"Tip-over"—the percentage of women or minority members that places them beyond being "tokens," generally believed to be 25 percent of the workforce

Tokenism—practice or policy of making only token acts, as in racial integration; the hiring of one individual so as to be able to demonstrate adherence to a policy

Uniformed patrol duties—duties of the vast majority of officers, whose uniformed presence denotes their authority and enforcement duties; in contrast to "plainclothes" or "undercover" duties

Use of deadly force—the utilization of a lethal weapon to kill another person to prevent serious injury or death to one's self or another person

Vicarious liability—legally responsible in the place of another, for example, a supervisor's legal responsibilities for the actions of those he or she supervises

"War stories"—experiences relayed by veteran officers to new officers

Women divisions—police units into which women were segregated

"Work the streets"—the ability to interact with the public safely and effectively

Written examination—an early step in the police selection process often done to assess reading, written communications, and math skills

Index